Higher Education in Contemporary India

Higher Education in Contemporary India

Policies, Practices and Perspectives

P. Satyanarayana

SHIPRA

Rs. 995, US$ 49.75

ISBN: 978-93-86262-11-0

First Published in India in 2017

Higher Education in Contemporary India: Policies, Practices and Perpectives

Published by:

SHIPRA PUBLICATIONS
LG 18-19, Pankaj Central Market,
I.P. Ext., Patparganj, Delhi 110092, India
Ph.: +91 11 22235152/6152
Email: info@shiprapublication.com
www.shiprapublication.com

Contents

GLIMPSES OF PAST

1. Background: Ancient, Medieval and Colonial Times 3

POLICIES AND PLANS

2. National Policies 11

3. Five Year Plans 21

INSTITUTIONAL PATTERN

4. Central, State, Deemed and Private Universities 31

5. Community Colleges 41

6. Ten Best Colleges 48

7. Academic Staff Colleges 54

8. National Institutional Ranking Framework 62

VARIED FORMS

9. Medical Education 73

10. Engineering Education 85

11. Management Education 95

12. Agricultural Education 102

13. Teacher Education 109

14. Legal Education 120

15. Women's Education 127

16. Distance Education 136

DIFFERENT DIMENSIONS

17. Autonomy 149
18. Accreditation 159
19. Financing 166
20. Regulatory Framework 177
21. Academia-Industry Interaction 181
22. Internationalisation 187
23. Information and Communication Technology (ICT) 197
24. Privatisation 205
25. Under-Represented Groups 212
26. Research 220
27. Rashtriya Uchchatar Shiksha Abhiyan (RUSA) 230

COMMISSIONS AND COMMITTEES

28. Some Important Commissions and Committees 243
References 250
Index 253

Glimpses of Past

1
Background: Ancient, Medieval and Colonial Times

The socio-historical journey of higher education in India has evolved through different periods, viz., ancient, medieval, colonial, post-independence, and contemporary. The institutions of higher education are recognised as the most important agency of social change involved in the human resource development of the country. The socio-historical journey of higher education started with an ancient system of education in the Vedic period. It was based on religious directives.

Ancient Times

The basic religions were Hinduism, Buddhism, and Jainism. In ancient India, there were two broad trends in educational systems—Brahminical education and Buddhist education. Brahminical education developed in the Vedic period. Rig Vedic education was thought to be an attempt to preserve contemporary religious texts through oral transmission.

The Rig Vedic educational institution consisted of small domestic school (*ashram*) run by a teacher (rishi), who admitted pupils for instructions in the literature in its possession. Women were allowed to participate in full religious rites and had access to educational facilities. In fact, women enjoyed equal status with men in all spheres of education during the Rig Vedic period. The later Vedic period saw continuity as well as some changes in the educational system. Three types of educational institutions existed in the later Vedic period (1000-600 B.C.). Firstly, there was the usual system under which the teacher, as a settled householder, admitted to his instruction pupils of a tender age. These pupils left their home for study after the *upanayana* or initiation ceremony. Secondly, debating circles and *parishads* were other types of institutions, where students discussed various aspects of knowledge. The third type of institution was represented by conferences summoned by kings in which the representatives of various schools participated.

The later Vedic period witnessed the crystallization of the *varna* system which was monopolized by the twice born castes in general, and by Brahmins in particular. Women still managed to have same influence in the sphere of education, but they were increasingly getting relegated to the background. Higher education was subservient to the requirements of priesthood and ritualistic religion. The external, material, and mechanical aspect of worship and sacrifice became the principal subjects of study. This was before the Upanishads, but the fact remains that usually in the days of the four Vedas, the teachers were all Brahmins, and came from the priestly class.

The post-Vedic early classical period (600-300 B.C.) saw the elaboration of rituals related to education. For instance, the pupils' first introduction of education was made by the performance of a ceremony called Vidyarambha. Theoretically, all the twice-born castes were allowed to receive education but, in practice it was monopolized by the Brahmins. *Arthashastra* (400-300 B.C.) details that the studentship of a prince should continue only up to sixteen years at which age he must marry. During this short period, he had to acquire the knowledge of religion, philosophy, agriculture, trade, and statecraft. The *Sushruta Samhita* provides detailed information about medical education and practice.

The nature of Buddhist education was religious as well as secular. The most important aspect of Buddhist education was that it remained open to all persons irrespective of castes except slaves, army deserters, the disabled, and the sick. It grew out of the teachings of the Buddha as classified as *vinaya* (monolithic discipline), *sutta* (group discourse), and *abhidhamma* work of experience and was in the hands of the monks. In some ways, aspects of these educational institutions can be compared with modern universities.

In this system of education, the viharas functioned as residential schools where various groups of students and teacher stayed together. Taxila was the most famous Buddhist seat of higher learning. It was famous especially for the school of Medicine, Law and Military Science which, by midway through the 6th century had acquired a reputation as a great centre of learning attracting scholars from distant parts of India. During the reign of Alexander, the Great, the fame of its philosophers had spread as far as Greece. Panini, the renowned Sanskrit Grammarian, and Kautilya, the author of the *Arthashastra*, were reputed to have studied in Taxila which flourished as a great educational centre until the middle of the 3rd century A.D.

In ancient India, the Rig Veda was the nucleus of the education system composed orally by the priestly tribes among the Aryans between 1500 and 1000 B.C. It was followed by the composition of three more Vedas—*Sama*, *Yajur*, and *Atharava*. The Brahmins had been the advisers and guides of the kings and emperors in the capacity as purohits. Therefore, the dominance of the Brahmins was reflected in the creation of a new set of religious scriptures called *Brahmanas*. Later *Aranyakas* and *Upanishads* were added to the *Brahmanas*. By 600 B.C. they, together with the Vedas and their six Vedangas, were studied in the Vedic schools by the Brahmins, the Kshastriyas, and the Vaisyas.

On the other hand, for ancient Indian Sudras in the Aryan society, the study of Vedas was forbidden, and they learnt their professional knowledge in agriculture and animal husbandry, spinning and weaving, fine arts and crafts through the expertise of their own families. Buddhism came to the forefront as a challenge to Brahmanism, possibly because it offered a simple way to reach salvation.

Medieval Times

The medieval era in the history of India signified a major phase of social and culture synthesis. In fact, the history of education in medieval India reflects a part of the wider study of the history of society, social history broadly interpreted with politics, economics, and religion. The medieval state in combination with the various other agencies such as Sufism and Bhakti ideology played a crucial role in the protracted process of integration and coexistence. Despite their diverse religious and cultures, these agencies brought the people together through their common experience in public as well as in private.

Early Indian education and many of its centres continued in the middle ages, but madrasa emerged as an important centre of education. Thus, the early Indian traditions of learning coexisted with the newly instituted madrasa, making both continuity and change important features of higher education during the period.

In medieval India there were usually three conduits through which knowledge was acquired. These were Maktab, Madrasa, and Khangah. While Maktab was a place where elementary education was imparted, higher learning was pursued at a madrasa, and religious education or theology was discussed at a Khangah, the birth place of Sufism or spiritualism in Islam.

By the 11th century A.D. madrasas or colleges had developed as the centres of higher education and learning with a distinctly religious bias. They were primarily theological institutions, providing instruction in language and other secular subjects as a subsidiary activity, and were supported or aided by the government of the day. The madrasas were generally attached to mosques in the same way as the Maktabs. The courses of instruction in the madrasas included grammar, logic, rhetoric, theology, metaphysics, literature, jurisprudence, and science. Some of the madrasas enjoyed the status of universities. The medium of instruction was Persian, but Arabic was obligatory for all Muslims. In the 12th century A.D. Lahore became a centre of Muslim learning.

Colonial Times

The development of education system during the British period was determined by the needs of the colonial powers. The end of the 18th century and the beginning of the 19th century was the period of consolidation in industrial capital in Europe and England. Corresponding to this, the emerging intellectual opinion argued for the spread of English language and culture in the colonies. The Utilitarians, Evangelists, and Liberals from their own standpoint, favoured the spread of English Education. The debate between the Anglicists and the Orientalists with regard to India was finally clinched with Lord Bentick asking Thomas Babington Macaulay for his opinion. In his famous Minute of February 2, 1835, Macaulay noted that selective natives must be educated "as interpreters between us and the millions whom we govern; a class of persons Indian in blood and colour, but English in tastes and opinion, in morals and intellect."

A month after Macaulay's note, Bentick ruled that "the great objective of the British Government was, henceforth, the promotion of European literature and science. All funds appropriated for the purpose of education would be best employed on education alone." There were at least three important reasons that had significant bearing on the ruling of Bentick. The first was the increasing opinion and the recognition of the fact that the British could derive political benefit from English education. Amongst others who held this opinion, was Charles E. Trevelyan who in 1838, noted that "the spirit of English literature cannot but be favourable to the English connection" and argued that this would stop Indians from treating Britishers as foreigners and make them, "intelligent and zealous cooperators."

Secondly, the framing of the education policy was guided by the practical administrative needs of the colonialists. At the time of passing the 1833 Charter Act, the East Indian Company was in serious financial difficulties, one method suggested was to cut down expenditure on European employees and instead employ Indians at much lower salaries. The 1833 Charter opened the lower order civil service jobs to Indians; but this required English educated clerks. Hence the policy of 1835.

Thirdly, English education was also seen as an important basis for expanding the British market in India by reining English values and tastes. As Macaulay noted "but wearing out broad cloth and working with our cutlery, they should not be too ignorant or too poor to value and buy English manufactures." Macaulay's note, Bentick's ruling, and the establishment and growth of English education in India was an expression of the direct needs of the ruling colonial power. The education system in India, a legacy that continues till date, originated not because of any individual opinion, but because of the contemporary needs of the Government.

In 1837, English replaced Persian as the official and court language, and in 1844 Hardinge announced preference for English educated Indians in the civil service. These two steps effectively sealed any growth of education other than English education.

The pursuance of these needs and the consequent rise in demand for English education led to the forward of the dispatch of Sir Charles Wood in 1854, which was popularly known as "Wood's Dispatch". This recommended the setting up of the Universities of Bombay, Calcutta, and Madras which were established in 1857. The recommendations reflected the needs of the ruling colonial powers to train a section of upper classes in higher education, and set up the administrative structure for education, which continues till date,

Macaulay reflects the view that English education was necessary for the Indian higher education system. On the other hand, McCully (1940) reported that Indians increasingly demanded an English style of higher education because it provided prestigious jobs in the British bureaucracy or in the growing commercial sector of the economy. Hence, the British themselves were convinced that they needed a class of educated Indians at the secondary level posts in the Government to act as intermediaries between the Raj and the Indian population. Similar views have been expressed by others that English education was wanted by the Indian urban elite, not only for employment and careers, but also because it spread the western secular education's special role in the social and political regeneration of India towards self-rule. The elite were the beneficiaries of this system and had a vested interest in its continuation.

The idea of establishing universities in India on the model of the London University (i.e. universities of the affiliating type), was first promoted in Sir Charles Wood's Dispatch of 1854 which has been described as the Magna Carta of English education in India. It described the aim of education in India as the diffusion of arts, science, philosophy, and literature of Europe, and the study of Indian languages. These recommendations also included law, medicine, and engineering and were followed by the establishment of universities at Calcutta, Bombay, and Madras in 1857 following the model of the University of London.

Both Macaulay's Minute of 1835 and Wood's Dispatch of 1854 laid down the basic objectives for the development of English education in India.

Twenty-five years after the establishment of the first three universities, there had been an increase in the number of colleges from 27 to 75. There was a demand for more universities and by 1923, there were 12. There was a steady growth in subsequent years, and by 1943 a need was felt for a comprehensive plan of educational development. The Sergeant Report of 1944 was the first attempt to formulate a national policy on education in India. It pointed out the failure of making university education relevant to communities' needs and suggested means for improvement. However, by the time India became independent in 1947, it had 18 universities and a total student strength of a little less than 0.2 million.

In brief, higher education in colonial India remained concentrated in and around the cities and towns, was more widespread among men than women, and amongst the higher castes. It would have been almost impossible to find a rural scheduled caste or scheduled tribe woman studying in a college. There were serious inequalities in the colonial system of higher education.

Higher education is the basis of future innovation and progress. Independent India inherited ownership of its system of higher education from the colonialists, but the need of the reconstruction of education was felt long before independence. However, it was only after independence that the national leadership had an independent opportunity to tackle the problem. Nehru's remarks to the educational conference of 1948 very strongly expressed the view that:

> Whenever conferences were called to form a plan for education in India, the tendency, as a rule, was to maintain the existing system with slight modification. This must not happen now. Great changes have taken place in the country and the education system must also be in keeping with them. The entire basis of education must be revolutionised.

What Nehru was emphasising was that the new education of the post-independence period must be made relevant to the new national goals of independent India. These national goals are found in the Indian Constitution. These national goals are: (a) democracy, (b) secularism, (c) elimination of poverty, (d) to create a socialist society, and (5) to create national integration. The nationalist sprit that had brought about the independence of the country became the motivating force behind a great number of changes that were initiated in the country. Nationalist leaders, faced with the socio-economic reality of India, were all firm in the belief that education had a revolutionary task to fulfill.

Policies and Plans

2
National Policies

India has always accorded high importance to education. The concern for the improvement of education had been at the top of India's development agenda since independence. Several commissions were appointed by the Government of India from time to time to formulate policies and programmes required to enhance access to and participation in education and improve quality of education. Important among them was the Education Commission (1964-66).

The Indian Education Commission, popularly known as Kothari Commission, was an ad hoc commission set up by the Government of India to examine all aspects of the educational sector of India, to evolve a general pattern of education and to advise guidelines and policies for the development of education in India. It was formed on July 14, 1964 under the chairmanship of D.S. Kothari, the then Chairman the University Grants Commission. The terms of the reference of the Commission were to formulate the general principles and guidelines for the development of education from primary level to the higher and to advise the government on a standard pattern of education in India. However, medical and legal studies were excluded from the purview of the Commission. The tenure of the Commission was from 1964 to 1966 and the report was submitted by the Commission on June 29, 1966.

The Commission, under the Chairmanship of D.S. Kothari was the sixth commission in India after independence and the first commission with comprehensive terms of reference on education. Apart from the core group, the Commission had a panel of overseas consultants numbering twenty and nineteen task forces, their sub-groups, and special panels of invitees. Nine thousand individuals covering educators, scholars, and scientists were interviewed and 2400 memoranda were examined by the commission, over a period spanning 21 months. The Commission submitted its 287-page report on June 29, 1966 to M.C. Chagla, the then minister of education. The report had four sub-sections:

- Section I: General issues
- Section II: Stages of education

- Section III: Recommendations and programmes
- Section IV: Additional papers

The four main themes of the Commission were:

1. Increase in productivity
2. Promoting social and national integration
3. Education and modernisation
4. Developing social, moral, and spiritual values

One of the main recommendations of the Commission was the standardization of educational system on 10+2+3 pattern, across the country. It advised that the pre-primary education which had different names such as kindergarten, Montessori and pre-basic should be renamed as pre-primary and the primary education (renamed as lower primary) to be up to the 4th standard. It further classified the schooling as upper primary or higher primary and high school (up to standard X). The undergraduate education was identified as XI and XII standards under the name higher secondary or pre-university. The graduate studies were recommended to be standardised as a three-year course.

The education system was categorized as first (primary education), second (secondary education), and third levels of education (higher studies).

The Commission recommended that a common public education system should be introduced, and that it should be vocationalized in general and special streams by introducing work experience as a part of education. It further stressed on the need to make work experience and social/national service an integral part of education. The Commission recommended that specialisation of subjects be started from higher secondary levels.

It also recommended that the days of instruction be increased to 234 for schools and 216 for colleges, and the working hours be fixed at not less than 1000 hours per academic year, preferably higher at 1100 or 1200 hours. It also advised reduction of national holidays. Linking of colleges to a number of schools in the neighbourhood, utilisation of school facilities eight hours a day all through the year, establishment of book banks, identification of talents and provision of scholarship, setting up of day study and residential facilities, and opportunities for students to earn while studying were some of the other recommendation of the Commission. It also emphasised the need for free education up to and including lower secondary level of education.

The Commission stressed the desirability of ensuring women's education and advised setting up of state and central level committees for oversight of women's education. It suggested establishment of schools and hostels for women and urged identification of ways to find job opportunities for women in the educational sector. Focusing on equalization of opportunities to all irrespective of caste, religion, and gender to achieve social and national integration, the schools were advised to provide education to backward classes on a priority basis and the minimum level of enrollment at a secondary school was advised to be not less than 360 every year. Two sets of curricula were prescribed—one at the state level and one at the national level. The schools were recommended to experiment with the curricula. It also proposed that three or four text books be prescribed for each subject, and moral and religious education be made a part of the curriculum.

It also recommended the establishment of guidance and counseling centres and a new approach in the evaluation of student performances. The Commission suggested incorporating the neighbourhood school system without social or religious segregation and a school complex system integrating primary and secondary levels of education. It put forward the suggestion that state and national boards of examination be set up and state level evaluation machinery be put in place.

The Commission recommended the establishment of Indian Education Service, along the lines of Indian Administrative Service, to bring in professional management to education sector. It proposed standardization and revision of the pay scales of the teaching, non teaching and administrative staff and prescribed minimum pay levels based on their location. It also advised standardization of pay scale working under different managements such as government, private and local bodies. The minimum scale was suggested to be in the ratio of 1:2:3 for teachers in the primary, secondary and higher levels of education sector. Another proposal was for the establishment of machinery for continuous on job training of the teaching staff and for efforts to raise the status of the teachers to attract talents into profession. It urged laws to be passed to legalize the educational standards and the educational expenditure to be raised from the then level of 2.9 percent of the gross domestic product (GDP) to six percent, to be achieved by the fiscal year, 1985-86. A significant suggestion was the issuance of a National Policy on Education by the Government of India, which should serve as a guideline for the state and local bodies in the design and implementation of their educational plans.

Formulation of a National Policy on Education was one of the important recommendations of the Commission. In 1968, the fourth Lok Sabha elected to office in 1967 under the leadership of Indira Gandhi, passed the bill. The policy covered many recommendations of the Kothari Commission such as free and compulsory education, status and pay scale revision of teachers, equalisation of educational opportunity, and science education.

Another recommendation of the Commission for the alignment of the educational system on the 10+2+3 pattern has been achieved by the government at the national level. The educational system has been modeled in accordance with the Commission's recommendation to stratify the sector with state and national bodies and a Central board, Board of Higher Secondary Education was set up in 1986.

Kothari commission and its recommendation are also reported to have influenced the 1986 revision of the National Policy on Education by the Rajiv Gandhi government. The guidelines laid out by the Commission were revisited by the National Knowledge Commission headed by Sam Pitroda in 2005.

1968 Education Policy

The report of the Education Commission was widely discussed and commented upon. The result was the emergence of the National Policy of Education in 1968.

The Government of India tried to implement the policy in the following ways:

1. Fulfillment of free and compulsory education.
2. Adequate and satisfactory status, enrolment and education of teachers.
3. Protection of academic freedom of teachers.
4. Due emphasis on teacher education.
5. Development of languages, Indian and international.
6. Equalisation of educational opportunities.
7. Correction of regional imbalances.
8. Promotion of social cohesion and national integration.
9. Emphasis on education of girls.
10. Expansion of educational facilities for the physically and mentally handicapped children.
11. Identification of talent and cultivation of excellence.
12. Emphasis on work experience and national service.
13. Growth of science education and research.
14. Emphasis on education for agriculture and industry.
15. Establishing agriculture universities in all states.
16. Relating practical training to technical education.
17. Continuous review of the agricultural, industrial, and other technical manpower needs.
18. Improving quality of textbooks.

19. Reforming examination framework.
20. Extension of secondary education.
21. Increasing facilities for technical and vocational education.
22. Expansion of university education.
23. Establishing new universities
24. Special attention to the organisation of postgraduate courses.
25. Establishing centres of advanced study.
26. Increasing support to research in universities.
27. Developing part-time education and correspondent courses.
28. Spreading literacy and adult education.
29. Emphasis on the education of practising farmers.
30. Developing games and sports.
31. Protecting the rights of minorities.
32. Following uniform educational structures (10+2+3) in all parts of the country.

1986 Education Policy

Having announced that a new policy was in development in January, 1985, the government of Prime Minister Rajiv Gandhi introduced a new National Policy on Education (NPE) in May, 1986. The new policy called for "special emphasis on the removal of disparities and to equalize educational opportunity," especially for Indian women, Scheduled Tribes (ST) and the Scheduled Caste (SC) communities. To achieve such a social integration, the policy called for expanding scholarships, adult education, recruiting, more teachers from the SCs, incentives for poor families to send their children to school regularly, development of new institutions and providing housing and services. The NPE called for a "child-centred approach" in primary education, and launched "operation blackboard" to improve primary school nationwide. The policy expanded the open university system with the Indira Gandhi National Open University (IGNOU), which was created in 1985. The policy also called for the creation of the "rural university" model, based on the philosophy of Mahatma Gandhi, to promote economic and social development at the grassroots level in rural India.

Some Salient Features of 1986 NPE

1. National system of education.
2. Education for equality.
3. Promotion of adult education.
4. Elementary education and operation blackboard.
5. Setting up Navodaya Vidyalayas.
6. Emphasising vocational training.

7. Recognising the status of the teacher.
8. Introduction of accountability in education.

NPE was adopted by the Indian parliament in May, 1986. In May, 1990 a Committee was set up under the chairmanship of Acharya Ramamurthy to review NPE and to make recommendations for its modifications. That Committee submitted its Report in December, 1990. At the request of the Central Advisory Board of Education (CABE), a Committee was set up in July, 1991 under the chairmanship of N.J. Reddy, Chief Minister of Andhra Pradesh, to consider modification in NPE taking into consideration the Report of the Ramamurthy Committee and other relevant developments on the Policy, and to recommend regarding modifications to be made in the NPE.

The 1986 NPE was modified in 1992 by the P.V. Narasimha Rao government. In 2005, Prime Minister Manmohan Singh adopted a new Policy based on the "Common Minimum Programme" of the United Progressive Alliance Government.

Since the formulation of earlier policies on education significant changes have taken place in India and the world at large. India's political, social, and economic development passed through a phase which necessitated a robust and forward looking educational system.

Significant changes have taken place in the education sector. The educational activities and learning process are no longer confined to the classroom. The educational process is not only mediated by classroom-based curriculum transaction but also by media, both electronic and print. Learners today have access to more current knowledge through non-institutionalised means.

The changing social context of education as well as the national concerns for achieving the goal of equity and inclusion demanded a changed approach to education.

Committee for Evolution of a National Education Policy 2016

The Government of India constituted a Committee for Evolution of the New Education Policy, which comprised of Shri T.S.R. Subramanian, former Cabinet Secretary as the Chairman and Smt. Shailaja Chandra, former Chief Secretary, NCT of Delhi, Shri Sevaram Sharma, former Home Secretary, UT of Delhi, Shri Sudhir Mankad, former Chief Secretary, Gujarat and Prof. J.S. Rajput, former Director, National Council for Educational Research and Training (NCERT) as members of the Committee.

The Committee for the evolution of a National Education Policy has submitted the report containing its recommendations to the Union Ministry of Human Resource Development (UMHRD) in June, 2016 under the name "Some Inputs for Draft National Education Policy—2016."

The Committee examined the large body of outcome documents, recommendations, and suggestions received from various consultations. The Committee also had several meetings with various stakeholders, held regional consultations and undertook field visits to educational institutions.

The online consultations on www.mygov.in portal were held from 26 January 2015 to 31 October 2015 and over 29,000 suggestions were received. The bottom-up consultative process across nearly all Gram Panchayats, Blocks, urban local bodies and districts of all 36 States/Union Territories were undertaken between May to October, 2015. Thematic consultations were conducted both by the ministry and also by the institutions like University Grants Commission, All India Council for Technical Education, National Council for Teacher Education, National Council for Teacher Educational Research and Training, and several centrally funded universities and institutions, autonomous bodies, attached offices. Also, all relevant stakeholders including experts, academics. industry representatives, civil society etc. were invited for deliberations on individual themes during July-October, 2015. Six zonal meeting were held by the Ministry of Human Resource Development in eastern, central, north-eastern, western, southern and northern zones covering all States and UTs in September and October 2015.

Major Suggestions

1. The main objective of the new National Policy on Education is to harness the full potential of a young vibrant population and equip it to contribute meaningfully to India's development.
2. The core objectives of this Policy is to provide information, knowledge, skills, and values; also to instill social attitudes which enable a student to become a good human being, a proud citizen, and contribute to the development of the country. Besides imparting quality education, the policy seeks to emphasise the need to foster an interest in India's history, culture and traditions, a respect for all religions and acceptance for the diversity that exists in India. Through education, the policy tries to create an understanding of the need to promote social cohesion and national integration which are essential for the country's progress. In the new technology-driven environment ever more students will become conversant with the tools of modern communication and technology. The Policy recognises the

immense opportunities for using these to promote education at every level.

3. Despite many gains, the Indian education system faces several problems, denting its credibility. The main factors include:
   - Absence of minimum standards in the provision of schooling facilities, processes, and student outcomes, and equity in educational opportunities;
   - Lack of professionalization in educational planning and management;
   - Absence of requisite disaggregated data, particularly at sub-national and institutional levels for evidence-based management of education;
   - Lack of competent and committed teachers, resulting in poor quality of education;
   - Substandard quality of teacher education and training;
   - A curriculum which encourages rote-based learning;
   - Malpractices in the examination system;
   - Neglect of skill and vocational education, overemphasis on acquiring dead-end qualifications which do not lead to employment;
   - Failure to make ICT functionally integral to the management of pedagogy of education;
   - Mushroom growth of private coaching classes and degree shops;
   - Corruption and politicization of education management at all levels;
   - Mediocre status of a majority of higher education institutions;
   - The pursuit of degree and qualification at any cost.
   - The new education Policy has addressed all these challenges.
4. The span of activities covered in the education sector is vast—apart from the central and state governments, the stakeholders include numerous institutions, parents, teachers, and students. In a climate of rising aspirations, the developments in the education sector require exceptional attention on a continuous basis. The problems faced by the education sector are complex and necessitate independent, considered, and mature response. The Ministry of HRD requires the assistance of a high-quality think tank in the form of a Standing Education Commission to study emerging challenges, evaluate and interpret policies and programmes, and provide information and guidance to the Ministry from time to time. The Commission should prepare a

National State of Education Report once in two years. The Commission should comprise of a limited number of experts and persons of eminence with special knowledge and experience of the education sector in India, supported by a small secretariat.

5. India has one of the largest systems of higher education in the country, with more than 700 universities, 37,000 colleges, and an enrolment of more than three crore students. The quality of many universities and colleges and the standard of education they provide are far from satisfactory. While there are some institutions like the IITs, IIMs, and a few others that have established a reputation as institutions of high quality, there are a large number of institutions which are mediocre, and some are no better than 'teaching shops'. The majority of higher education institutions fall in between these two extremes.
6. The process of according recognition of higher education institutions' general and technical needs require considerable revamping. Accreditation is an effective system for assessing the quality of higher education institutions. Accreditation validates and provides assurance that the quality of education provided by the institutions is of satisfactory standard. Assessment and accreditation enhances the reputation and acceptability of the institution and the value of the degrees conferred by it. At present accreditation is not compulsory for all higher education institutions. It is required only for receiving grants from the University Grants Commission (UGC). According to the latest information available, 140 universities got themselves accredited by the National Assessment and Accreditation Council (NAAC); but only 32 per cent were rated as 'A' grade or above. Most universities have been rated average. Quality and excellence in colleges clearly leaves much to be desired. A credible system of accreditation covering all institutions of higher education needs to be instituted.
7. Many private universities and colleges, professional and otherwise, flourish under the patronage of influential people backed by money power with little interest in education, taking advantage of a lax or corrupt regulatory environment. The proliferation of privately run 'teaching shops' and so-called non-profit institutions, ill-equipped and operating with unqualified staff, is a disturbing development and needs to be addressed urgently. It is necessary to weed them out through a process of accreditation for which transparent benchmarks have to be applied.

8. At present, accreditation is mandatory only for general stream higher education institutions receiving grants-in-aid from the UGC. Accreditation should be made mandatory for all institutions of higher education, including technical education, medicine and agriculture, both in public and private sectors.
9. Most of the older universities were created by law either by the centre or the states. Though technically these universities are autonomous, in actual practice the intervention by governments is extensive. There is a need to remove such interventions and to give freedom to universities to focus on improving their academic performance through their own initiative.
10. Although India's overall share of research publication in the world has risen in the past decade, the quality of research has not made a significant mark. Barring a few pockets of excellence like IITs, IIMs, and a few top universities and institutions, the system is marked by mediocrity. Research minded students and faculty prefer to go aboard as they do not find the research climate in our institutions conducive. It is estimated that nearly three lakh students go abroad every year to study in the world's best universities, spending more than $10 billion, which is twice the allocation of the Union budget in higher education. Favourable conditions need to be created in the country to promote high quality research.
11. Over the next decade at least 100 new centres for excellence, in the field of higher education both in public and private sector need to be established. If this is successfully accomplished, it will pave the way for high quality research and innovation to be undertaken. A regulatory regime which can oversee and encourage the establishment of such institutions of excellence needs to be put in place.

It is hoped that the Central Government would soon formulate a progressive New National Educational Policy, taking into consideration the suggestions made by several committees and commissions and representatives of Private Sector.

3
Five Year Plans

Since 1947, Indian development has been premised on the concept of planning. This has been carried through Five Year Plans, developed, executed, and monitored by the Planning Commission. With the Prime Minister as Chairman, the Commission has a nominated Deputy Chairman, who holds the rank of a Cabinet Minister. The Eleventh Plan completed its term in March, 1212 and the Twelfth Plan is currently underway. The new government led by Narendra Modi, elected in 2014, announced the dissolution of the Planning Commission and its replacement by a think tank called NITI Aayog, an acronym for National Institute for Transforming India.

Five Year Plans

First Plan	(1951-1956)	Second Plan	(1956-1961)
Third Plan	(1961-1966)	Fourth Plan	(1969-1974)
Fifth Plan	(1974-1979)	Rolling Plan	(1978-1980)
Sixth Plan	(1980-1985)	Seventh Plan	(1985-1990)
Annual Plans	(1990-1992)	Eighth Plan	(1992-1997)
Ninth Plan	(1997-2002)	Tenth Plan	(2002-2007)
Eleventh Plan	(2007-2012)	Twelfth Plan	(2012-2017)

An analysis of the past Five Year Plans indicates that, there have been continuous efforts to strengthen the base by developing infrastructure, improving quality through several programmes and schemes, introducing reforms in content, and evaluation and encouraging creation of new knowledge through research. The focus of the Fifth Five Year Plan was on infrastructure development; the Sixth Plan onwards the focus shifted to consolidation and quality improvement. The Seventh Plan laid emphasis on research and academic development. It was from this plan onwards that the development of centres of excellence and area study programmes got special attention. From the Eighth Plan onwards, the need for differential funding was recognised. It was envisaged that the developing departments would be provided necessary funds to bring their facilities and activities up to an optimum level for their teaching and general research programmes. The Ninth Plan aimed at gearing the system of higher education to meet the challenges arising out of the major social, economic, and technological changes. The focus of the Tenth plan was on quality and relevance of higher education, research and development, management in financing, and the use of the new information and communication technologies. The Tenth plan provided the basis for higher education in the 21st century.

The Elevnth Plan laid renewed emphasis on higher education and the three targets of broadening access, making higher education inclusive, and promoting improvements in quality. In the Elevnth Plan, the share of education in total plan outlay increased from mere 6.7 per cent in the Tenth Plan to 19.4 per cent of which 30 per cent was earmarked for higher education. This was a nine-fold increase over the Tenth Plan, viz. Rs. 84,943 crores against Rs. 9,500 crores

Enrolment by Faculty during the Tenth Plan (lakh)

Faculty	*2007-08*		*2011-12*		*Increase*
	Total	*%*	*Total*	*%*	
Arts	59.3	38.34	61.8	30.6	2.48
Science	27.37	17.75	31.3	15.5	3.9
Commerce & Management	24.41	15.83	29.9	14.8	5.46
Education	7.32	4.75	12	5.92	4.63
Engineering	24.14	15.65	49	24.3	24.82
Medicine, Nursing & Pharmacy	6.86	4.45	10.9	5.41	4.05
Agriculture & Veterinary Science	1	0.65	1.21	0.6	0.21
Law	2.69	1.74	3.27	1.62	0.58
Others	1.11	0.72	2.74	1.29	1.63
Total	**154.2**	**100**	**202**	**100**	**47.79**

Source: ASHE—Annual Status of Higher Education in States and UTs, 2012.

Number of Universities, Colleges, Students, and Teaching Staff Enrolment during last four decades

Year	*Universities*	*Colleges*	*Students enrolment (in millions)*	*Teaching staff enrolment (in millions)*
1970-71	103	3604	2	NA
1980-81	133	4722	2.8	0.19
1990-91	190	7346	4.9	0.26
2000-01	256	12806	8.4	0.41
2006-07	387	21170	16.6	0.82
2011-12	659	33023	25.9	NA
CAGR	4.6	5.6	6.4	4.9

Sources: Higher Education in India: Twelfth Five Year Plan (2012-2017).

Principles, Objectives, Goals, and Strategies of the Twelfth Plan

Higher education in India is passing through a phase of unprecedented expansion, marked by an explosion in the volume of students, a substantial expansion in the number of institutions, and a quantum jump in the level of public funding. The enormity of the challenge of providing equal opportunities for quality higher education to ever-growing number of students is also a historic opportunity for correcting sectoral and social imbalances, reinvigorating institutions, crossing international benchmarks of excellence, and extending the frontiers of knowledge. The Twelfth FYP shall focus on utilising this historic opportunity for expansion of excellence, and achieving equal access to quality higher education.

India has made enormous strides in achieving these goals in more than six decades since independence, and the success milestones of its higher education system are recognised globally. Yet, considerable challenges remain. To meet these challenges, the University Grants Commission called for a major thrust for expansion of higher education, and promotion of greater regional and social equity in the Eleventh FYP. During this Plan, provision was made for setting up of 16 new central universities and 374 model colleges in low gross enrolment ratio (GER) districts. The Government of India provided for concomitant expansion with equity through implementation of the recommendation of the oversight committee. There was also a continued focus on achieving quality and supporting reforms in higher education and promoting excellence.

All adopted measure yielded results with a significant increase in enrolment and reduction in overall social group disparities. However, as Twelfth FYP document states, considerable challenges still remain. Access to higher education is still less than the minimum international threshold levels, distribution of institutions is skewed, enrolment in public universities is largely concentrated in the conventional disciplines; whereas in the private self-financed institutions, the student enrolment is overwhelmingly in the market-driven disciplines.

Much greater challenges continue to exist with respect to quality and the provision of relevant education. Curricular reforms leading to regular revision and upgrading of curricula, introduction of semester system, choice-based credit system, and examination reforms are yet to take place in all higher educational institutions across the country. Exceptions apart, the majority of our higher education institutions perform poorly in the area of quality on a relative global scale.

To accomplish a "quantum jump" in achieving the triple objective of access and expansion, equity and inclusion, and quality and excellence, with an emphasis on consolidation and optimal use of infrastructure already created during the Eleventh FYP, the Twelfth FYP focused on the following strategies:

- The focus is towards access through expansion by consolidation and better utilisation of the existing infrastructure, upgrading of the infrastructure as and where necessary, and creation of new institutions primarily to meet the objective of regional equity.
- Increasing and enhancing access through a mission mode national programme, Rashtriya Uchch Shiksha Abhiyan (RUSA) aims to achieve 25 per cent national level GER which will include: (a) upgrading of autonomous colleges, colleges with potential for excellence, and A grade accredited colleges by the National Assessment and Accreditation Council (NAAC), as university-level institutions; (b) promoting evening universities/evening colleges; (c) introduction of undergraduate programmes in the universities as integrated undergraduate/postgraduate (UG/PG) programmes; (d) enhancing the intake capacity of the existing institutions of higher education; (e) developing the 'college cluster universities' regionally; and (f) establishing 'meta university complexes' in association with public/private sector undertakings as a part of their corporate-social responsibility, on an industry-academic mode.
- The strategy for promoting equity at all levels, and in all branches of higher education, from enrolment to graduation/post-graduation, shall be through new schemes for financial support of social deprived groups, minorities and women, alone with significant remedial support for such students and faculty.
- Schemes for reducing regional/disciplinary/gender imbalances will include: (a) setting up of large number of polytechnics (1000); (b) completing the establishment of 374 model colleges in the identified educationally backward areas of low GER districts; (c) establishment of 800 constituent colleges in the already existing 40 central universities; and (d) establishment of 20 exclusive universities for women.
- The system of financial support to girl students and students from SC/ST, minorities and other backward category (OBC) category is considerable enhanced at all levels of higher education and for all branches, including professional and technical education. Financial support will be expanded in the form of scholarships, transport/rent allowance, book banks, and fee-plus-scholarship system for professional students.

- In order to retain students from deprived social groups in the higher education system, post-doctoral scholarship will be enhanced and a fast-track methodology implemented.
- There will be strengthening of infrastructure to provide access, and retain women students, differently-abled students, and students from socially deprived backgrounds.
- A major emphasis will be the strengthening of the remedial system for students from socially deprived backgrounds in order to enable their retention and ensure better performance.
- Equal opportunity cells, which were initiated in the Eleventh FYP, will be set up in all institutions, including institutions covered under Section 2(f) of the UGC Act. These will monitor and oversee the implementation of policies and programmes for the weaker section and their progress in their respective institutions in achieving social inclusion.
- Promotion of quality would be through a greater focus on performance, curricula reforms, better human resources management, schemes to promote high quality research, and technology-assisted monitoring mechanism. National science experimentation facilities, particularly in the cutting edge areas, will be set up as inter-university centres and university-housed networking centres to provide international quality resource support to all researchers and PG students.
- Faculty being the single most critical factor responsible for the overall quality and excellence in higher education, it is a matter of grave concern that a large number of faculty positions remain perennially vacant due to either non-availability of suitably qualified persons or due to procedural restrictions/fund constraints in state universities/colleges. In order to ensure that the expansion drive in higher education is sustained, initiatives shall be taken to attract and retain the best talents as faculty resources by creating conducive working ambience, and by making teaching and research a lucrative career destination through continuous central assistance.
- The capacity building and capability enhancement, keeping in tune with modern-day requirement of the faculty resources through the faculty talent promotion scheme by upgrading the Academic Staff Colleges (ASCs) as Faculty Development Centres (FDCs) with redefined roles and responsibilities, would be another priority.
- Equally important shall be the initiative for leadership development and institutional management programmes at all

levels from top to bottom, for those who may be currently holding the leadership, management and administrative position. For those in the leadership tiers who need to be readied to take over such leadership positions in colleges and universities in future, a separate leadership mentoring programme is envisaged through dedicated/competent centres.

- Support for curricular and academic reforms to improve student choices, technology-assisted participatory teaching-learning process and increasing the provision or relevant education, with an emphasis on feedback-based holistic examination/evaluation system.
- Minimising the affiliating burden of the existing universities by implementing the affiliation reform package development by the UGC during the Eleventh FYP in a multipronged approach would be another added dimension of promoting access with quality and relevance.
- For promoting private sector participation in higher education, newer models based on quality shall be explored, supported, and incentivized by well-defined policies, norms, and monitoring mechanism. The initiative would also include maximising the potential of public private partnership (PPP) in higher education not only for setting up new universities and colleges, but also for creating/sharing quality infrastructure and physical facilities in the existing colleges and universities.
- For promoting skill-based education and to improve competence, a fresh impetus to vocational education shall be given with due regards to National Vocational Education Qualification Framework (NVEQF), and the initiative is to be supported and incentivised through well-defined policies and monitoring mechanisms.
- Reforming the financing system of higher educational institutions by the UGC such as to promote the culture of accountability, improve performance and better resource use efficiency and at the same time respecting the academic autonomy.
- For better coordination and speedy implementation of the Twelfth FYP priorities, the UGC, as an organisation, will have to be restructured and modernised, and rejuvenated as a vibrant academic, administrative, and fund providing/monitoring body through the introduction of new management system of good governance which is a layer above e-governance, with transparency and accountability on the one hand, and by roping in eminent academics on full-time basis as advisers on the other

hand, besides lateral entry/deputation—mediated administrative talent infusion.

- State Councils of Higher Education have so far been established only in a few states as interface bodies between the state governments, the universities of the state, and the national bodies/ councils like the UGC/All India Council for Technical Education (AICTE), etc. In order to facilitate national level coordination of the higher education schemes/policies and their speedy implementation, all states will be encouraged and incentivised to establish and activate these Councils. Similarly, the College Development Councils (CDCs) of the universities will be made more effective in channelizing the UGC scheme to colleges through the CDCs, supported appropriately by the UGC.
- Universities and colleges being the end-users of the public funds, provided by either the central or the state government, shall have to be made accountable for the funds. To that end a New Educational Management System will be introduced whereby their accountability would be assessed more in terms of their performance and outcomes, and less in terms of insistence on adherence to elaborate process and procedure.
- State universities and colleges affiliated thereto account for an overwhelmingly large number of enrolments in higher education, and it is this sector that has been least attended to in terms of resource support and subject to external influence and pressures in the name of accountability. Enhanced resource support to this sector based on the commitment of the state governments to provide these institutions greater autonomy and operational flexibility shall be a priority during the Twelfth FYP.
- A large number of new central universities and model colleges that were established during the Eleventh FYP would require continued and accelerated support, because during this Plan they are likely to quicken the pace of their development and operational work. Any resource constraints at this juncture would be detrimental to their growth and development.
- The Twelfth FYP document provides the details of the present trends, prevailing issues and challenges, projected goals and the planned strategies for the Twelfth FYP with schemes and programmes under the three major heads of access, equity and quality with interlaced components of relevance, value-education, and creativity.

Institutional Pattern

4
Central, State, Deemed and Private Universities

The higher education system in India includes both private and public universities. Public universities are supported by the Government of India and the state governments, while private universities are mostly supported by various bodies and societies. Universities in India are recognised by the University Grants Commission (UGC), which draws its power from the University Grants Commission Act, 1956. In addition, 15 professional councils were established, controlling different aspects of accreditation and coordination.

The types of universities include:

- *Central universities,* or Union universities, are established by an Act of Parliament and are under the purview of the Department of Higher Education in the Union Human Resource Development Ministry. The UGC lists 47 central universities.
- *State universities* are run by the state government of each of the states and Union Territories of India, and are usually established by a local legislative assembly Act. As of 25 May, 2016, the UGC listed 347 state universities. The oldest establishment date listed by the UGC is 1857, shared by the University of Mumbai, the University of Madras, and the University of Calcutta. That most state universities are "affiliating universities" in that they administer a large number of "affiliated colleges" (many located in very small towns) that typically offer a range of undergraduate courses, but may also offer postgraduate courses. More established colleges may even offer Ph.D. programmes in some departments with the approval of the affiliating university.
- *Deemed university* or "Deemed to be University", is a status of autonomy granted by the Department of Higher Education on the advice of the UGC, under Section 3 of the UGC Act. As of 25 May, 2016, the UGC listed 130 deemed universities. According to this list, the first institute to be granted deemed

university status was Indian Institute of Science, at Bengaluru which was granted this status on 12 May 1958. The same listing by the UGC covers several institutes. For examples, the listing for Homi Bhabha National Institute covers the Institute of Mathematical Sciences, the Indira Gandhi Centre for Atomic Research and other institutes.

- *Private universities* are approved by the UGC. They can grant degrees, but they are not allowed to have off-campus affiliated colleges. The UGC list of private universities as on 25 May 2016 listed 237 private universities.

India has 754 universities. There are universities of some kind in each of the 29 states of India as well as three of the Union Territories: Chandigarh, Delhi, and Puducherry. The state with the most universities is Rajasthan with 71 universities. Tamil Nadu is the state with the most deemed universities, numbering 30. Gujarat and West Bengal have the most state universities, 25 each and Uttar Pradesh has 24 State universities. Rajasthan has the most private universities—41. Uttar Pradesh has six central universities and Delhi has five central universities.

Apart from the above universities, other institutions are granted the permission to autonomously award degrees. These institutes do not affiliate colleges, and are not officially called universities, but are autonomous organisations or autonomous institutes. They fall under the administrative control of the Department of Higher Education. These organisations include the Indian Institutes of Technology, the National Institutes of Technology, the Indian Institutes of Science Education and Research, the Indian Institutes of Engineering Science and Technology, the Indian Institutes of Management the National Law Schools, the All India Institute of Medical Sciences, and other autonomous institutes.

The regions with the most central universities in India are Delhi (namely University of Delhi, Jamia Millia Islamia, Jawaharlal Nehru University, IGNOU, South Asian University) and Uttar Pradesh also with five central universities namely BHU, AMU, Allahabad University, BBAU, Rajiv Gandhi National Aviation Institute. There are central universities in all of the states of India except Goa, Andhra Pradesh, and UT of Chandigarh. Of the Union Territories, there are central universities in Delhi and Puducherry.

Central Universities

The British government in India passed Acts in 1857 to establish

State	Central universities	State universities	Deemed universities	Private universities	Total
Andhra Pradesh	0	20	5	0	25
Arunachal Pradesh	1	0	1	7	9
Assam	2	12	0	4	18
Bihar	3	15	2	0	19
Chandigarh	0	1	1	0	2
Chhattisgarh	1	13	2	8	22
Delhi	5	7	10	0	22
Goa	0	1	0	0	1
Gujarat	1	25	2	24	52
Haryana	1	14	6	19	40
Himachal Pradesh	1	4	0	17	22
Jammu and Kashmir	2	7	1	0	10
Jharkhand	1	7	2	3	13
Karnataka	1	25	15	12	52
Kerala	1	13	2	0	16
Madhya Pradesh	2	21	3	20	44
Maharashtra	1	21	21	5	48
Manipur	2	0	0	1	3
Meghalaya	1	0	0	8	9
Mizoram	1	0	0	1	2
Nagaland	1	0	0	2	3
Odisha	1	13	2	3	19
Puducherry	1	0	1	0	2
Punjab	1	9	2	13	25
Rajasthan	1	21	8	41	71
Sikkim	1	0	0	5	6
Tamil Nadu	2	22	30	0	52
Telangana	3	16	2	0	21
Tripura	1	1	0	1	3
Uttar Pradesh	6	24	10	24	63
Uttarkhand	1	10	4	11	25
West Bengal	1	25	1	8	35
Total	**47**	**347**	**130**	**237**	**754**

universities at Calcutta, Bombay, and Madras. So also, the universities of Punjab (1882), Allahabad (1920), Banaras (1916), Patna (1917), and Aligarh (1920) were established by the central legislature. They were central universities when established. In fact, the Calcutta University had the status of Central University for a long time as it was located in the capital of the country and the Governor-General was its chancellor. It continues to be a central university even after the capital was later shifted to Delhi.

Later, all universities except Banaras Hindu University were transferred to the provincial governments. When Delhi University was set up in 1922, it was outside the jurisdiction of provincial government. Hence it came under central legislature and in 1935, by the Government of India Act, these three universities (Aligarh, Banaras, Delhi) were included in List-1 and remained central universities.

When the Constitution was framed, there were heated discussions on listing education under Union or State jurisdiction, and finally it found a place in all the three lists—Union, State, and Concurrent. Central universities have unique objectives of serving specific needs, apart from being institutions of national importance, attracting students and faculty from all over the country.

Visva Bharati was set up in 1951 as a central university and the objectives of the University were clearly enunciated as the objectives under which Tagore had founded the Visva Bharati at Santiniketan in 1921.

The objectives of Visva Bharati are:

i. To study the mind of man in its realisation of different aspects of truth from diverse points of view.
ii. To bring into more intimate relations with one another through patient study and research the different culture of the east on the basis of the underlying unity.
iii. To approach the west from the standpoint of such unity of life and thought of Asia.
iv. To seek to realise in a common fellowship of study the meeting of the east and the west, and thus ultimately to strengthen the fundamental conditions of world peace through the establishment of free communication of ideas between the two hemispheres; and
v. With such ideals in view to provide at Santinikentan aforesaid a centre of culture where research into a study of religion, literature, history science, and art of Hindu, Buddhist, Jain, Islamic, Sikh, Christian, and other civilisations may be pursued along with the culture of the West for true spiritual realisation, in amity, good fellowship, and cooperation between the thinkers and scholars of both Eastern and Western countries, free from all antagonism of race, nationality, creed or caste.

Overall Objectives of Central Universities

The Banaras Hindu University Inquiry Committee (1969) enunciated in its Report the objectives and role of central universities as follows:

> "In this connection there is one point of some importance to which we wish to refer. The Banaras Hindu University like the Aligarh Muslim University, the Delhi University, Vishwa Bharati, and Jawaharlal Nehru University are central universities and the Union Government fully finances, through the UGC, the expenditure incurred by these institutions. The question which

> arises is what should be the specific features of a central university? Central universities should not be described as central merely because the central government finances them. They should have a distinctive character of their own.
>
> "The central universities should seek to supplement, and not always duplicate the facilities and achievements of state universities. The state universities, though they should function in every possible way as all-India institutions, have a basic responsibility to address the needs of the state and the local community. Sometimes these may not coincide exactly with the order of priorities and demands of other parts of the country or the country as a whole. However, in the case of central universities, their role and responsibility is clear—it is to function effectively and vigorously on an all-India basis to help build up a corporate intellectual life in the country and to further national integration. Broadly speaking, the central universities should provide courses which need facilities (in terms of staff and equipment) ordinarily beyond the reach of state universities, or for which the demand would be too small if limited only to the requirements of an individual state. There is another aspect which we would like to refer as it has reference to the special function and responsibilities of central universities. It is well known that in our country, just as some areas are economically backward, so are some areas educationally backward, and we feel that the central universities should regard it as a part of their special function to contribute towards removal of imbalances from the academic life of our country and take suitable action to help deserving students from educationally backward areas. In order to achieve this object such facilities as may be necessary should be made available to the central universities."

The Report of the Committee to enquire into the working of the central universities (1984) commented:

> "The central universities are in a state of perpetual crisis and are faced with problems some of which are beyond their competence to solve. We have to ask many questions in order to appreciate the causes of crisis. Is it due to lack of clarity in understanding the aims of university education on the part of the people, the academics, or the decision makers? ... Unfortunately, the intellectual, cultural and ethical values, which the universities are expect to uphold and preserve are easily subordinated to lesser concerns on the part of the university community."

State Universities

State universities are still the backbone of higher education. Majority of students get enrolled there. State governments are to shoulder the responsibility of maintaining and developing them. Presently, many colleges are affiliated to state universities. This has burdened many universities with the management of academic content, examination, and quality maintenance issues. Good affiliating colleges should be converted into autonomous colleges. There is a view that the optimum size of a university has not only a quantitative, but also a qualitative dimension.

Stage-wise Enrolment by Type of Institution

Higher Education Institutions	*Ph.D.*	*M. Phil.*	*Post-Graduate*	*Under-Graduate*	*Diploma/ Certificate*	*Total*
Central Universities	20.04	6.52	10.92	6.36	8.55	7.03
Institutes of National Importance	14.96	0.37	1.08	0.34	1.17	0.50
State Universities	42.25	83.45	80.32	90.22	78.04	88.49
Deemed Universities-Public	7.43	2.07	1.41	0.31	1.49	0.50
Deemed Universities-Private	11.61	5.08	3.92	1.81	3.16	2.14
Private Universities	3.70	2.51	2.34	0.95	7.58	1.33
Others	0.01	0.00	0.01	0.01	0.00	0.01
Total	**100.00**	**100.00**	**100.00**	**100.00**	**100.00**	**100.00**

Enrolment by Level of Study in Central Universities

Level of Study	*Central University*
Ph.D.	3.16
M. Phil	0.32
Post Graduate	14.68
Under Graduate	78.12
Diploma + Certificate	3.72
Total	**100.00**

Sources: MHRD (2012-13).

It is high time that academics, as a collective body, start reflecting on the university college system from within. Three systemic problems can be mentioned instantaneously: (1) subtended and unprofessional faculty, lack of up-to-date libraries and other supportive online resources; (2) uninspiring teaching methodologies, obsolete, and irrelevant syllabus coupled with an obsessive orientation to examination; and (3) a contempt for merit and scholarship.

What is interesting is the manner in which academic practice is structured in the typical university. There is little chance that someone who has managed to get admission will not come out with a degree. What is more remarkable is that, given the already low levels of academic work that is required of students, an undergraduate student normally has to work harder than a typical Master of Arts (M.A.) student to get his degree. The M.A. student, once admitted has a higher probability of finishing the course even with less of an academic input. And if s/he manages to get into a Ph.D. programme, a degree is assured with the most minimal inputs by the student. This illustrates the anomaly in our state universities. Similar conditions prevail in the recruitment and promotion of faculty. At the entry point itself there is a deficit of professional and academic skills of those who are in state universities and colleges. Once someone enters as a lecturer in any university, it is highly unlikely that the person will not rise, given time to become reader and then a professor, not withstanding academic achievements or lack of these. Instead of the pursuit of knowledge, the chase for power and petty politicking has become the principal axis of the state university system. Even at the cost of advocating nihilism, it may be stated that in the prevailing anomalous conditions there is no escape for the Indian state universities.

National Policy on Education, 1986 and RUSA, 2013 proposed the establishment of State Council of Higher Education in all states to increase the coordination among state and centre, and also among college and state universities. National Knowledge Commission, 2008 argued that the existing governance and regulation have an adverse effect on the development of the higher education system. Knowledge Commission proposed the establishment of an independent regulatory authority for higher education. The Yash Pal Committee also recommended replacing multiple bodies for accreditation with a single regulatory body.

Deemed Universities

The main idea behind the concept of 'deemed university' is to promote, strengthen, and bring those institutions under the purview of UGC, which for historical or any other circumstances are not universities; yet are maintaining high standards of work in specialised academic fields comparable to a university. The UGC Act provides for the possibility of an institution being granted a deemed university status under Section 3 of the Act.

Till 1970, only seven institutions were notified as deemed to be universities. Between 1970 and 2000, 36 more were granted the status of deemed to be universities. Now, the total number is 130. This unusual growth has created a problem of equity, quality, and excellence. Various committees constituted by UGC, MHRD, and other bodies suggested measures for strengthening private deemed universities and resolving quality issues.

The Yash Pal Committee expressed great concern over the mushrooming of deemed universities. Though the deemed universities do not have affiliating powers; many of them have a number of campuses spread throughout the country. The Yash Pal Committee suggested that in view of misuse of the provision for deemed university status; the granting of such status should be put on hold till unambiguous and national guidelines are evolved. The committee further suggested that institutions wishing to get deemed university status should demonstrate special capabilities as was originally intended.

Private Universities

Private universities are mostly supported by various bodies and societies. They are regulated under UGC Establishment and Maintenance of Standards in Private Universities Regulation, 2003. They are established by an Act of local legislative assembly and listed by the UGC in the gazette upon receiving the copy of the Act. As confirmed by the ruling of the Supreme Court, recognition by the UGC is required for the university to operate. Also, as per the 2003 regulation, the UGC sends committees to inspect the private universities and publishes their inspection report. The earliest date of notification is that of Sikkim Manipal University, 11 October 1995. The earliest inspection report is that of Nirma University of Science and Technology, 15 May 2004. Private universities were established in 22 of the 29 states of India. and in none of the Union territories. The State with the most of private universities listed is Rajasthan. There are no private universities in Andhra Pradesh, Bihar, Goa, J&K, Kerala, Tamil Nadu, Telangana, Puducherry, NCR Delhi, and UT of Chandigarh.

Private universities are competent to award degrees as specified by UGC under 22 of the UGC Act, with the approval of the statutory councils, wherever required through their main campus. Whenever the approval of the statutory council is not a prerequite to start a programme, the universities are required to maintain the minimum standards regarding academic and physical infrastructure as laid down by the concerned statutory council. They cannot affiliate an institution or college. They cannot establish off-campus centres beyond the territorial jurisdictions of the concerned state. However, they can establish off-campus centres within the concerned state after five years of functioning as a private university recognised by the UGC, and with the prior approval of the UGC. A private university shall provide the relevant information relating to the first degree/diploma programmes, including the curriculum structure, contents, teaching and learning process, examination and evaluation system, and the eligibility criteria for admission of students, to the UGC on a Proforma prescribed by the UGC prior to beginning these programmes. UGC gives clearance before starting the programme by the university.

Philip Altbach, who has studied higher education around the world for nearly five decades, notes that, with some exceptions, "there are no successful private research universities outside of the U.S. and Japan."

While private institutions do have the potential to make a contribution in the production of new knowledge, it is quite unlikely that they will actually do so in the foreseeable future.

It is also unlikely that India's private institutions will emulate the American or Japanese models. This is because the majority of private institutions are run by two sets of entrepreneurial social groups—business people and politicians—who are in the game for one simple reason: higher education is a great business opportunity.

Not surprisingly, private institutions have proliferated across the country to meet the high demand for education, especially in professional streams such as engineering and management. Labeled "teaching factories" by their detractors, they charge high fees, and often demand a lump sum by one name or another.

Here is the list of top 10 private and deemed multidisciplinary universities in India. The list is made by a survey conducted by *The Week* and Hansen research for the year 2015.

Rank	*Name of the Institution*	*Places*
1.	Manipal University	Manipal
2.	Amity University	Noida
3.	Symbiosis International University	Pune
4.	Banashali Vidyapeeth University	Banashali
5.	Amity Viswa University	Coimbatore
6.	SRM University	Chennai
7.	Christ University	Benguluru
8.	D.Y. Patil University	Mumbai
9.	SASTRA University	Thanjavur
10.	SVKM's NMIMS University	Mumbai

Establishing Research Universities

The idea of establishing research universities by RUSA (Rashtriya Uchhater Shiksha Abhiyan) is welcome. It may elevate the status of existing promising universities or set up new ones. In any case, the idea behind the concept is excellent. Setting up of research universities requires well defined vision and perspective. It should be based on developing a bond between research and education. Research should extend the boundaries of education, and education in turn nurture creativity and innovative outlook among learners. They should work in close collaboration with various sectors: government, society, business, industry, etc.

Organisation for Economic Cooperate and Development (OECD) reports that out of 50 world class universities, 40 are in America with the highest research input. Though we have more than 700 universities, none of these is included in top 100 universities of the world. We have models of research universities in developed countries, various features of which can be adapted and followed.

Establishing Navratna Universities

Some Indian universities have enormous potential to reach world standards in teaching and research. Identification of such universities, based on stringent parameters identified by a Committee of Vice-Chancellors, could be taken up during the Twelfth FYP. The salient features that may determine a university's eligibility to be rated "Navaratna" could be: (a) the number of programmes offered and departments existing in the university; (b) the rate of expansion during the last five years; (c) visibility assessed by the number of students seeking admission; (d) plurality and demographic diversity of faculty and students; (e) number of SAP departments, CAS advancements, national facilities, centres of excellence, (f) extramural funding and research projects carried out, (g) number and quality of publications in impact factor journals, Average Citation Index, Average H Index (h) international collaborations. Such top universities to be identified in the Twelfth FYP will function under total autonomy and relaxation of rigid regulations in respect of faculty, appointment of overseas professors, and international partnership. Such universities may have to be provided an annual additional grant of 50.00 crore over and above the normal grant provided for five years.

Fake Universities in India

Statewise list of fake universities according to UGC.

- Maithili University/Vishwavidyalaya, Darbhanga, Bihar.
- Commercial University Ltd. Daryaganj, Delhi.
- United Nations University, Delhi.
- Vocational University, Delhi.
- ADR-Centric Juridical University, New Delhi.
- Indian Institute of Science and Engineering, New Delhi,
- Badaganvi Sarkar World Open University Education Society, Gokak, Belgaum.
- St. John's University, Kishanattam, Kerala.
- Raja Arabic University, Nagpur, Maharashtra.
- D.D.B. Sanskriti University, Pututr, Trichi, Tamil Nadu.
- Institute of Alternative Medicine and Research, Calcutta.
- Gurukul Vishwavidyala, Vrindavan, Uttar Pradesh.

5
Community Colleges

There is a worldwide shift from conventional education system to competence based qualification system. With a view to make the skills acquired by the learners acceptable nationally, the curricula and system of certification should align with the National Occupation Standards. In order to facilitate offering of nationally standardised skill related programmes, the Government of India notified the National Skills Qualification Framework (NSQF) on 27 December 2013. It is a nationally integrated education and competency-based skill framework which provides for multiple pathways, both within vocational education and between general and vocational education, to link one level of learning to another higher level and enable learners to progress to higher levels from any starting point in the education and/or skill system. It permits individuals to accumulate their knowledge and skills and convert them, through testing and certification by the competent authorities, into higher level of certification which could be a certificate, diploma, advanced diploma, a degree, or a PG diploma in common parlance.

The Twelfth Five Year Plan Document of the Planning Commission has also laid a special emphasis on expansion of skill-based programmes in higher education. It recommends setting up of community colleges (CC) to serve multiple needs including: (i) career oriented education and skills to students interested in directly entering the workforce; (ii) training and education programmes for local employees; (iii) high-touch remedial education for secondary school graduates not ready to enroll in traditional colleges giving them a path to transfer to three or four years institutions; and (iv) general interest courses for the community for personal development and interest. The Plan Document also states that community colleges will be located to facilitate easy access to underprivileged students, and such colleges could either be established as affiliated colleges of universities or as entirely autonomous institutions.

The community colleges model, as envisaged, will be accessible to a large number of individuals of the community, offer low cost and high quality education locally, that encompasses both skills development as well as traditional coursework, thereby providing opportunities to the learners to move directly to the employment sector or more into higher education. It provides a flexible and open education system which also caters to community-based life-long learning needs. It has a synergistic relationship between the community, learner, and the job market.

The idea of establishing such colleges in the country was unanimously endorsed in the Conference of State Education Ministers held on 22 February 2012 and a Committee of Education Ministers of nine States was constituted to finalise the concept and framework of the community college scheme. The Committee, after wide consultations with all concerned, presented its report to the Government of India which received the concurrence of the state education ministers in the conference held on 6 June 2012. The Government of India accepted this report and decided to introduce this scheme during the Twelfth Five Year Plan.

Objectives

The main objectives of scheme are:

- To make higher education relevant to the learner and the community;
- To integrate relevant skills into the higher education system;
- To provide skill based education to students currently pursuing higher education, but actually interested in entering the workforce at the earliest opportunity;
- To provide employable and certifiable skill based on National Occupational Standards (NOSs) with necessary general education to Senior Secondary School pass-outs, with general education and/or vocational education background.
- To provide for upgradation and certification of traditional/ acquired skills of the learners irrespective of their age;
- To provide opportunities for community-based life-long learning by offering courses of general interest to the community for personal development and interest;
- To provide opportunities for vertical mobility to move to higher education in future;
- To offer bridge courses to certify holders of general/vocational education, so as to bring them at par with appropriate NSQF level;
- To provide entrepreneurial orientation along with require skill training for self-employment and entrepreneurship development.

Target/Eligibility

- The existing universities and colleges recognised by the UGC under section 2(f) and 12 (B) of UGC Act, 1956 and receiving general development assistance are eligible for implementing the Scheme of CC. The eligible universities and colleges may submit the proposal under the Scheme to the UGC.

- Self-financing institutions recognised under 2 (f) and 12 (B) of the UGC Act 1956, and not receiving general development assistance from the UGC may also be considered for approval under the scheme. They will abide by the guidelines of UGC as amended from time to time, but will not be entitled for any financial assistance under the scheme.
- The CC should not be a part of departments of a university/ college and it should have a separate entity within the institution.
- The government/society/trust or a company may also set up an independent community college, to implement the scheme and may offer courses as per the extant guidelines. The financial assistance to such community colleges will be governed as per the prevailing policy of the Commission.

Selection of Community Colleges

- While selecting the host institution for the CC, preference will be given to such colleges/universities which have proximity to the local industry partners, address local job requirements, and/ or youth aspirations of the region. Considering an autonomous college as host institution of the CC, may have added advantages for curriculum design, assessment and governance, and therefore, will be accorded priority under the scheme.
- The proposals will be invited in a prescribed Proforma from the interested universities/colleges by issuing a public notice on the UGC website. The proposals will be submitted within specified time, enclosing therewith a detailed DPR, proposed action plan, and itemized budget estimates. The proposal will be placed before an expert committee for evaluation. If required, UGC may a constitute a screening committee to shortlist the proposals. The UGC may also decide to arrange an interface of the institutions with the expert committee. Based on the merit of the proposal/interface, the expert committee will recommend institutions under the scheme.

Governance of Community Colleges

- Each CC will constitute a separate Board of Management (BoM) for its effective governance which will include representative(s) of the affiliating university, relevant industries, relevant Sector

Skills Council(s), and nodal officer(s) of CC. For the purpose of brevity, henceforth the word "industry" will be used to signify all the sectors of the economy including manufacturing, mining, services, agriculture, and allied sectors. The Vice Chancellor of the university or Chairman/President of the managing committee of the college will be the Chairman of the BoM and the Principal of the college shall be its Member-Secretary, and representatives from the partner industry and SSC as its Co-Chairpersons. BoM will meet periodically to review the functioning of the CC and, thereafter, as and when required, but at least once in six months.

- The Board of Studies (BoS) would have representatives from the college, university to which the college is affiliated, partner industries and relevant Sector Skill Council(s). The Principal of the CC shall be the Chairperson, while the local head of one of the partner industries shall be the Co-Chairperson. The BoS shall decide the programmes to be offered by the CC, depending upon the industry needs, skill gaps studies done by NSDC or such other credible sources, and finalise the curriculum in modular form in consultation with the partner industry and relevant SSC.

Programmes and Curricula in Community Colleges

- In order to make education relevant and to create "industry fit" skilled workforce, the CCs will have to be in constant dialogue with the industry and respective Sector Skill Council(s) so that they remain updated on the requirements of the workforce for the local economy. These colleges should also preserve and promote the cultural heritage of the region, be it art, craft, handicraft, music, architecture, or any such things, through appropriately designed curriculum with proper assurance of employment including self-employment and entrepreneurship development.
- As the CBSE and many other school boards are initiating skill based vocational courses with certification at NSQF Level 4 for students completing 10+2, there may be three types of learners getting admissions to first semester of CC courses:
  Category—1: Students who have already acquired NSQF certification level 4 in a particular industry sector and opted for admission in the courses under CC in the same trade with job role for which he/she previously certified at school level.
  Category—2: Students who have acquired NSQF certification level 4, but may like to change their trade and may enter into CC in a different industry sector.

Category—3: Students who have passed 10+2 examination with conventional schooling, without any background of vocational training.

The community college will develop curriculum and arrange for skill intensive training/teaching for the learners belonging to the category -2 and -3 as above during the first six months. They will be assessed and certified for NSQF level 4 of skill competency by concerned SSC at the end of first semester. However, learners belonging to category-1 will require such certification as they already have NSQF level-4 certificates in same industry sector/job role required for specified skill credits.

All the learners continuing to Diploma courses or further will be treated at par from second semester onwards. Students may exit after six months with a CC certificate (NSQF level-4) or may continue for diploma or advanced diploma level courses.

- The practical/hands-on portion of the skills component of the curriculum shall be transacted in face to face mode.
- The CCs will offer credit-based modular programmes, wherein banking of credits for skill and general education components shall be permitted so as to enable multiple exit and entry. This would enable the learner to seek employment after any level of Course and join back as and when feasible to upgrade her/his qualification/skill competency either to move higher in her/his job or in the higher education system. This will also provide the learner an opportunity for vertical mobility to second year of B. Voc. degree programme after a one-year diploma and to third year of B. Voc. degree programmes after two-year advanced diploma course.
- Recognition of Prior Learning (RPL): CC may also provide for Recognition of Prior Learning (RPL) framework for job roles at NSQF level-4 onwards by conducting assessment and certification through respective SSC(s)/Directorate of General of Employment and Training (DGET).
- Relevance of programmes offered along with that of the curriculum is important. Therefore, monitoring, evaluation, and updating of the curriculum needs to be done periodically in consultation with all stakeholders, particularly the industries and SSCs, keeping in view their requirements and changes in NOSs. The CCs shall incorporate these as a continuous and dynamic process, inbuilt in their system.
- All the programmes offered under CC will be full time courses and should not be conducted as add-on programmes.

- The CCs may like to appropriate use Technology to improve the effectiveness of the delivery of courses.

Infrastructure and Faculty in Community Colleges

- The CCs approved under existing institutions with UGC funding shall operate in the identified building and premises of existing colleges/universities. They may use industry sites and/or National Skill Development Corporation (NSDC) approved training partners whenever required for imparting necessary skills. The CCs set-up as under 3.4 should have proper building/ infrastructure created for the purpose before starting the courses. Each CC needs to have adequate laboratory/workshop facilities for face-to-face delivery of skill and hands-on practice either owned, arranged through tie up with the partner industry, or NSDC approved training partners.
- In the CCs, the faculty would typically consist of existing faculty with the institution and a pool of guest/visiting/part-time faculty taken from either the industry or open market or National Skill Development Corporation (NSDC) approved training partners for imparting skills. The mix of permanent/part-time/guest/ visiting/adjunct faculty would be decided by the host institution with approval of BoM, depending on the local needs and availability. The laboratory staff/instructors will be planned and approved by BoM, as per the need. Remuneration to the guest faculty may be paid under this scheme at the locally prevalent rates, but not exceeding the rates prescribed by UGC. However, there will be no cap on the total payment to a particular faculty in a month.
- The CC may also have a part time nodal officer for overall coordination of all the courses, liaising with the industry, SSCs, and other stakeholders. The host institution may not insist on the prescribed minimum workload for the faculty, who will be given the responsibility of a nodal officer.
- For guest lecturer/part time faculty etc., sufficient knowledge of the sector, training/ teaching skills along with relevant industry experience of minimum 2-3 years is desirable.
- The standard of knowledge and skills of the faculty also need continuous updating through appropriate training and exposure programmes in collaboration with the university, technical education institutes, SSCs, and industry.

Admission, Fee, and Scholarships

- The minimum educational qualification for admission into CC under this scheme will be class 12 pass or equivalent from any recognised board or university.
- Equal weightage should be given to vocational subjects at +2 levels while considering the students for admission into CC for recognition of skills credits.
- While deciding criteria for admission into any particular trade, the CCs will consider students having background in relevant stream at 10+2 level. For admission to the programmes offered by the CCs preference should be given to the learners living in the local community. Reservation to SC, ST, OBC, and PwD categories will be available as per the extant national/state policy. There shall be no age bar for admission in the community colleges.

6
Ten Best Colleges
The Week-*Hansa Research Survey, 2016*

Arts Colleges

Rank 2016		
1.	Lady Shri Ram College for Women	Delhi
2.	St. Stephen's College	Delhi
3.	Loyola College	Chennai
4.	St. Xavier's College	Mumbai
5.	Hindu College	Delhi
6.	Madras Christian College (MCC)	Chennai
7.	Miranda House	Delhi
8.	St. Xavier's College	Kolkata
9.	Christ University	Bengaluru
10.	Hans Raj College	Delhi

Science Colleges

Rank 2016		
1.	St. Stephen's College	Delhi
2.	Loyola College	Chennai
3.	Hindu College	Delhi
4.	Hans Raj College	Delhi
5.	St. Xavier's College	Mumbai
6.	St. Xavier's College	Kolkata
7.	Madras Christian College (MCC)	Chennai
8.	Fergusson College	Pune
9.	Ramjas College	Delhi
10.	Miranda House	Delhi

Commerce Colleges

Rank 2016		
1.	Shri Ram College of Commerce	Delhi
2.	Loyola College	Chennai
3.	Lady Shri Ram College for Women	Delhi
4.	St. Xavier's College	Kolkata

5.	Hindu College	Delhi
6.	Christ University	Bangalore
7.	Hans Raj College	Delhi
8.	Madras Christian College (MCC)	Chennai
9.	Narsee Monjee College of Commerce and Economic	Mumbai
10.	Ethiraj College for Women	Chennai

Engineering Colleges

Rank 2016, Government (G) Private (P)

1.	G Indian Institute of Technology (IIT)	Delhi
2.	G Indian Institute of Technology (IIT)	Mumbai
3.	G Indian Institute of Technology (IIT)	Kharagpur
4.	G Indian Institute of Technology (IIT)	Chennai
5.	G Indian Institute of Technology (IIT)	Kanpur
6.	G Indian Institute of Technology (IIT)	Roorkee
7.	P Birla Institute of Technology & Science (BITS)	Pilani
8.	G Indian Institute of Technology (IIT)	Guwahati
9.	G Delhi Technological University (DTU)	Delhi
10.	G Indian Institute of Technology (Banaras Hindu University)	Varanasi

Private Engineering Colleges

Rank 2016

1.	Birla Institute of Technology & Science (BITS)	Pilani
2.	International Institute of Information & Technology (IIIT)	Hyderabad
3.	Birla Institute of Technology (BIT), Mesra	Ranchi
4.	Vellore Institute of Technology (VIT)	Vellore
5.	Thapar University	Patiala
6.	Veermata Jijabai Technology Institute (VJTI)	Mumbai
7.	RV College of Engineering	Bengaluru
8.	PSG College of Technology	Coimbatore
9.	Manipal Institute of Technology	Manipal
10.	BMS College of Engineering	Bengaluru

Medical Colleges

Rank 2016, Government (G) Private (P)

1.	G All India Institute of Medical Sciences (AIIMS)	Delhi
2.	P Christian Medical College	Vellore
3.	G Armed Forces Medical College (AFMC)	Pune
4.	G Jawaharlal Institute of Postgraduate Medical Education & Research (JIPMER)	Puducherry
5.	Maulana Azad Medical College (MAMC)	Delhi
6.	Institute of Medical Science	Varanasi
7.	Grant Medical College	Mumbai
8.	Lady Hardinge Medical College	Delhi
9.	Kasturba Medical College	Manipal
10.	Bangalore Medical College & Research Institute	Bengaluru

Private Medical Colleges

Rank 2016

1.	Christian Medical College (CMC)	Vellore
2.	Kasturba Medical College (KMC)	Manipal
3.	St John's Medical College	Bengaluru
4.	Sri Ramachandra Medical College & Research Institute	Chennai
5.	Amrita Institute of Medical Sciences Research Centre	Kochi
6.	Mahatma Gandhi Institute of Medical Sciences	Wardha
7.	Dayanand Medical College & Hospital (DMC)	Ludhiana
8.	Christian Medical College (CMC)	Ludhiana
9.	Kasturba Medical College (KMC)	Mangalore
10.	MS Ramaia Medical College	Bengaluru

Law Colleges

Rank 2016

1.	G National Law School of India University (NLSIU)	Bengaluru
2.	G National Academic of Legal Studies & Research (NALSAR) University of Law	Hyderabad

3.	G Faculty of Law, University of Delhi	Delhi
4.	G National Law Institute University (NLIU)	Bhopal
5.	G National Law University	Jodhpur
6.	G The West Bengal National University of Judicial Science (WBNUJS)	Kolkata
7.	G Gujarat National Law University (GNLU)	Gandinagar
8.	G Law School, Banaras Hindu University	Varanasi
9.	P ILS Law College	Pune
10.	G Government Law College	Mumbai

Private Law Colleges

Rank 2016

1.	ILS Law College	Pune
2.	Symbiosis Law School	Pune
3.	Amity Law School, GGSIP University Delhi	Noida
4.	Army Institute of Law (AIL)	Mohali
5.	New Law College, Bharati Vidyapeeth Deemed University	Pune
6.	Institute of Law, Nirma University	Ahmedabad
7.	School of Law, Christ University	Bengaluru
8.	CMR Law School	Bengaluru
9.	Kerala Law Academy Law College	Thiruvananthapuram
10.	KC Law College (Kishinchand Chellaran Law College)	Mumbai

Hotel Management Colleges

Rank 2016 Government (G) Private (P)

1.	G Institute of Hotel Management, Catering & Nutrition, Pusa	Delhi
2.	P Welcome Group Graduate School of Hotel Administration	Manipal
3.	G Institute of Hotel Management, Catering Technology & Applied Nutrition	Mumbai
4.	G Institute of Hotel Management Catering Technology & Applied Nutrition	Chennai
5.	G Institute of Hotel Management	Bengaluru

6.	P Institute of Hotel Management	Aurangabad
7.	P Institute of Hotel Management, Catering Technology & Applied Nutrition	Kolkata
8.	G Institute of Hotel Management, Catering Technology & Applied Nutrition	Hyderabad
9.	G Institute of Hotel Management, Catering Technology	Thiruvananthapuram
10.	G Institute of Hotel Management	Ahmedabad

Private Hotel Management Colleges

Rank 2016		
1.	Welcome group Graduate School of Hotel Administration	Manipal
2.	Institute of Hotel Management	Aurangabad
3.	Amity Institute of Hotel Management, Catering Technology	Bengaluru
4.	Banarsidas Chandiwala Institute of Hotel Management and Catering Technology	Delhi
5.	International Institute of Hotel Management	Kolkata
6.	Department of Hotel Management, Christ University	Bengaluru
7.	Acharya Institute of Management & Sciences	Bengaluru
8.	NSHM School of Hotel Management	Durgapur
9.	Amity School of Hospitality	Noida
10.	Amrapali Institute of Hotel Management	Nainital

Fashion Technology Colleges

Rank 2016		
1.	National Institute of Fashion Technology (NIFT)	Delhi
2.	National Institute of Design (NID)	Ahmedabad
3.	National Institute of Fashion Technology (NIFT)	Mumbai
4.	Pearl Academy	Delhi
5.	National Institute of Fashion Technology (NIFT)	Bengaluru

6.	National Institute of Fashion Technology (NIFT)	Chennai
7.	National Institute of Fashion Technology (NIFT)	Kolkata
8.	National Institute of Fashion Technology (NIFT)	Hyderabad
9.	Amity School of Fashion Technology	Noida
10.	Raffles Millennium International	Delhi

Social Work Colleges

Rank 2016

1.	Tata Institute of Social Science (TISS)	Mumbai
2.	Department of Social Work, University of Delhi	Delhi
3.	Department of Social Work, Jamia Millia Islamia	Delhi
4.	Madras School of Social Work	Chennai
5.	Colleges of Social Work, Nirmala Niketan	Mumbai
6.	Loyola College of Social Sciences	Thiruvananthapuram
7.	Karve Institute of Social Service	Pune
8.	Department of Social Work, Christ University	Bengaluru
9.	Faculty of Social Work, MS University of Baroda	Vadodara
10.	Roda Mistry College of Social Work & Research Centre	Hyderabad

7
Academic Staff Colleges

The National Policy on Education (NPE) 1986 in its programme of action makes a pointed reference to the crucial link between teacher's motivation and the quality of education.

The NPE recognised the need for improving the quality of teaching and proposed to provide opportunities for professional and career development, so that teachers may fulfill their role and responsibility within the system of higher education. It was proposed to enhance their motivation, skills, and knowledge through systematic orientation in specific subjects, techniques and methodologies, and thereby inculcate in them the right kind of values that would in turn encourage them to take initiatives for innovative creative work.

Keeping the above objectives in view, the following steps were proposed:

(a) To organise specially designed orientation programmes (OPs) in pedagogy, educational psychology and philosophy, and socio-economic and political concerns for all new entrants at the level of lecturers;

(b) To organise such orientation programmes and refresher courses (RCs) for serving teachers, covering every teacher at least once in three to five years;

(c) To organise specially designed orientation programmes/refresher courses in IT for new entrants as well as for in-service teachers; and

(d) To encourage teachers to participate in seminars, symposia, workshop, etc.

In order to achieve the above, a scheme of setting up Academic Staff Colleges (ASCs) in suitable universities in the country was initiated by the University Grants Commission (UGC).

Objectives of the Academic Staff College

The objectives of the Academic Staff College (ASC) are to enable newly appointed lecturers to:

- Understand the significance of education in general, and higher education in particular, in the global and Indian context;
- Understand the linkages between education and socio-economic and cultural development, with particular reference to the Indian polity where democracy, secularism, and social equity are the basic tenets of society;
- Acquire and improve art of teaching at the college/university level to achieve goals of higher education;
- Keep abreast of the latest development in their specific subjects;
- Understand the organisation and management of a college/ university and to perceive the role of teachers in the total system;
- Utilise opportunities for development of personality, initiative, and creativity; and
- Promote computer literacy as well use of ICT in teaching and learning process.

Philosophy

The ASCs' main philosophy is to keep in mind that the teacher is central to the system. While it is universally accepted that the teacher is the pivot of the educational system, our system does not provide adequate opportunities for their professional development. It is, therefore, necessary to develop inbuilt mechanisms to provide opportunities for teachers within the framework of knowledge society. It is also accepted that a teacher must not be confined only to transmitting information. She/he must also orient students to meet the challenges of life, to become not merely trained professionals, but also better citizens.

It was believed in the past that a college/university teacher learnt the art of teaching on the job by emulating outstanding models such as his/ her own teachers or senior colleagues. The stock-in-trade of the college/ university teacher has always motivated the students. Today, it is no longer adequate to expect a newly appointed teacher to acquire the art of teaching by emulating his/her peers.

Expansion of the Education System

From the very beginning our country had moved away from an elitist approach to higher education. We can truly claim that our system of higher education is mass based. This is a great achieved in a developing country.

While the expansion of the system of higher education is creditable, it has been achieved at a cost to itself. As the system moved away from the idea of higher education of the select few to higher education for all, there has been a decline in overall standards. Initially this was inevitable, but is nonetheless disturbing, especially when one considers the rapid advances being made in knowledge and the explosion of information worldwide. This trend must be reversed. It places greater responsibilities on teachers, and we owe it to them and to ourselves to make it possible for them to perform better in these changing times.

Educational Technology and Orientation in IT

New methods of teaching and educational technology along with development in information technology (IT) have made the job of a teacher both exact and demanding. Now, it has been decided to give a bigger thrust to e-content development. In order to create Internet savvy as well as computer literate teachers, to create e-content assemblers and creators, the University Grants Commission is launching specially designed orientation programmes/refresher courses in these subjects.

The special orientation programme in IT is to create Internet literate people from amongst new entrants as well as in-service teachers and to make them familiar with use of software tools irrespective of the subject/ discipline they are teaching. Acquisition of knowledge is a two-way process between the teachers and the taught and, therefore, collectively they must advance the frontiers of knowledge.

Knowledge Expansion

Furthermore, there has been knowledge explosion in every discipline. A college/university teacher has to continuously update his/her chosen field of expertise, or run the risk of becoming totally outdated in a very short period of time.

While the really motivated and industrious teachers use their own resources to keep themselves abreast of new knowledge and to train themselves in the latest processes, methodologies and techniques of teaching, it is necessary to provide systematic and organised orientation programmes for the large number of teachers at the college and university level.

Orientation of Newly Appointed Lecturers

The concept of an orientation programme emphasises teachers as agents of socio-economic change and national development, and underlines the need to make them skill-oriented teachers.

The philosophy and objectives of the orientation courses are significantly different from the traditional B.Ed. and M.Ed. programmes.

Flexible Orientation Programme

The orientation programmes envisaged under this scheme must not be rigid. Under the programme, it is intended to inculcate in young lecturers the quality of self-reliance through their awareness of the social, intellectual, and moral environment. The programme should enable the teachers to discover themselves and their potential through a positive appreciation of their role in the total social, intellectual, and moral universe within which they function and of which they are important members. Only in a country where teachers are able to fulfill their responsibility with awareness and confidence, does the education system become relevant and dynamic.

Orientation Relevant to Indian Conditions

The orientation programmes must engender in the teacher awareness of the problems that the Indian society faces, and that education is the solution to these problems.

It must also focus on the achievement of the goals set out in the Indian Constitution. Matters relating to subject knowledge and pedagogy, although important in them, would only become meaningful when understood in the total context of national development.

Active Involvement of Decision-makers and Leaders in Higher Education

It is equally important to recognise that no scheme for orientation of teachers can succeed if the decision-makers and administrators of higher education do not understand the importance of such schemes.

Therefore, along with the courses for newly appointed teachers, orientation programmes for heads of departments, principals, deans, officers, etc. must be organised with a view to acquainting the top-level administrators with what teachers are learning in the orientation programmes. This exposure will enable the decision-makers to actively participate in the scheme. At the same time, these administrators would be able to modify their own roles as supervisors of higher education by demanding newer role behaviour from the teachers.

Exchange of Ideas in Academic and Educational Environment

An Academic Staff College with adequate number of teachers and resource persons is required to create a good academic and educational environment in the university. This will also help the UGC-ASC/RCCs (Refresher Course Centres) to have a place for exchanging ideas and topics of interest in the subject area. Lectures from participating teachers may be arranged for mutual benefit. The UGC-ASC/RCC may also request the relevant university department to organise lectures by eminent resource persons for the benefit of other students and researchers. This may create a decent amount of academic interest in the UGC-ASC/RCC. The Director/

Coordinator of the UGC-ASC/RCC should prepare a plan well in advance, including the list of names of eminent persons to be invited as resource persons, for the concerned department/school to take suitable measures.

Function of an ASC

The functions of an Academic Staff College will be to plan, organise, implement, monitor, and evaluate orientation courses for newly appointed college/university lecturers. An ASC will also organise refresher courses for serving teachers, and orientation programmes for senior administrators and heads of departments, principals, officers, etc. Specifically, an ASC will:

- Formulate a programme of orientation along broad guidelines given above;
- Identify resources persons in various fields of specialisation for running the orientation programmes and refresher courses, and familiarise such resource persons with the philosophy and guidelines for the courses;
- Set up a documentation-centre-cum-library for reference and source materials necessary for the courses;
- Produce specially designed material required for effective implementation of the courses;
- Organise, monitor, and evaluate the courses for teachers;
- Create a culture of learning and self-improvement among teachers so that it becomes an integral part of the education system at the tertiary level;
- Organise orientation programmes for senior administrators, heads of departments, principals, deans, and other decision-makers of familiarise them with the appropriate modification of the management systems at various levels;
- Provide opportunities for teachers in service to exchange experiences with their peers and to mutually learn from each other;
- Provide a forum for serving teachers to keep themselves abreast of the latest advances in various subjects;
- Provide opportunities to further widen their knowledge, and to pursue research studies;
- Provide an introduction to new methods and innovations in higher education so that the participants can in turn develop their own innovative methods of instruction;
- Publish relevant research papers etc. for enhancing the teaching and research capabilities of teachers; and

- Conduct capability enhancement programmes for non academic staff so as to strengthen the teaching-learning environment.

The concept of in-service training and continuing education in India was first mooted by the Radhakrishnan Commission in 1949. The commission stated that "teacher competence is one of the crucial factors and [they] should be given continuous training for the improvement of their performance." Subsequently, the first National Conference of the Principals of Training Colleges held in Baroda in 1951, identified three types of courses to cater to different interest group among the teachers—(i) Short term courses for untrained teachers; (ii) Refresher courses for trained teachers; and (iii) advanced level training in the field of their interest. The Kothari Commission in 1964-66 also reiterated the importance of in-service teachers' training in higher education by pointing out the necessity of regular orientation courses every year for a few weeks in every college. As a follow-up, the UGC created some facilities in the form of seminars, fellowships, summer schools, and orientation courses for teachers in higher education.

National Education Policy, 1986

The National Policy of Education (NPE), 1986 pointed out that teachers are not given adequate opportunities for professional and career development, and are not sufficiently oriented to the experiential methodologies for teaching/learning, or the value of innovative and creative work to fulfill their roles and responsibilities effectively. In order to overcome these deficiencies, it was proposed that specially designed orientation and refresher courses be organised for teachers as 'in-service training'. As a result, the academic staff orientation scheme, later known as Academic Staff College scheme was initiated by the UGC in 1987.

Inception of Academic Staff Colleges

The main philosophy behind the establishment of Academic Staff Colleges is to provide adequate opportunities for the professional development of teachers in higher education system which is ever expanding. These colleges are seen as inbuilt mechanisms to provide opportunities for teachers within the framework of knowledge explosion worldwide in the recent past. It is impossible to cope with the vast amounts of new information, technology and methods, without resorting to acceleration and organised modes of continuing education. Academic Staff Colleges provide an opportunity for the teachers to update their knowledge in subject, technology, and new methods in various areas of studies. In the first phase 45 Academic Staff Colleges (ASCs) were established during the Seventh Five Year Plan period (1985-90), which has now increased to 66 spread across the country.

NAAC Review of ASCs

To gauge the effectiveness of Academic Staff College programmes, the Ministry of Human Resource Development and University Grants Commission organised a review of all Academic Staff Colleges through National Assessment and Accreditation Council in 2012.

Observations

After a vast nationwide survey, and based on peer team ASC visit reports, the NAAC prepared a 'Report of NAAC Review Committee on Academic Staff Colleges in 2012. NAAC observed that—only 19.69 percent of the ASCs are performing according to the objectives set by the UGC. The others could not perform because of the constraints at policy level and system level.

Recommendations

Considering the challenges and constraints confronted by the ASCs in satisfactory functioning, the NAAC Review Committee unanimously felt need to strengthen and recommended certain measures to MHRD and UGC for consideration. The recommendations are—The Academic Staff Colleges (ASCs) be renamed Human Resource Development Centres (HRDCs) to cater to the needs of academic, research, and administrative staff of the higher education sector; Need to add more HRDCs considering the size and magnitude of Indian higher education system.

How to Strengthen ASCs

Some measures for strengthening ASCs are:

- The best training practices can be benchmarked against the practices prevailing in the world class teachers' training institutions so as to make the ASCs professionally competitive;
- ASCs can also be thought of working as a link between academia and industry. Persons from the industry can be trained at ASCs. They can also work as a centre to fetch consultancy projects for the host university and the client institutions in the catchment area;
- A consistent communication should be maintained with the client institutions by ASCs so as to get sufficient number of participants;
- Competent resource persons are key for the success of ASCs. Certain parameters need to be chalked out so as to ensure that only the right people are invited as resources persons;

- Training calendar needs to be prepared in a timely manner and widely published;
- Training objectives must be in line with vision and mission of ASC and host university, and other participating institutions;
- The syllabi/contents of the orientation programme and refresher course must be reviewed at a reasonable interval to keep pace with new developments;
- Enough institutional support should be extended to the trained employees to put learning into practice;
- Changing nomenclature from ASC to HRDC by UGC can only be justified when there is ample concern for effective functioning of ASCs/HRDCs on the part of sponsoring agency, the UGC;
- Director ASC ought to have the qualities—D-Devoted, I-Involved, R-Rigorous, E-Energetic, T-Trained, O-Orator, R-Resourceful. Director should have strong managerial skills in conceptualization, human relations, technical, communication, decision making, motivational ability, and problem solving. He/she should possess a strong sense of commitment and be good at planning, organising, directing and controlling;
- The guidelines prescribed by NAAC are quite rigorous and comprehensive. If ASCs duly adhere to them carefully and considerately, their functioning would undoubtedly be efficacious.

New Initiatives of UGC in Twelfth Plan

The new Twelfth Plan Guidelines of UGC announced restructuring of Academic Staff Colleges to revitalise the staff development programmes. The ASCs have been renamed Human Resource Development Centre (HRDC). In addition Regional Centres for Capacity Building (RCCB) have also been created. Several initiatives to create linkages and sharing of resources with premier institutions/research labs for staff development have been created.

The Twelfth Five Year Plan aptly emphasised the concerns of a large pool of non-permanent faculty involved in higher education and suggested improving their recruitment practices, performance, working conditions, and also faculty training. Twelfth Plan document further suggested supplementing ASCs with Teaching Learning Centres (TLCs) in order to perfectly deliver the job, which ASCs could not do in the past two decades. Establishment of 50 specialised TLC training centres have been proposed during the Twelfth Plan period. The success of reforms depends on adequate implementation of the proposed guidelines by the ASCs (HRDCs/RCCBs) and UGC.

8
National Institutional Ranking Framework

The process of framing the National Institutional Ranking Framework (NIRF) began on October 9, 2014 with the constitution of a 16-member core committee under the chairmanship of Secretary, Ministry of Human Resource Development. The terms of reference of the committee were to suggest a reliable, transparent, and authentic national framework for performance measurement, ranking of institutions for higher education, and to recommend institutional mechanisms, processes, and timelines for implementation of the National Institutional Ranking Framework. The framework was given a final shape subsequent to intense discussions and deliberations during a series of meetings of the committee, and exchange with peers and stakeholders through many online discussions.

The National Institutional Ranking Frameworks (NIRF) for engineering and management categories were unveiled by the Minister for Human Resource Development on September 29, 2015. Soon after, the NIRF for ranking of the pharmacy and architecture institutions as well as for colleges and universities were released. The NIRF envisaged separate rankings for different categories of institutions in their own respective peer groups. Further, within each discipline, there was provision for separate ranking in two categories—institutions that are engaged in research and teaching (Category A), and those engaged mainly in teaching (Category B).

The final framework identified nearly 22 parameters under five major heads, several of them are similar to those employed globally, such as excellence in teaching, learning and research. However, there are a few which are India-centric, reflecting aspirations of the rising number of young people of a vast nation. Country-specific parameters relevant to the Indian situation include regional and international diversity, outreach, gender equity and inclusion of disadvantaged sections of society.

NIRF Parameters for Ranking of Institutions

The NIRF provides for ranking of institutions under five broad generic parameters, namely: i) teaching, learning, and resources; ii) research, consulting, and collaborative performance; iii) graduate outcome; iv) outreach and inclusivity; and v) perception.

Teaching, Learning, and Resources (TLR)

Faculty Student Ratio (FSR)—permanent faculty
Faculty Student Ratio—visiting faculty
Metric for Faculty with Ph.D and Experience (FQE)
Metric for Library, Studio, and Laboratory Facilities (LL)
Metric for Sports and Extracurricular Facilities (SEC)
Metric for Teaching and Innovation (TI)

Research Productivity, Impact, and IPR (RPII)

Combined Metric for Publications (PU)
Combined Metric for Citations (CI)
Intellectual Property Right and Patents (IPR)
Percent of Collaborative Publications and Patents (CP)
Footprint of Projects and Professional Practice (FPPP)

Graduation Outcomes (GO)

Performance in University Examinations (PUE)
Performance in Public Examinations (PPE)
Performance in placement, higher studies, and entrepreneurship (PHE)
Mean salary for employment (MS)

Outreach and Inclusivity (OI)

Outreach footprint—continuing education, service (CES)
Percentage of students from other states/countries (RD)
Percentage of women students and faculty (WS)
Percentage of economically and socially disadvantaged students (ESDS)
Faculties for physically challenged/ differently abled persons

Perception (PR)

Process for peer rating in category (PR) and applications to seat ratio (SR)

Collaborators

National Board of Accreditation (NBA)

The National Board of Accreditation (NBA) was assigned the responsibility for inviting applications for ranking of institutions for all the six disciplines using NIRF framework, and for anchoring the effort for "Indian Rankings 2016." NBA also serves the Implementation Core Committee (ICC) constituted by the MHRD as well as all other committees set up to examine the data for all five sets of parameters under each of the six disciplines.

All India Council for Technical Education (AICTE)

The AICTE was instrumental in providing authenticated data on institutions that are approved for offering graduate and postgraduate level courses in four disciplines, namely engineering, management, pharmacy, and architecture. The AICTE also encouraged institutions to apply for ranking under NIRF framework.

University Grants Commission (UGC)

The UGC provided authenticated data on colleges and universities under its purview. The UGC also encouraged universities and colleges to apply for ranking under NIRF framework.

Information and Library Network Centre

The services of INFLIBNET Centre were taken for developing the NIRF web portal as well as for providing data on publications, citations, and collaborations.

Academic Partners

Web of Science (Thomson Reuters), Scoops (Elsevier) and Indian Citation Index was used for retrieving data on publications, citations, and collaborations. These three publishers contacted to help out the process of retrieving data for some of the institutions who had applied for ranking through NIRF.

Analysis of Ranking Results

Engineering (Category A-Research and Teaching)

The IITs (old and new) lead the league tables for engineering (Category A-Research and Teaching) occupying the first eleven positions. Predictably, the first five IITs, established during 1950s and early 1960s, take the first five positions led by IIT Madras in the top slot with a weighted score of 89.42, followed by IIT Bombay, IIT Kharagpur, IIT Delhi, IIT Kanpur with weighted scores of 87.67, 83.91, 82.03, and 81.07 respectively. In addition to the five old IITs, five more IITs secured distinction in terms of weighted score, viz., IIT Roorkee (rank 6; weighted score: 78.68), IIT Hyderabad (rank 7; weighted score: 77.23), IIT Gandhinagar (rank 8; weighted score: 75.21), IIT Ropar (rank 9; weighted score: 74.89) and IIT Patna (rank 10; weighted score: 74.68). However, IIT Guwahati with a weighted score of 74.63 missed the distinction marks by a whisker. Remaining five IITs are interspersed between ranks 14 and 26. It is encouraging to note that 12 NITs find their places amongst first 50 institutions led by NIT, Tiruchirappalli at rank 12 and 10 NITs are interspersed between ranks 51 to 92. The Vellore Institute of Technology (rank 13) and PSG College of Technology, Coimbatore (rank 24) get the distinction of being two private institutions occupying top slots amongst the IITs and NITs.

Rising Stars: IIT Hyderabad, IIT Gandhinagar, IIT Ropar, IIT Patna (ranks 7 to 10), IIT Indore (rank 16), IIT Mandi (rank 20), IIT Jodhpur (rank 25) and IIT Bhubaneswar (rank 26), set up in 2008-2009, can truly be considered as rising stars since all these new IITs secured positions within the first thirty slots. Generally, institutions funded by the central government directly are head and shoulders above the others, be they privately-funded or state government funded institutions. While this is clearly on expected lines, it also brings out the significant gap between these institutions and the others. Clearly there are deeper lessons to learn here. Having said that, there are interesting new institutions, which are slowly but surely creeping into the top slots. We should certainly watch out for them in the years to come. It is also possible to argue that some of the parameters like funding for library and laboratories, load the dice in their favour, and it would be interesting to see how some of these institutions perform on "outputs" and "outcomes" on a per rupee investment scale.

Management (Category A-Research and Teaching)

Predictably IIMs hog the top slots amongst the management institutions. The first six ranks are occupied by IIMs led by IIM Bangalore at 1st rank with a weighted score of 93.042, closely followed by IIM Ahmadabad (rank 2), IIM Calcutta (rank 3) and IIM Lucknow (rank 4) with weighted scores of 89.92, 87.45, and 86.13 respectively. IIM Udaipur and IIM Kozhikode are at 5 and 6 positions respectively with weighted score of 84.23 and 81.97 respectively. The remaining seven IIMs are interspersed between ranks 10 and 28. International Management Institute, New Delhi, a private institution is at rank 7 with a weighted score of 81.78.

In addition to top seven management institutions mentioned above, seven more management institutions secured distinction in terms of weighted scores. These institution are: Indian institute of Forest Management (rank 8; weighted score: 81.01); Department of Management Studies, IIT Kanpur (rank 9; weighted score: 79.44); IIM Indore (rank 10; weighted score: 78.68); Management Studies, IIT Kanpur (rank 9; weighted score: 79.44); IIM Indore (rank 10; weighted score: 78.63); Management Development Institute (rank 11; weighted score: 77.45); International Management Institute, Kolkata (rank 12; weighted score: 77.14); Xavier Labour Relations Institute (XLRI) Jemshedpore (rank 13; weighted score: 75.30) and IIM Tiruchirappalli (rank 14; weighted score: 75.24).

Management Schools of IIT Kanpur (rank 9), Vellore Institute of Technology (rank 17) and Birla Institute of Technology, Pilani (rank 25) have also claimed top slots amongst the management institutions. Several private management institutions also claim top slots in the ranking including: International Management Institute, New Delhi (rank 7), Tyagaraja School of Management Madurai (rank 15) and S.P. Jain Institute of Management and Research Mumbai (rank 16).

Rising Stars: Indian Institute of Management, Udaipur (rank 5), International Management Institute, Kolkata (rank 12), Indian Institute of Management, Tiruchirappalli (rank 14), Indian Institute of Management (rank 20), Indian Institute of Management, Kashipur (rank 21), and Indian Institute of Management, Ranchi (rank 28), set up between 2007 and 2011, which have taken positions in the top 30 slots, are amongst the rising stars.

Pharmacy (Category A—Research and Teaching)

Low scores characterise the league table for Pharmacy (Category A—Research and Teaching). Manipal College of Pharmaceutical Sciences Manipal at rank 1 with a weighted score of 77.87 closely followed by University Institute of Pharmaceutical Sciences, Chandigarh at 2 rank weighed score of 77.10. Jamia Hamdard (rank 3), Poona College of Pharmacy, Pune (rank 4) and Institute of Pharmacy, Nirma University (rank 5) obtained weighted scores of 71.39, 70.93, and 69.76 respectively.

Universities

Indian Institute of Science (IISc), Bengaluru is ranked as the first amongst universities with a weighted score of 91.81 closely followed by Institute of Chemical Technology, Mumbai, formerly University Department of Chemical Technology (UDCT), University of Mumbai, which stands at rank 2 with a weighted score of 87.58. Ranks 3 to 8 are occupied by the traditional, multi-disciplinary universities led by Jawaharlal Nehru University (JNU), New Delhi (rank 3), followed by University of Hyderabad (rank 4), Tezpur University (rank 5), University of Delhi (rank 6), Banaras Hindu University (rank 7), and Indian Institute of Space Science and Technology Thiruvananthapuram (rank 8) with weighted scores ranging from 86.46 (JNU) to 78.83 (IISST). Birla Institute of Technology and Sciences (BITS) Pilani at 9th position with a weighted score of 76.85 is closely followed by Aligarh Muslim University at rank 10 with a weighted score of 76.62.

Visva Bharati (rank 11; weighted score: 76.11) and Punjab University (rank 12; weighted score: 76.07) also secured a distinction in terms of weighted score while two other universities namely, Pondicherry University (rank 13; weighted score: 74.44) and Bharathiar University (rank 14; weighted score: 74.32) come very close.

It is noteworthy that King George Medical University, Lucknow (rank 16), Bidhan Chandra Krishi Vishvavidyalaya (rank 31), Tamil Nadu Veterinary and Animal Science University (rank 36), Tamil Nadu Agricultural University (rank 39), are discipline-specific institutions performing research and imparting education in medical, agricultural, veterinary, animal sciences, etc. could find their places amongst multi-disciplinary universities and technological institutions. This demonstrates that the ranking parameters and the metric are generic enough to suit all kinds of educational institutions.

Computation of Scores and Ranking: Top 25 in Each Category

Rankings are based on the information and data provided by the institutions. Data on publications and citations have been taken from standard indexing and citation sources, viz., Scopus (Elsevier Science), Web of Sciences (Thomson Reuters) and the Indian Citation Index. Perception data has been compiled from inputs from general public and peers. NIRF has done limited validations of the data. However, responsibility for the accuracy and authenticity of the data lies with the concerned institutions supplying it. Data are available on the NIRF portal.

India Rankings 2016: Engineering Category "A"

Name	*City*	*Rank*
Indian Institute of Technology, Madras	Chennai	1
Indian Institute of Technology, Bombay	Bombay	2
Indian Institute of Technology, Kharagpur	Kharagpur	3
Indian Institute of Technology, Delhi	New Delhi	4
Indian Institute of Technology, Kanpur	Kanpur	5
Indian Institute of Technology, Roorkee	Roorkee	6
Indian Institute of Technology, Hyderabad	Hyderabad	7
Indian Institute of Technology, Gandhinagar	Ahmedabad	8
Indian Institute of Technology, Ropar	Rupnagar	9
Indian Institute of Technology, Patna	Patna	10
Indian Institute of Technology, Guwahati	Guwahati	11
National Institute of Technology, Tiruchirappalli	Tiruchirappalli	12
Vellore Institute of Technology, Vellore	Vellore	13
Indian Institute of Technology (BHU), Varanasi	Varanasi	14
Sardar Vallabhbhai National Institute of Technology, Surat	Surat	15
Indian Institute of Technology, Indore	Indore	16
Birla Institute of Technology, Ranchi	Ranchi	17
Visvesvarya National Institute of Technology, Nagpur	Nagpur	18
National Institute of Technology, Rourkela	Rourkela	19
Indian Institute of Technology, Mandi	Mandi	20
College of Engineering, Pune	Pune	21
National Institute of Technology, Karnataka	Mangalore	22
Motilal Nehru National Institute of Technology, Allahabad	Allahabad	23

PSG College of Technology, Coimbatore	Coimbatore	24
Indian Institute of Technology, Jodhpur	Jodhpur	25

India Ranking 2016: Management Category "A"

Name	*City*	*Rank*
Indian Institute of Management, Bengaluru	Bengaluru	1
Indian Institute of Management, Ahmedabad	Ahmedabad	2
Indian Institute of Management, Calcutta	Kolkata	3
Indian Institute of Management, Lucknow	Lucknow	4
Indian Institute of Management, Udaipur	Udaipur	5
Indian Institute of Management, Kozhikode	Kozhikode	6
International Management Institute, New Delhi	New Delhi	7
Indian Institute of forest Management, Bhopal	Bhopal	8
Indian Institute of Technology, Kanpur	Kanpur	9
Indian Institute of Management, Indore	Indore	10
Management Development institute, Gurgaon	Gurgaon	11
International Management Institute, Kolkata	Kolkata	12
Xavier Labour Relation Institute (XLR), Jamshedpur	Jamshedpur	13
Indian Institute of Management, Tiruchirappalli	Tiruchirappalli	14
Thiagarajar School of Management, Madurai	Madurai	15
S.P. Jain Institute of Management & Research, Mumbai	Mumbai	16
Vellore Institute of Technology, Vellore	Vellore	17
Indian Institute of Management, Raipur	Raipur	18
Indian Institute of Management, Rohtak	Rohtak	19
Rajiv Gandhi Institute of Management, Shillong	Shillong	20
Institute of Management, Kashipur	Kashipur	21
Indian Institute of Information Technology & Management, Gwalior	Gwalior	22
Fore School of Management, New Delhi	New Delhi	23
Lal Bahadur Shastri Institute of Management, New Delhi	New Delhi	24
Birla Institute of Technology, Mesra	Ranchi	25

India Ranking 2016: Pharmacy Category "A"

Name	*City*	*Rank*
Manipal College of Pharmaceutical Sciences, Manipal	Manipal	1
University Institute of Pharmaceutical Sciences, Chandigarh	Chandigarh	2
Jamia Hamdard, New Delhi	New Delhi	3
Poona College of Pharmacy, Pune	Pune	4
Institute of Pharmacy, Nirma University, Ahmedabad	Ahmedabad	5
Bombay University of Pharmacy, Mumbai	Mumbai	6

Birla Institute of Technology, Mesra	Ranchi	7
Amrita School of Pharmacy, Kochi	Kochi	8
JSS College of Pharmacy, Ootacamund	Ootacamund	9
JSS College of Pharmacy, Mysore	Mysore	10
PSG College of Pharmacy, Coimbatore	Coimbatore	11
L.M. College of Pharmacy, Ahmedabad	Ahmedbad	12
AL Ameen College of Pharmacy, Bengaluru	Bengaluru	13
R. C. Patel Institute of Pharmaceutical Education & Research, Shirpur	Shirpur	14
H.K.E.S.S Matoshree Taradevi Rampur Institute of Pharmaceutical Science, Gulbarga	Gulbarga	15
University College of Pharmaceutical Science, Warangal	Warangal	16
Chitkara College of Pharmacy, Rajpura	Rajpura	17
N.G.S.M Institute of Pharmaceutical Science, Mangalore	Mangalore	18
School of Pharmacy, Solan	Solan	19
Raghavendra Institute of Pharmaceutical Education & Research (RIPER), Anantapur	Anantapur	20
S.E.T's College of Pharmacy, Dharwad	Dharwad	21
University Institute of Pharmacy, Raipur	Raipur	22
Goa College of Pharmacy, Panaji	Panaji	23
H.R. Patel Institute of Pharmaceutical Education and Research, Shirpur	Shirpur	24
Bharat Vidyapeeth College of Pharmacy, Kolhapur	Kolhapur	25

India Ranking 2016: Universities

Name	City	Rank
Indian Institute of Science, Bengaluru	Bengaluru	1
Institute of Chemical Technology, Mumbai	Mumbai	2
Jawaharlal Nehru University, New Delhi	New Delhi	3
University of Hyderabad, Hyderabad	Hyderabad	4
Tezpur University, Tezpur	Tezpur	5
University of Delhi, Delhi	Delhi	6
Banaras Hindu University, Varanasi	Varanasi	7
Indian Institute of Space Science and Technology, Thiruvananthapuram	Thiruvananthapuram	8
Birla Institute of Technology & Science, Pilani	Pilani	9
Aligarh Muslim University, Aligarh	Aligarh	10
Visva Bharati, Kolkata	Kolkata	11
Panjab University, Chandigarh	Chandigarh	12
Pondicherry University, Puducherry	Puducherry	13
Bharathiar University, Coimbatore	Coimbatore	14
North Eastern Hill University, Shillong	Shillong	15
King Georges Medical University, Lucknow	Lucknow	16
Homi Bhabha National Institute, Mumbai	Mumbai	17

Jamia Hamdard, New Delhi	New Delhi	18
Amrita Vishwa Vidyapeetham, Coimbatore	Coimbatore	19
Goa University, Goa	Goa	20
Guru Gobind Singh Indraprastha University, New Delhi	New Delhi	21
Guwahati University, Guwahati	Guwahati	22
International Institute of Information Technology, Hyderabad	Hyderabad	23
Guru Jambeshwar University of Science & technology Hissar	Hissar	24
Guru Nanak Dev University, Amritsar	Amritsar	25

Interestingly, before finalising the NIRF, the government had approached some international agencies for India-specific rankings so Indian colleges could be brought up on an international institutional ranking platform. "The government created the NIFR platform as international bodies refused to do something for Indian colleges," says A.R. Bhalerao, principal, Bharati Vidyapeeth College of Engineering, Pune. "The government had approached Times Higher Education (THE) and QS Ranking, which are known for their global college rankings, to include some India-specific parameters in their rankings, but they refused. So the government started NIRF, which is a good measure to judge Indian colleges." Many feel the NIRF ranking will help the government decide on funding colleges based on their performance.

> "It will help the government take a calibrated approach," say a senior IIT professor on the condition of anonymity. "A large number of government-funded colleges are reputedly at the bottom of the charts. They pay little attention to factors like proper faculty or infrastructure, or updating their systems. These will come to light now. Once you link their funding to performance, they will have to improve their performance and that will reflect in their ranking."

There are, of course, many who feel a lot more needs to be done to properly streamline the NIRF rankings and make them logically consistent with the colleges' comparative performance. Experts point at several anomalies in the approach followed in the first year that needs to be corrected. That process may have begun. The government has now set up a panel to look into the ranking exercise so it can be improved in next year's edition. But unless some balance is brought in and the rankings present a logical picture, it will be an exercise in futility. The HRD Ministry must tread carefully and do the right thing. We all know who the ultimate sufferers will be.

Varied Forms

9
Medical Education

The path leading to the history of medical education in India is a very interesting journey. Long before the world started talking about Harvard and Cambridge, when the Royal College of Surgeons was unheard of, India had given birth to a civilisation that gave immense importance to the medical sciences as well as doctors. The country has produced a number of competent physicians. Gurukuls of Vedic period provided training in medical science. It has been claimed that students came from distant lands to study medicine in Nalanda and Taxila. Most of the rulers took steps to encourage medical education. However, it was only after the arrival of the British that modern medicine was introduced. The first medical college was set up in 1835 in Kolkata. Many more were established in the 19th century.

It is indeed a matter of pride that our institutions have produced many world class physicians. However, paradoxically, more than half of the children in India are not immunized and less than half of the women here receive proper prenatal care during pregnancy. The doctor-patient ratio is nowhere near the WHO standards, the lack of doctors in rural areas, and a high number of appalling statistics clearly depict that the Indian medical education system has many fundamental defects.

India is one of the countries where there is high demand for medical seats. More than six lakh students sit for the pre-medical entrance tests every year. Only about 45000 are fortunate enough to secure a seat. It has often been pointed out that the method of selection of doctors-to-be is highly defective. Though the examination system has been changing from year to year, the fundamental examination pattern has remained more or less the same. Aspirants are screened on the basis of the answers they give to multiple choice questions (MCQs). These tests often turn out to be mere test of memory. True knowledge is seldom assessed through these MCQs. The humanitarian attitude much needed to become a doctor is not evaluated. Hence, the medical education system in India presently allows anyone who can memorise and store a large amount of information to be a doctor. Nobody seems to be interested in creating socially committed compassionate healers.

Growth of Medical Colleges

India has witnessed a rapid growth in the medical education sector—one of the largest in the world. Starting with 28 teaching institutions at the undergraduate level in 1950, we have reached a total of 384 colleges in 2014, with a total intake capacity of about 50,000 medical students. Traditionally, medical colleges in India were largely funded by the government and the contribution of private sector was negligible. But with the implementation of new economic policy of 1991, broadly known as structural adjustment programme, the trend shifted towards private funding of medical education and the growth of private medical colleges has been phenomenal. The private medical colleges have increased by 405 percent (from 41 to 209) in the last two and half decades (1990 to 2014); whereas the government-run medical colleges have increased only 72 percent (from 102 to 176), with an overall growth of 169 percent during this period. The share of private sector in total number of medical colleges has increased from 3.6 percent in 1950 to 54.3 percent in 2014. Similarly, the enrolment share in these colleges currently accounts for more than half (52.1 percent), in comparison to merely 1.4 percent in 1950. The annual average growth rate of private medical institutions during 1950 to 2014 is 8.7 percent compared to three percent in government sector, with a more or less similar intake capacity. In India this growth has been driven largely by developments in the private sector, and in some states it grew to such a level that in relative size, the public sector became infinitesimally small.

Although the involvement of private sector in medical education has spread all over the country, the distribution is found to be quite uneven across different regions. In total, the five southern states—Andhra Pradesh, Telangana, Karnataka, Kerala, and Tamil Nadu—with 21 percent of India's total population have nearly half of the medical schools (43.6 percent) and intake capacity (46.3 percent). In contrast, 12 states from eastern and northern region accounting for 45.3 percent of India's population have only about one-fourth of the total medical institutions and their intake. It is astonishing to note that in Jharkhand, all the three existing medical institutions were established during the 1960s and no more colleges were added to the list afterwards. Similarly, only about 2.8 percent of the medical colleges (11 in number) with the total intake capacity of 2.2 percent (1126 students) are located in the eight north-eastern states. The population share of these states in 3.76 percent as per 2011 Census of India. Interestingly, most of these states with fewer medical institutions and intakes (Bihar, Chhattisgarh, Jharkhand, Odisha, Madhya Pradesh, Rajasthan, Uttar Pradesh, and Assam) are also the empowered action group states that was formed by the Ministry of Health and Family Welfare in March 2001, especially to ensure population stabilisation and intersectoral convergence. It is noteworthy that these are the states with high fertility rates and weak socio-demographic indicators. Overall, the number of medical institutions and their intake capacity is much higher in states with better health indicators that reflect the distorted distribution of the country's production capacity of health workers.

Trends in Medical Education, 1950-2014

Year		*Government*	*Institutions Private*	*Total*	*Government*	*Intake capacity Private*	*Total*
1950	Number	27	1	28	4175	60	4235
	Share	94.4	3.6	100	98.6	1.4	100
1960	Number	56	4	60	7725	610	8335
	Share	93.3	6.7	100	92.7	7.3	100
1970	Number	89	10	99	10925	1350	12275
	Share	96	10.1	100	89	11	100
1980	Number	87.3	14	110	11425	1820	13245
	Share	102	12.7	100	86.3	13.7	100
1990	Number	71.3	41	143	11800	4785	16585
	Share	115	28.7	100	71.1	28.9	100
2000	Number	65.3	61	176	12720	6635	19355
	Share	121	34.7	100	65.7	34.3	100
2004	Number	54.8	100	221	13320	10685	24005
	Share	176	45.2	100	55.5	44.5	100
2014	Number	45.7	209	385	24038	26055	50093
	Share		54.3	100	47.9	52.1	100
CAGR (1950-2014)		3.0	8.7	4.2	2.8	10.0	3.9

The more detailed analysis, by region and ownership, of medical schools shows that in 2014, around two-thirds of the total medical colleges in the southern region are owned by private sector. In three states—Karnataka, Kerala, and Puducherry—the share is more than 70 percent. Similar trend is also observed for students' intake in this region. Interestingly, the intake of students for MBBS course in private medical colleges in Puducherry and Karnataka is around 80 percent of the total. Likewise, about 54 percent of the total medical colleges in the western region are privately managed, and in Goa the share is 60 percent. In contrast only about 29.2 percent of the total medical colleges and 22.6 percent of the total students' intake in eastern region are from the private sector and a more or less similar trend is also observed in the north-eastern region. In Bihar, Jharkhand, and West Bengal medical education is largely provided by the public sector and the presence of private sector is quite negligible. Also, only around 20 percent of the MBBS students in Delhi and Jammu and Kashmir (two states from northern region) have the option to enroll in private medical colleges. In Chandigarh, the students interested in pursuing medical education completely rely on the private colleges in India is largely due to rapid growth of the private sector that is concentrated in a few states.

Region-wise Institutions and Intakes in Government and Private Medical Colleges in India, 2014

Region	*Institution*			*Intake*		
	Government	*Private*	*Total*	*Government*	*Private*	*Total*
Southern	33.93	66.07	100 (168)	34.02	65.98	100 (23195)
Western	46.15	53.85	100 (78)	52.47	47.53	100 (10825)
Northern	51.47	48.53	100 (68)	58.66	41.34	100 (7607)
Eastern	70.73	29.27	100 (41)	77.35	22.65	100 (4900)
Central	57.89	42.11	100 (19)	54.92	45.08	100 (2440)
North-Eastern	72.73	27.27	100 (11)	77.80	22.20	100 (1126)
India	45.71	54.29	100 (385)	47.99	52.1	100 (50093)

State-wise Number of Required and Existing Medical Colleges, 2014

State/UT	*Population 2014 (P) (in millions)*	*Medical colleges required @one per 5 million population*	*Existing number of medical colleges in 2014*	*Difference*
States with more colleges than required				
Andhra Pradesh	86.95	17	43	26
Delhi	20.9	4	8	4
Gujarat	61.33	12	22	10
Karnataka	61.21	12	46	34
Kerala	35.26	7	25	18
Maharashtra	117.2	23	44	21
Puducherry	1.573	1	9	8
Punjab	28.57	6	10	4
Tamil Nadu	68.65	14	45	31
States with fewer colleges than required				
Assam	31.69	6	5	-1
Bihar	101.5	20	13	-7
Jharkhand	32.77	7	3	-4
Madhya Pradesh	75.61	15	13	-2
Rajasthan	70.97	14	11	-3
Uttar Pradesh	211.2	42	31	-11

Medical Colleges in India

S. No.	State/ Union Territory	Number of Colleges offering MBBS	State-run Colleges	Private Colleges	Govt. College seats	Private Colleges Seats	Total no. of seats
1.	Andhra Pradesh	40	15	28	2400	3850	6250
2.	Assam	5	5	0	626	0	626
3.	Bihar	11	7	4	540	369	909
4.	Chandigarh	1	1	0	50	0	50
5.	Chhattisgarh	5	4	1	400	100	500
6.	Delhi	7	5	2	800	200	1000
7.	Goa	1	1	0	150	0	150
8.	Gujarat	22	9	13	1530	1400	2930
9.	Haryana	6	2	4	300	400	700
10.	Himachal Pradesh	2	2	0	200	0	200
11.	Jammu and Kashmir	4	3	1			400
12.	Jharkhand	3	3	0	250	0	250
13.	Karnataka	43	11	32	1350	4655	6005
14.	Kerala	24	6	18	1000	1850	2850
15.	Madhya Pradesh	11	5	6	660	900	1560
16.	Maharashtra	43	19	24	2200	2995	5195
17.	Manipur	2	2	0	200	0	200
18.	Odisha	6	3	3	550	300	850
19.	Puducherry	9	2	7	225	900	1125
20.	Punjab	9	3	6	350	645	995
21.	Rajasthan	10	7	3	900	400	1300
22.	Sikkim	1	0	1	0	100	100
23.	Tamil Nadu	42	19	20	2205	2850	5055
23.	Tripura	2	1	1	100	100	200
25.	Uttar Pradesh	27	12	15	1449	1800	3249
26.	Uttarakhand	4	2	2	200	250	450
27.	West Bengal	14	13	2	1650	300	1950
SI	South India	154	52	102	6830	13705	20535
WI	West India	63	34	43	4540	5295	9835
NI	North India	81	37	33	4499	3745	8244
EI	East India	47	37	10	411	1010	5026
	Total	**381**	**160**	**188**	**25085**	**38715**	**63800**

In India also, there is considerable variation in the density of the health workforce between rural and urban regions. The density of total health workforce (doctors, nurse and midwife, dentist, pharmacist, and other medical staff) per 10,000 populations in urban area is approximately four times higher compared to the rural area, i.e. 42.03 for urban region and 10.78 for rural region. Most importantly, the difference in the density is highest among doctors, 13.34 in urban region and 3.28 in rural region. About 74 percent of graduate doctors living in urban areas serve only 28 percent of the national population, while the rural population is largely unserved. Due to critical shortage of doctors, unqualified practitioners play an important role in the delivery of health care to a large section of society. Healthcare being largely a demand driven service, in rural areas of many Indian states, the shortage of allopathic doctors is met through Ayurveda, Yoga and Naturopathy, Unani, Siddha and homeopathy (AYUSH) doctors, and Rural Medical Practitioners (RMPs), who lack formal allopathic training. Up to 63 percent of clinicians practicing in rural India had inadequate or no medical training. The situation is particularly alarming because a relatively small fraction of the country's health workforce is available in areas where majority of the population resides.

Quality of Medical Education

Developing an effective healthcare delivery system and ensuring universal access to healthcare in a country immensely dependent on the nature and quality of medical manpower it produces is critical. But it is an oft-repeated criticism that medical colleges in India are producing graduates who are not well-equipped to tackle the healthcare needs of the society. It has been argued that the unregulated growth of medical education in the private sector and poorly implemented regulations relating to admissions, faculty strength, and infrastructure in medical colleges adversely impacts the quality of training in India's medical institutions.

Medical Apex Bodies

These are the apex bodies that govern the Medical profession and allied services in the country:

- Medical Council of India (MCI)
- Dental Council of India (DCI)
- Pharmacy Council of India (PCI)
- National Board of Examination (NAT Board)

Medical Council of India (MCI)

The Medical Council of India (MCI) is the apex statutory body for medical education in India. It is responsible for establishing and maintaining high standards of medical education and recognition of medical qualifications in India. However, in practice, it is only a recommendatory body, without genuine autonomy and authority, which has led to the unregulated expansion of private medical colleges that are supplying low quality human resources for the health sector. The system of regulation practiced by MCI is neither adequate nor appropriate to meet the needs of the profession, and over the years it has led to a progressive decline in medical education. It has also failed to provide a synergistic approach in addressing the need for human resources for health in India by coordinating with the other professional councils like Indian Nursing Council and the Pharmacy Council. Although it is widely advocated that privatisation of medical education is a powerful tool to support public health system by producing the required health professionals; at the same time it should be monitored with stringent implementation of the rules set by MCI so that the health of the nation is not compromised in the long run. The NKC National Knowledge Commission working group report on medical education strongly recommended amendments to the Indian Medical Council Act to make MCI a truly autonomous statutory body and not simply as a recommendatory body to the central government.

NITI Aayog Pitches for New Medical Education Regulator

NITI Aayog is likely to propose the scrapping of the Medical Council of India (MCI), which will be replaced by a National Medical Commission (NMC). The new body will act as the regulator and also advise the government on policy and curriculum preparation for medical colleges across the country.

To bring in professionalism and world-class medical infrastructure, the new body will be assisted by four impendent boards—an undergraduate medical board, postgraduate board, assessment and rating board, and a board of medical register that will keep a record of people qualified to practice as doctors.

A medical advisory council will be formed with four boards, representatives from states, two members from union territories, and NMC members.

"The new model is aimed at ending the 'license raj' that exists in the allocation of license to set up medical colleges," a source in NITI Aayog said.

The committee has suggested replacing the current system of 'electing' candidates to the MCI with 'selecting' by a high-level search-cum-selection committee. It is also likely to propose the introduction of competition and merit among the medical colleges through an exit interview of the students.

"The changes are aimed at improving career, enterprise, and ethics in medical colleges, since the MCI has failed as a regulator and allowed corruption," said a senior NITI Aayog official.

Shortages of Teachers

It is well known that there is a 30 to 40 percent shortage of medical teachers across India leading to unhealthy practices at the time of MCI inspection to fulfill the prescribed norms. Several suggestions have been made by N. Anantha Krishnan of JIPMER, Puducherry:

1. Relaxing the eligibility criteria for teachers.
2. Special weightage and incentives for teachers in areas with critical shortage.
3. Teaching weightage to specialists and medical officers with postgraduate degrees working in medical colleges and participating in teaching-learning activities to enable them to join the teaching profession.
4. Recognition of foreign qualification now under reciprocal de-recognition.
5. Employing retired teachers on a part-time basis as a short term measure
6. Sharing of faculty between adjacent medical colleges in disciplines with critical shortage.
7. Reintroduction of the honorary system to utilise the services of qualified personnel willing to work in medical colleges for a short time every day.
8. Removal of all restriction on the number of non-medical teachers in pre- and selected paraclinical disciplines.
9. Special incentives to candidates for joining postgraduate programmes in pre- and paraclinical disciplines.
10. Alteration of the student-teacher ratio from the current 1:1 to 2:1 or 3:1, depending on the needs and characteristics of individual subjects.
11. Increasing the retirement age of teaching to 70 years as has been done by the Dental Council of India.
12. Recognition of diplomas of national board (DNB) so that DNB qualified professionals would be able to enter the teaching profession.

Continuing Medical Education

Indian Medical Association (IMA) says their doctors desperately need to be up-to-date with the latest drugs, equipment, and medical practices; but legislation to make this a requirement has made little progress. The Medical Council of India is campaigning for continuing medical education (CME) to be made compulsory, as it is in the U.K. and USA, for the country's 615000 registered doctors. It has proposed a draft amendment to a law that would standardise medical practice across the country while making sure it is up to date with the latest developments. If passed into law, mandatory CME for registered doctors in India could set a precedent.

Despite the lack of legal incentive for doctors to attend regular refresher courses, CME has been catching on in India over the last three years partly due to the efforts of regional medical associations.

The Delhi Medical Council, which represents 24000 doctors in the capital, made it mandatory two years ago for members to complete 100 hours of CME every five years before they can be re-registered as doctors. CME programmes have also been held in Belgaum, Mangalore, Madurai, Manipal, and Tirunelveli in the south; Dharamshala, Aligarh, and Muzaffarnagar in the north; Bhopal, Nagpur, and Jaipur in the west; and Cuttack, Patna, and Guwahati in the east. However, doctors in many rural areas are still missing out as they have little or no access to such courses. CME is a requirement for the registration of health professionals in many developed countries, such as the United States of America.

Faculty Development

Faculty development (FD) is a planned programme: (i) to improve an individual's knowledge and skill in teaching, education research and educational administration; and (ii) to prepare institutions and faculty members for their various roles. In medical education, faculty development deals with the sensitization and training of teachers in carrying out their professional tasks, which lead to improvement in the quality of teaching and learning that contributes to the competence of health professionals. Faculty development has assumed a lot of significance, because of its role in capacity building. The theme of faculty development is how best to sensitize, equip, and empower teachers for discharging their professional responsibilities.

Teaching is a demanding and complex task. George Miller observed, "It is curious that so many of our most important responsibilities are undertaken without significant preparation. Marriage, parenthood and teaching (in medical schools) are probably most ubiquitous." It is necessary for the present day teacher to be aware of and become part of far reaching changes that are taking place in medical education. The changes are: shift from conventional role of teacher, changes in learning styles, innovative curriculum models, and changes in assessment philosophy, methods, and tools.

1. Additional roles of teachers: Conventionally, the role of a medical teacher was confined to 'information giving,' viz., passing on a wealth of biomedical information to the students assuming that the students would be able to do their jobs well, once placed in a situation. The teacher in the present scenario is expected to play multiple roles such as:

- Facilitator (of learning)
- Curriculum and course planner
- Resource material creator
- Student assessor

- Mentor
- Programme evaluator

2. Changing learning styles: Medical students need to be effective lifelong learners in order to continue to develop personally and practice professionally. This demands encouragement of diverse learning styles. Application of adult learning principles, student autonomy, self-learning, experiential learning, reflective learning, computer assisted learning, distance learning, e-learning, use of skill learning laboratories are some of the areas requiring expertise, which are not readily available for most teachers.

3. Innovative curriculum models: While many medical schools abroad are offering innovative curricula such as 'Problem based curriculum (PBL),' 'Integrated curriculum,' 'Cell biology curriculum,' 'Competency based curriculum,' and 'Hybrid curriculum;' in India we are still following traditional subject based curriculum. Shifting to a new curriculum requires skills and competence that cannot be taken for granted.

4. New Assessment methods and tools: The traditional methods of assessment have been challenged. Dissatisfaction has been expressed over their validity and reliability. Several new methods and tools are now available, the use of which requires special training. To name a few:

- OSCE and OSPE
- OSLER (Objective Structured Long Examination Record)
- Mini CEX (Mini Case Evaluation Exercise)
- CbD (Case based Discussion)
- DOPs (Direct Observation of Procedures)
- Portfolio
- Multi Source Feedback
- Patient Satisfaction Questionnaire

The focus of student assessment has shifted to the use of multiple methods for testing a wide gamut of learning outcomes, such as higher cognitive abilities, communication skills, IT skills, and professionalism including ethical behaviour. Many of the methods lay emphasis on frequent assessment of learning outcomes through predetermined agreed assessment criteria, using observation check-lists, or rating scales for scoring. It is, therefore, essential for our teachers to be aware of these new developments and suitable adopt them in our medical education system.

Recent Developments

Medical Council of India's vision 2015 document: The Medical Council of India's (MCI) vision 2015 draft has proposed some sweeping reforms.

The report cites three main reasons for India's healthcare woes—storages of physicians (both general practitioners and specialists), inequitable distribution of manpower and resources, and deficiencies in the quality of medical education. They have proposed the following reforms: Increased numbers of doctors, curricular reform, laying emphasis on primary healthcare and family medicine, and strengthening of medical institutions by investing in technology. However, the steps that have been taken in this direction are far from adequate to achieve the objectives set, while many dilutions have already happened.

NHSRC BILL, 2011

The National Commission for Human Resources for Health (NCHRH) was proposed to be an overarching regulatory body for medical education and allied health sciences with the dual purpose of reforming the current regulatory framework, and enhancing the supply of skilled manpower in the health sector. NCHRH was supposed to prescribe, monitor, and promote standards of health professional education. But the very fact that the Commission was designed to subsume the existing councils of India, led to widespread opposition from the medical profession citing dilution of autonomous nature of the council. The parliamentary standing committee later rejected this bill.

National Eligibility cum Entrance Test (NEET)

NEET was introduced via a notification by the Medical Council of India in response to a public interest litigation filed by prospective medical student demanding a single entrance test. This was also seen as an opportunity to curb illegal capitation fees as well as bring uniformity in medical education across India. However, this notification was quashed recently in the Supreme Court of India on the ground that it violated the rights of state and private institutions to administer such institutions.

Medical education got a shot in the arm when the Supreme Court, later, gave its nod to hold NEET for admission to medical colleges across the country, be they private or government colleges, or deemed universities. The Supreme Court constituted a committee under retired Chief Justice of India R.M. Lodha to oversee the functioning of MCI. The court arrived at this decision based on Ranjit Roy Committee recommendations and the 92nd Parliamentary Standing Committee report on the functioning of MCI.

Commission and Task Forces

The National Knowledge Commission (NKC) observed that medical education in the country was mostly directionless, unregulated, and non-standardised. The NKC report strongly recommended amendments of Indian Medical Council Act to make Medical Council of India (MCI) a "truly autonomous statutory body and not simply as a recommending body to the Central government."

Another document is the Report of the "Task Force on Medical Education for the National Rural Health Mission" constituted by the Ministry of Health and Family Welfare, Government of India. Revamping medical education with reference to the requirements of medical professionals was the first objective of the terms of reference of the Task Force. In the light of the changing epidemiological scenario, the Report emphasised the need for revitalizing the healthcare system in the country with special focus on primary healthcare. The Task Force recommended restructuring the curriculum to match the community need, and to adopt training methods which focus on attainment of clinical competence, through an integrated approach, preferably a modular one. The Report also explored the scope of increasing medical manpower.

All these reports recognised that the standard and quality of medical education in India is much below the desired level, and admitted the need for reforming the medical education system to produce doctors with enhanced skills and competencies to address the health needs and challenges in the present day's scenario.

Medical Structural Reforms Needed

Major structural reforms needed in Indian medical education are:

1. Need assessment of medical colleges
2. Ensure quality in medical education and research in the country
3. The curricula and syllabi of medical education should be revised
4. Evolving competency-based curriculum
5. Standing mechanism for curriculum update
6. Clinical skills lab in all medical colleges
7. Faculty development programme
8. True independent status to Medical Council of India
9. Diligent use of information technology
10. Promote new specialties in medical education department
11. Emergency medicine as a separate department
12. Establish Medical Grants commission (MGC)
13. National eligibility entrance test for admission
14. Appropriate weightage to the qualifying examination
15. Age of entry to medical colleges
16. Inter-disciplinary studies
17. Public health as a core subject

10
Engineering Education

After gaining independence from Britain in 1947, Prime Minister Nehru conceived the vision of present day engineers and engineering education for the ultimate economic development of the country. He immediately asked the planners and educationists to plan and establish engineering institutions of various levels all over the country with the help of willing developed economies like USA, Germany, U.K. and Sweden.

The first three decades saw engineering polytechnics, regional colleges, national institutes, and universities come up in India, that led Indians to emerge as a leading group of people. An earlier underdeveloped country, but today Indians are among the top in the world in the field of computers, software, internet, etc., expert engineers, and biggest entrepreneurs operating in the leading economies. Hitherto emphasis had been on producing theoretically taught engineers with focus on theory and research aspects, sidelining more emphasis on practical training and educating them as global engineers. This concept is now being changed. More and more new institutions are being set up which are going to be citadels of global engineering education in the 21st century.

Brief History of Engineering Education

Pre-independence period: The British rulers set up four engineering colleges in the four corners of India—Roorkee (1847), Shibpur (1856), Guindy (1794) and Poona (1854) to train the engineers needed for the civil and other engineering activities of the day. These four engineering colleges had a total enrolment of 608 students during 1884-85. Each had a glorious record, having produced some of the outstanding engineers of India. Two other prominent institutions were set up nearly 100 years ago—Indian Institute of Science by the House of Tatas (1908) and Banaras Hindu University (BHU) by Pandit Madan Mohan Malaviya (1916)—which grew to become important institutions. At the time of independence, there were only 24 engineering degree colleges with a total intake capacity of 2570 students.

Another major step taken in the pre-independence era was the creation of the N.R. Sarkar Committee in 1945, which submitted a preliminary report recommending the setting up of four higher technical institutions with broad-based education, patterned after the Massachusetts Institute of Technology, USA, in the four regions of the country.

Post-independence period: "The scientific approach has changed the world completely. I think that if the world is to solve its problems, it will inevitable have to be through the means of science. The world will ultimately be saved, if it is to be saved, by the method and approach of science," said Pandit Jawaharlal Nehru. Implementing the Sarkar Committee recommendations, five IITs were established at Kharagpur (1951), Bombay (1958), Madras (1959), Kanpur (1960) and Delhi (1961) as institutions of national importance by an Act of Parliament. After a gap of over three decades, the sixth IIT was established at Guwahati (1995); while the Engineering College at Roorkee was first made a University and then the seventh IIT (2001). In 2008, four more IITs were established at Patna, Jodhpur, Hyderabad, and Gandhinagar followed in 2009 by four more at Ropar, Bhubaneswar, Mandi, and Indore, making a total of 15 IITs. The oldest IITs are mentoring the newer ones.

The recent eight IITs have limited undergraduate (UG) enrolments to about 100 each, and only nominal admissions at the Master's and Ph.D. level at present. In the next few years, when they grow to their full size, the 15 IITs will admit about 15,000 UG, 10,000 Master's and at least 8,000 Ph.D. students per year. The Institute of Technology at BHU has been elevated as an IIT. Thus there are 16 IITs now. Clearly, IITs contribute a small fraction of engineering graduates in India.

In the next tier of institutions, there are 20 regional engineering colleges (RECs) which were recently renamed National Institutes of Technology (NITs) with central government funding and greater autonomy. It is proposed that 10 more NITs be setup soon making a total of 30 NITs. The 20 NITs admitted 9297 UG and 4569 postgraduate students in 2007-08 (mostly for a master's degree, rather than diplomas).

Then, there are a large number of state government engineering colleges, often affiliated to a university, and having a limited or no autonomy about curriculum, examinations, degree granting, etc. the great demand for engineering and technical education has led to the mushrooming of the large number of private engineering colleges, many started by politicians or as money-making ventures.

This phenomenal growth has led to a steep decrease in quality, though some of them are accredited by the All India Council of Technical Education (AICTE) or other bodies, but they lack autonomy in most matters.

The U.R. Rao Committee Report

In 2002, a five-member committee headed by U.R. Rao, a prominent scientist and former chair of the India Space Research Organisation (ISRO), was established by the Ministry of Human Resources Development (MHRD) to review the performance of the AICTE. Submitted to the government in September, 2003 the committee's report, "Revitalising Technical Education," describes a technical sector that is expanding at an unsustainable level and is in drastic need of regulation to ensure academic standards are improved.

When issued, the report sparked deep controversy and gained global coverage due one of its more minor and tangential recommendation—cutting fees at the Indian Institutes of Management. The report's main findings and recommendations centre on the following areas:

- There are too many institutions due to unregulated growth, especially in the private sector
- Institutions are proliferating in geographical pockets, leading to oversupply in some markets and shortages in others
- Not enough qualified faculty, and not nearly enough doctorates coming through the system
- Weak quality assurance structures, especially accreditation procedures
- Lack of cooperation and interaction between industry and the classroom
- High levels of unemployment and underemployment among engineering graduates
- The graduate growth rate is far exceeding the economy's growth rate
- Colleges are not meeting the skilled manpower needs of industry
- Exorbitant tuition fees at many private colleges.

The Accreditation Shortfall

In the fields that the AICTE regulates (engineering, technology, management, architect, town planning, pharmacy, applied arts and crafts, hotel management and catering), institutional and programme accreditation is the responsibility of the National Board of Accreditation (NBA), an autonomous body under the umbrella of the AICTE.

Although accreditation is mandatory, less than 10 percent of institutions in the technical sectors are actually accredited. Data provided in the Rao report reveals a large gap that exists between the AICTE system of recognition and accreditation. In May, 2003 just 985 programmes from 202 institutions under the purview of the AICTE had been accredited. At that time there were approximately 14,000 programmes at 3,589 approved degree-granting institutions, and 1,608 approved diploma institutions. The data appears to reveal a general lack of belief in the accreditation process.

Part of the reason for this could be that institutions might have to wait indefinitely to seek accreditation. The Rao report recommends a tightening of regulatory standards, not only to increase the percentage of accredited institutions; but also to weed out substandard institutions. Institutions would be actively required to seek accreditation, and those institutions that fall below minimum standards would be given a probationary period to resolve problems or face cuts in intake or outright closure.

In the field of engineering, the accreditation conundrum is particularly troubling for those that would like to see the Indian engineering sector improve its international credibility through membership of the Washington Accord, a multilateral agreement representing agencies that accredit engineering programmes in 12 member countries and accept one another's standards as equally high standards. The agreement recommends that graduates of accredited programmes be recognised as having met the academic requirements for entry to the practice of engineering in any member country.

Admission to the Washington Accord would lend much greater weight to NBA accreditation as students graduating from NBA-accredited programmes would enjoy increased international employment and credit-transfer opportunities.

On January 9, 2015, AICTE, CII, and World Bank organised a workshop on "Implementing Strategies for Engineering Education in India towards 2025."

The Workshop's comments on the performance of the vast majority of engineering institutions in 2015 include:

- Largely affiliated colleges are following the curriculum of universities;
- Only a small number of autonomous colleges are emerging;
- Focus of most of the institutions is undergraduate teaching and the post-graduate programmes are weak;
- Employers are not happy with engineering talent pool;
- Very little focus on research;
- Absence of academic framework to constantly respond to the changing needs of the economic environment;
- No serious engagement between education providers and employers;

- Lack of enterprising character/innovation mindset;
- Lack of systemic capacity building effort in education and research;
- Accreditation is more of a compliance rather than an improvement tool;
- 95 to 100 percent revenue from government disbursement and/or student fees;
- No participation in regional development;
- Low key entrepreneurship promotion activities.

The Workshop's goal was to come up with recommendations for how a significant number of engineering institutions would be able to improve their performance from the current dismal stage of development to the aspirational stage of high-performing engineering institutions over the next ten years.

How high-performing engineering institutions should aspire to be in 2025:

- Institutions with full academic autonomy and adequate financial autonomy;
- Excellent teaching and research-intensive/research-led/research-informed institution;
- Adaption of academic framework that is responsive to stakeholders' needs;
- More experiential/practice based curriculum creating relevant student experiences;
- Student learning outcomes in tune with employers' expectations;
- Strong link with industry in design, development, and delivery of the courses/programmes;
- Employers satisfied with quality of the talent pool;
- Faculty training that is strongly linked to institutional processes and aspirations;
- Effective ICT technology adaption to enhance student learning and faculty competence;
- Strong post-graduate and research programmes;
- Enhanced capability for industry consultancy and IPR generation;
- Led by strong academic leaders and administrators who continually drive institutional aspirations;
- At least 30 percent of expenditure met by revenue generated by other than government subsidies and/or student fees;
- Contributing to the regional socio-economic development through entrepreneurship and innovation activities;

- Centres of excellence in priority areas for the college.

The workshop suggested following five steps that can transform India's engineering education by 2025:

- Strengthen governance and leadership.
- Improve quality of teaching, learning and research.
- Faster stronger industry-institute collaborations.
- Encourage innovation and entrepreneurships.
- Make a concerted national initiative to improve engineering education.

It is essential for engineering education system to keep itself updated with the global requirements in the present knowledge era. In view of the changing scenario, some of the imperative requirements for the engineering education system suggested by the Vice-Chancellor of Madan Mohan Malaviya University of Technology are as follows:

- Regulators of engineering education should evolve suitable framework for producing technical human resource with capability to meet the present day challenges.
- All engineering education institutions should conduct their self-assessment in respect to the goals set by the regulators of engineering education.
- Establish suitable mechanism for creating a pool of good quality faculty/human resources.
- Adoption of suitable teaching pedagogy for improvement in teaching methods and practices.
- Creating student-centric learning ambience for high quality classroom and laboratory teaching, which is better than the available digital content so that the student-teacher contact type education is strengthened.
- Update the curriculum so that it can help in achieving the present day goals of the engineering community.
- Enhance meaningful collaborations with industry for better interaction to improve the quality of engineering students.
- Creation of suitable IT enabled outreach system for strengthening the engineering education.
- Supplement teaching content with the relevant digital content in the routine teaching.
- Industry should adapt and rope in relevant academic institution(s) for the regular interaction with academia and offer requisite opportunities to the budding technocrats—either through mutual consent or through certain legislative provisions.

India's higher technical education is good in small pockets, but far from world class. The bulk of it is of poor quality, producing graduates many of whom are unemployable. The main reason for this pathetic situation is rapid expansion of the education system without adequate number of qualified teachers, shortage or absence of infrastructure, and lack of autonomy in all aspects of the technical education system. Other contribution factors are: poor linkage with industry, poor visibility in terms of publications, patents, new products, and low or no international collaboration in teaching and research.

In order to rectify this pathetic situation and enable India to have at least a few world-class institutions calls for some hard decisions. Recognising that India does not have the resources to raise too many institutions to world class level, it is essential to identify a small number of the best institutions to start with, and provide all the support needed in terms of world-class faculty; outstanding students; large postgraduate and research programmes; excellent infrastructure; totally independent Boards of Governors with no government participation and interference; freedom to raise corpus funds from alumni (here and abroad), industry, and business for enhancing of salaries of faculty and improve infrastructure; and build extensive international collaboration at the faculty, student, and research levels. The directors should be eminent scholars, and chosen by the respective Boards. They should not be burdened with mundane tasks such as campus residential maintenance, etc. The initial five institutions can be chosen from among the seven original IITs, I.I. Sc., Institute of Chemical Technology, Mumbai, among others. At the end of three years, these institutions will be critically evaluated by international groups of experts in terms academic content, research quality and quantity, publications and patents, and awards and funding received. In the second round, other institutions will also compete so that a set of ten institutions are nurtured to raise their standing in the world knowledge community. This process will be continued every three years. The initial goal is that at least some institutions break into the top 100 world-class academia, and in the next round for some to find a place among the top 50 and so on. At the end of the first decade, one or more institutions should be among the top 20 in the world. China, Singapore, South Korea, etc. have followed this strenuous exercise and demonstrated that their select institutions did climb the stringent quality ladder, based on massive support and unlimited freedom.

The second crisis issue concerns shortage of qualified teachers. Responding to great demand for technical education, engineering colleges have mushroomed (mostly in the private sector) leading to teacher shortage. This issue is also linked to few people going in for postgraduate education, preferring an industrial job. Every possible means should be employed to increase the output of engineers with Ph.D. and Master's degrees. The number of Ph.Ds. guided, number and quality of publications should be major factors in the evaluation of faculty from abroad, and adjunct teachers from industry and R&D institutions, improving the salaries of teachers based on performance, obtaining and securing star teachers with substantially larger emoluments, etc. Another major step in this direction is a more imaginative use of ICT to make good lecture and course material more widely available to the technical education system.

Competition Success Review (CSR-GHRDC) Engineering College Survey, 2016

The survey was carried out with prime purpose of evaluating the performance of engineering institutes, to reveal vital and detailed information for the advantages of all stakeholders. The methodology comprised of evaluation of the following areas: (1) physical and academic infrastructure; (2) faculty, publications, research, consultancy, curriculum development delivery system; (3) admission, curriculum and delivery system; (4) placement, social responsibility, and industry interface. As many as 140 colleges across the country provided their data. Rating and ranking of all participating colleges in India was done. The categorization of institutes was done into rating groups. The division of categories is defined as:

1. Top Leading Engineering Colleges of Super Excellence.
2. Top Engineering Colleges of Super Excellence
3. Top Engineering Colleges of Eminence
4. Top Outstanding Engineering Colleges of Excellence
5. Top Engineering Colleges of Excellence
6. Top Promising Engineering Colleges

Ranking of Top Engineering Colleges

Ranking of Top Leading Engineering Colleges of Super Excellence

1. Indian Institute of Technology, Kharagpur, West Bengal
2. Indian Institute of Technology (BHU), Varanasi, Uttar Pradesh

Ranking Of Top Engineering Colleges Of Super Excellence

1. Delhi Technological University (formerly Delhi College of Engineering), Shahabad Daulatpur, New Delhi
2. National Institute of Technology, Surathkal, Karnataka

3. College of Engineering, Pune, Maharashtra
4. Thapar University, Patiala, Punjab
5. Motilal Nehru National Institute of Technology, Allahabad, Uttar Pradesh
6. National Institute of Technology, Rourkela, Odisha
7. PEC University of Technology, Chandigarh, Punjab
8. SRM Engineering College, SRM University, Kattankulathur, Tamil Nadu
9. Jawaharlal Nehru Technological University Hyderabad, College of Engineering, Hyderabad, Telangana
10. Dhirubhai Ambani Insitute of Information and Communication Technology (DA-IICT), Gandhinagar, Gujarat
11. Institute of Technology, Nirma University, Ahmedabad, Gujarat
12. SSN College of Engineering, Chennai, Tamil Nadu

Total Number of Engineering Colleges and Engineering Seats in each State of India

AICTE Approved Institutes for Engineering for the Academic Year: 2016-2017

State	*UG Colleges*	*Seats*	*PG Colleges*	*Seats*
Andaman and Nicobar Islands	1	90	–	–
Andhra Pradesh	328	172476	281	26950
Arunachal Pradesh	–	–	1	–
Assam	18	5055	9	528
Bihar	31	10130	4	204
Chandigarh	3	915	5	608
Chhattisgarh	49	22604	27	1652
Delhi	16	8395	8	1514
Goa	5	1260	2	174
Gujarat	126	68447	70	6694
Haryana	144	58557	116	9360
Karnataka	192	100565	135	12896
Kerala	164	62398	116	9479
Madhya Pradesh	211	98247	150	11462
Maharashtra	372	154254	247	20432
Manipur	1	115	1	40
Meghalaya	1	420	–	–
Nagaland	1	240	–	–
Odisha	96	46133	52	305
Puducherry	18	8910	11	841

State	*UG Colleges*	*Seats*	*PG Colleges*	*Seats*
Punjab	103	43790	62	4262
Rajasthan	130	58013	57	3538
Sikkim	1	780	1	54
Tamil Nadu	527	279397	398	34475
Telangana	284	141118	256	32086
Tripura	2	600	1	102
Uttar Pradesh	296	142972	135	8747
Uttarakhand	31	12405	20	1279
West Bengal	91	37263	51	4423
Total	**3,289**	**15,53,809**	**2,234**	**1,97,018**

Sources: www. aicte.imdia.org
www.mhrd.gov.in
www.indiastury.com

11
Management Education

Management education has a long history in India dating back to the 19th century. Early business schools focused on the commercial side of business, seeking to fulfill the needs of the then British government. India's first business school, i.e. Commercial School of Pachiappa Charities was set up in 1886 in Chennai, then called Madras.

In 1903, the British government initiated secondary school level commerce classes at the Presidency College in Calcutta with a focus on secretarial practice, business communication, shorthand, typing, correspondence, and accounting.

The first college level business school was founded in 1913 in Mumbai i.e. Sydenham College, soon followed by another college in Delhi in 1920, the Commerce College, which later on was renamed as Shri Ram College of Commerce.

In Indian Institute of Social Science founded in the year 1948 was India's first management programme with an intention to train manpower to create and spread the knowledge required for managing industrial enterprises in India. The Catholic community founded Xavier Labour Relations Institute (XLRI) at Jamshedpur in 1949.

Indian Institute of Social Welfare and Business Management (IISWBM) was set up in 1953 at Calcutta. That was considered as India's first official management institute.

Encouraged by the results, the Government of India obtained a grant from the Fort Foundation in 1961 to set up two Indian Institutes of Management (IIMs)—one at Calcutta (West Bengal) and the other at Ahmedabad (Gujarat). This grant was focused on helping spread American management education knowledge and models to other nations, and had an intensive collaboration with an American business school for facilitating the transfer of learning.

- The IIM, Calcutta was established in collaboration with the Sloan School of Management (MIT) for faculty and pedagogy development in the year 1961, with the intention of focusing on the quantitative and operational aspects of management.
- IIM, Ahmedabad was founded in 1962, and pioneered the case

method of teaching in India with an emphasis on qualitative strategic integration.

- The mission of the IIMs was to professionalise Indian management education through teaching, research, training, institution-building, and consulting with the support of expertise developed by the pioneering IIMs.
- Two more IIMs were founded in Bangalore (Karnataka), and in Lucknow (Uttar Pradesh) in 1973.
- The Indian Institute of Forest Management was set up in 1982 in Bhopal (Madhya Pradesh) as a leader in specialised management education for the entire forestry system in India with the help of IIM, Ahmedabad.
- In the late 1990's, two more IIMs were set up, one at Kozhikode (Kerala) and the other at Indore (Madhya Pradesh).

Present Structure of Indian Management Education

The present structure is divided into six categories:

1. Indian Institutes of Management.
2. University departments of management studies, correspondence and part-time courses.
3. Colleges and institutes affiliated to universities.
4. Government or private institutes approved by AICTE.
5. Private colleges or colleges not affiliated to any university and not approved by AICTE.
6. Private colleges or institutes offering MBA courses in India in collaboration with foreign universities, where degree and diploma certificates are awarded by foreign universities.

Growth of B-Schools in India

Year	*No. of B-Schools*
1950-1980	118
1981-2000	673
2001-2005	700 (approximately)
2006-2007	1,400 and more
2007-2012	1,600 (approximately)

Distribution of Schools across Categories

Categories	*Approximate Nos.*
Government and quasi-government B. Schools	20
University Department	200
Private autonomous B-Schools	200
University affiliated colleges	1000
Others	200

B-Schools 1950-2011

Period	*No. of B-Schools added*	*Average Annual Addition*
1950-1980 (30 yrs.)	118	4
1980-1995 (15 yrs.)	304	20
1995-2000 (5 yrs.)	322	64
2000-2006 (6 yrs.)	1017	169
2006-2011 (5 yrs.)	2883	577

There are over 1,700 business schools in the country today distributed over different states as follows:

State	*Number*	*Percentage*
Andhra Pradesh	239	13.5
Bihar	14	0.8
Delhi	60	3.4
Gujarat	50	2.8
Haryana	34	1.9
Karnataka	116	6.6
Kerala	247	14.0
Madhya Pradesh	51	2.9
Maharashtra	202	11.5
Odisha	247	14.0
Punjab	25	1.4
Rajasthan	56	3.2
Tamil Nadu	139	7.9
Uttar Pradesh	181	10.9
Uttarakhand	18	1.0
West Bengal	47	2.9
*Others	35	1.9
Total	**1761**	**100.0**

* Others: Himachal Pradesh, Assam, Chhattisgarh, J&K, Jharkhand, Manipur, Meghalaya, Goa.

Sources: www.indiastudycentre.com
www.indiaedumrt.com
www.iosrjournalss.org
www.mbrd.gov.in

It can be observed from the above statistics that AICTE allowed a mindless expansion of B-Schools during 2006-11, a period in which both the global and Indian economies witnessed severe recession and a slump in demand for MBAs. It is owing to the faulty working of AICTE that we are now on the verge of a B-Schools' bubble burst. It has already started, and according to a statement of AICTE's Chairman, 65 B-Schools are under closure. The *Times of India* has recently reported that three lacs seats of engineering and management courses could not be filled up during 2011-12.

Drawbacks of Indian Management Education

Management experts pointed out the following drawbacks in Indian management education (Balaji, 2013)

1. Insufficient availability of specialised experts and qualified faculty.
2. Lack of industry-based specialisation.
3. Lower infrastructure.
4. Burden with heavy subjects.
5. Lack of necessary guidance to the students.
6. Lack of updated and industry-based syllabus.
7. Lack of admissions in management research.
8. Lack of inter-disciplinary approach.
9. Lack of specified authorities for quality research in management studies.
10. Insufficient grants for research.
11. The courses remain too theoretical and do not equip students with the right attitudes, skills and knowledge (ASK) required for them to be employable.
12. Students are not properly educated either to fit the industry requirements or to be entrepreneurial to start and grow small and medium companies. Students only get a degree, but not the industry-relevant qualification
13. Neither the institution nor the students are clear as to what kind of "product specification" is achieved at the end of the two years of study i.e., the quality of students produced and their ASK levels.
14. More than 85 percent of the students who complete their MBA/PGDM are not industry ready.
15. Just as customers would like to know about the specifications and quality before buying any "product," industry would also like to know and be assured of the product specification (quality) of the graduates/postgraduates it is going to hire.

How to Overcome the Drawbacks?

The following are some the ways:

- Provide decent salaries and professional ambience to faculties.
- Send the faculties regularly for training programmes to update their skills and abilities.
- Develop right mindset and attitude. Focus on quality of education, not quantity.

- There have to be interactive sessions for the students, rather than merely teaching what is mentioned in the books
- You cannot become a crackshot unless you lose some ammunition.
- The students have to be exposed to the industry through interface so that they understand the practical problems in corporate world. This boosts more confidence among the students.
- MBA is a professional degree and it should train and groom the students to be true professionals to take on the challenges being faced in the business environment.
- Make accreditation mandatory to ensure quality of education.
- Take stringent action against the illegal and unauthorised MBA colleges.
- Use online courses and other e-learning methods to increase training opportunities for field and local staff.
- Provide training in other languages besides English.
- Ensure that training is provided even in emergency situations.

Committees

The Government of India appointed various committees for time to time to critically review management education in India. The important ones are:

1. Kurian Committee—1991.
2. Iswar Dayal Committee—2001.
3. Management Education Review Committee—2009.
4. U.R. Rao Committee on Faculty Development—2004.
5. All India Management Association (AIMA)—2005.

The National Knowledge Commission was set up by the Prime Minister in 2005 and it appointed a Working Group on Management Education under the Chairmanship of S.L. Rao. The Working Group studied various committees' reports and the current status of business education in India and pointed out the following major challenges faced by Indian management education:

1. Though India produces a large number of graduates perhaps second to only the U.S., still a scholarly debate on curriculum pedagogy and innovation is negligible.
2. Most institutes depend on curricula and materials developed elsewhere, and have not developed an intrinsic capacity to respond to and evolve with changing needs of various sectors of industry.

3. Many institutions still are unable to fulfill the mandatory changes imposed on them, such as upgrading of the curriculum by the universities or the board of management studies.
4. Management institutions in India are today estimated to be graduating approximately 1 lac (+) students annually. However, what proportion of the total requirement will be for the increasingly more expensive graduates in management, and what proportion would be for the less expensive lower levels of managers is not yet clear. Again there is a need to raise the number from the current level of 1 lac (+) managers to about 3 lacs (+) managers a year over the next 10-15 years.
5. With the opening up of trade and cross border movement of goods and service, the country needs a paradigm shift in management education and management training for working professionals.
6. Presently, management education is treated as sub-department of engineering by AICTE, rather than recognising that management itself is an independent subject.

Though the various committees have suggested improvements for the betterment and qualitative improvement of management education, no significant changes have been made, except a few minor changes in the top ranking B-Schools. Now it is time to face the following challenges to respond to the global competition.

1. Ensure quality faculty.
2. Promote research culture.
3. Faculty development programmes.
4. Develop reading materials relevant to Indian context.
5. Develop interaction with industry.
6. Evolve a proper system of accreditation and rating.
7. Create an independent institutional mechanism.
8. Corporate governance of B-schools.
9. Need to broaden specialization areas of study.
10. Create a global mindset.
11. Internationalise management education.

The present business education is in a bad shape and needs to be reinvented with changing times. It is unfortunate that India with a billion plus population could not produce global leaders like Jack Welch, Peter F. Drucker, Bill Gates, Michel Dell. It is time India took a relook at the methodology of management education. It is also time Indian B-schools took stock of the situation and set their houses in order. The silver lining in the dark cloud of management education in India is the Indian School of Business (ISB) at Hyderabad which is ranked as the 15th best business school in the world surpassing other premier management institutions like IIMs. There is a strong need to focus management education globally (i.e. think globally, but act locally).

As business is becoming global, day by day, there is an increasing need for the B-school to provide global managers. Therefore, it has become necessary that management education should become more global, (G. Saha). Hence:

1. The business schools must admit international students to the programme. The Indian management institutes have no international participation.
2. The B-schools should induct a few international faculty members and provide an opportunity to the students to listen to how other country's business culture and systems function.
3. The B-schools should provide active programmes of students and faculty exchange with advanced countries.
4. Ensure that at least 25 percent of the curriculum deals with international subjects like international economics, international marketing, international financial management, and international business management etc.
5. Indian B-schools should collaborate with some well known foreign B-schools by which Indian students can do part of their education in those institutes.
6. Lastly, the B-schools need to also collaborate with some foreign placement consultancies to make sure at least some students can obtain jobs abroad.

12
Agricultural Education

India is an agricultural country. Agriculture and its allied activities act as main source of livelihood for more than 80 percent population of rural India. It provides employment to approximately 52 percent of labour. Its contribution to the gross domestic product (GDP) is between 14 to 15 percent. At the time of independence, India faced food grain shortage. India has achieved spectacular growth in agriculture sector since 1966. India today is self-sufficient in food grain, despite population increase. The food grain production in India increased from 51 million tonnes in 1950 to about 245 million tonnes in 2011-12. This growth in itself represents a remarkable achievement in the history of world agriculture. India has achieved significant growth in agriculture, milk production, pisciculture, and production of oilseeds, fruits, and vegetables owing to green, white, blue, and yellow revolutions. All these revolutions have brought prosperity for the farmers. Many factors are responsible for these achievements, namely, conducive government policies, receptivity of the farmers, and also establishment of higher agricultural education institutions. The new breed of skilled human resources was instrumental in generating new technologies, and in its assessment, refinement, and finally its dissemination to the farming community through extension methods.

In order to sustain, diversify, and realise the potential of agriculture sectors, it is necessary to develop skilled human resources. Agricultural human resource development is a continuous process undertaken by agricultural universities. Agricultural universities impart education in the various disciplines of agriculture, namely, agriculture, agricultural engineering, forestry, horticulture, veterinary and animal husbandry, dairy science, food technology, fisheries science, agriculture information technology, agro-business management etc. It imparts education at diploma, graduation, master's, and doctoral levels. At present there are 53 state agricultural universities (SAUs), five deemed to be universities, one central agricultural university, and four central universities with agricultural faculty. All these educational institutions get financial and technical support from Indian Council of Agricultural Research (ICAR), New Delhi.

Evolution of Agricultural Education in India

There was no formal system for agricultural education until 1877, when the first Agricultural College was established at Saidapet, which later shifted to Coimbatore. In some other parts of the country agricultural education started as a part of engineering colleges like Bengal Engineering College (then known as Civil Engineering College), Shibpur, which started agricultural education as part of the formal curriculum in 1898. It was only in the beginning of the 20th century that the need for formal agricultural research and education on a large scale was realised with the establishment of the Imperial Agricultural Research Institute (IARI) at Pusa, in 1905, where the agricultural education programme of the Civil Engineering College, Shibpur, had shifted a year earlier. Establishment of IARI in 1905 was followed by the establishment of colleges at Kanpur, Nagpur, Lyallpur, and Coimbatore in 1906, Pune in 1907, and Sabour in 1908.

Right from its inception, IARI has been developing trained manpower for the country, and training officers of the department of agriculture. High demand for such trainings led to the start of formal training courses leading to two year Diploma of Associateship of IARI from 1923 to 1957. The Associateship of IARI was recognised as equivalent to the M.Sc. degree of Indian universities by the ministry of education in 1949. The Associates of IARI became the backbone of the National Agricultural Research System (NARS). The institute shifted to its present location in New Delhi in 1936, and it was renamed Indian Agricultural Research Institute (IARI) in 1947.

Immediately after independence in 1947, the Government of India formed the University Education Commission under the Chairmanship of Dr. S. Radhakrishnan, who identified agricultural education as a major issue, and recommended establishment of 'rural universities.' Located in rural settings, the rural universities were to consist of a ring of small residential undergraduate colleges with specialised main university courses for postgraduate education at the centre. The rural universities were proposed to be autonomous and free to develop their own programmes, syllabi, curricula, and regulations to teach all subjects, including literature, history, philosophy, psychology, social sciences, mathematics, and the natural sciences. The concept of rural university was very similar to the land grant colleges. Subsequently, two joint Indo-American Teams of Agricultural Research Education (in 1954-55 and 1959-60) also endorsed the recommendation of the University Education Commission and suggested establishment of agricultural universities in various states of the country on the pattern of the land grant colleges of the USA.

In 1958, the University Grants Commission accorded the status of a Deemed to be University to IARI, to impart postgraduate education leading to M.Sc. and Ph.D. degrees. This was the beginning of reorganisation and modernisation of higher agricultural education in the country.

The first state agricultural university (SAU) was established in 1960 at Pantnagar, as UP was the only state which developed a blue-print to establish an SAU on a 1600-acre government farm (the Tarai State Farm). Government agreed to the setting up of the State Agricultural University at Pantnagar only as an experimental measure. Soon, new SAUs were established at Bhubaneshwar and Ludhiana (1962), Jabalpur (1964), Bangalore (1065), and other places. Today there are 66 universities/ institutions imparting agricultural education in the country.

The salient features of the SAUs are: (a) integration of teaching, research, and extension functions at all levels, (b) course-credit pattern of education with continuous internal evaluation, (c) teaching through constituent colleges with no provision for affiliated colleges, (d) organisational and operational autonomy, and other features related to overall improvement in social and economic conditions of rural areas. Later the Education Commission (1964-66) recommended establishment of at least one agricultural university in each state. The Indian Council of Agricultural Research developed a model in 1966, which could be adopted with such changes as were deemed necessary by the newly developed agricultural university.

There is no system in place, which can appraise the performance of SAUs. In 2014, Tamil Nadu Agricultural University (TNAU) was the best SAU at 74 position, followed by IARI at 138 position, and CS Haryana Agricultural University (HAU) at 254 position amongst the Indian universities in the web ranking.

Top Eleven Agricultural Universities in India, 2014

Institute/University	*Rank Indian University Web Ranking*
Tamil Nadu Agricultural University	74
Indian Agricultural Research Institute	138
CS Haryana Agricultural University	254
Assam Agricultural University	260
University of Agricultural Sciences, Dharwad	268
Kerala Veterinary and Animal Sciences University	278
Odisha University of Agriculture and Technology	293

YS Parmar University of Horticulture and Forestry	294
Rajasthan Agricultural University, Bikaner	301
Veterinary and Animal Sciences University, Ludhiana	303
Indian Veterinary Institute	304

It has been observed that pace and quality of technology generation and human resources development in many of the SAUs has gone down. The reasons for this slackening are inadequate state funding, reduced faculty strength, inadequate faculty development programmes, lack of modern infrastructure for education and research, etc. Establishment of new state agricultural universities and new faculties/colleges without providing necessary financial and faculty support has aggravated the problem.

Directly Visible Aspects/Issues

In general, agricultural education at graduate level is not a first or preferred choice for students. Generally, the bright students opt first for medicine and engineering as the case may be. Barring a few exceptions, only those who do not get admission in these preferred branches seek admission in agricultural colleges.

India is an agricultural country and agricultural education is directly and totally responsible to meet the most important need of human beings i.e. food. Therefore, some effectual action needs to be taken up by the government to attract bright students in the field of agricultural. Some challenges which the SAUs are facing are listed below:

Financial difficulties: Agricultural is a state subject. Therefore, the statutory responsibility for agricultural vests with the state government. The SAUs receive their annual budget from the state government. It is seen that the major portion of budget grants (85 percent) is utilised to meet the salary component of the university leaving only a limited grant portion (15 percent) for other operational expenses. Therefore, SAUs face difficulties in maintaining buildings, practical laboratories, infrastructure, etc. This ultimately affects the quality of agricultural education. This situation needs to be overcome by providing sufficient budget to meet all kinds of necessary expenses to the SAUs. Ideally, the budget grant for salaries and operational expanses should be 60:40.

Unfilled vacancies: In most of the SAUs a significant number of faculty positions are vacant. The vacant positions of faculty arise due to recruitment ban, and retirements. Many of such vacant positions are also abolished by respective state governments. This leads to heavy work load on existing faculties which may lead to poor performance in teaching and no time left for research or extension activities. To overcome the problem, the SAUs should take initiative in terms of recruitment process at appropriate time. Agricultural education being a professional discipline, the state government should also provide adequate financial support to fill up the vacant positions on a priority basis.

Inbreeding: There is very high inbreeding in the staff recruitment. Moreover, staff turnover in academics is very low which reduces opportunity to introduce new blood in the faculty.

Lack of autonomy: Agricultural universities are established by state governments. Thus although they are autonomous but they do not enjoy any kind of autonomy in real sense. For all major decisions SAUs are required to obtain permission/clearance from state government. There is also considerable political interference even in day to day activities. This lack of autonomy ultimately affects the quality of education. In order to prepare first-rate agricultural graduates real autonomy should be provided to all the SAUs by respective state governments.

Poor centre-state relationships: Since SAUs are established by the state government, it tries to retain its control over them. At the same time ICAR also helps SAUs by providing development grant. ICAR also monitors the utilisation of its grants. Sometimes it creates administrative issue/problems in SAUs with regard to certain policy decisions. In order to have uniformity throughout India, and overcome such administrative problems arising due to two controlling authorities, agricultural education and research may be appended to the concurrent list of the Constitution and leave it with the state thereby placing SAUs under direct control of ICAR.

Indirect Aspects/Issues

The main aim of agricultural education is to prepare human resources for agriculture sector. In addition to the above mentioned direct issues, agriculture education also faces some of the following indirect issues.

Poverty, unemployment, and malnutrition among agricultural dependent population: Global food demand is expected to double by 2050 and at the same time natural resources are continuously reducing and deteriorating. Inadequate attention to agriculture has led to increase in prices of food products, thus making it inaccessible to poor people. Poverty is closely associated with malnutrition. India has a large number of poor people (250 million out of approximately 1000 million worldwide). Approximately 75 percent of poor people reside in villages. Most of them are small and marginal landholders and landless labourers. They overcrowd agriculture for their livelihood with limited or marginal productivity. Moreover, they overexploit natural resources for their subsistence. Harmonizing science and technological (S & T) inputs is probably the only solution to nurture rural livelihood without degrading natural resources. Education and training for capacity building to gain access to employment will be essential. Therefore, to overcome this challenge, in addition to awarding formal degrees, SAUs will be required to initiate job driven vocational programmes to build avenues for off-farm activities.

Integration of agricultural education and job creation: In India almost every graduate desires a white collar job, preferably in the government sector. But due to financial crunch and the government's resolve to phase out nonperforming assets, job opportunities in this sector have also reduced. Therefore, it is essential to prepare graduates and postgraduates who create their own work and provide work to others. Agricultural education, being a professional discipline, can satisfy these conditions. Although the present course curricula of agriculture and allied faculties as suggested by ICAR do satisfy this need, but still there is scope for reorienting them to address stakeholders' concerns and needs.

Demand of stakeholders: Farmers and consumers as major stakeholders of agricultural system would be more aware of usefulness and relevance of S & T findings. Their expectations and concern would form an integral part of agricultural S & T activities and programmes.

Improvement of Agricultural Education: Many proposals to improve the state of agricultural education have been put forward by eminent persons and discussed at relevant fora also. Some progress is evident due to such efforts, but still further actions are required to make it responsive to the present needs. Improving the quality and relevance of agricultural education requires a fundamental change of approach in governance and control, financial sustainability, accountability, autonomy, transparency, and meritocracy.

The following recommendations can be implemented to bring agricultural education in tune with present needs.

- ICAR guidelines should be binding on state authorities to have uniformity in all the agricultural universities in different states throughout India. ICAR should play a leadership role in improving the overall governance of the SAUs by ensuring adherence to the provisions of the model act for agricultural universities.
- Despite provision of adequate funds from state government as well as ICAR, agricultural universities should be encouraged to be self-sufficient.
- Agriculture universities should be granted full autonomy and avoid political interference. Functioning of any university is

influenced to a great extent by the Vice-Chancellor. Selection of each Vice-Chancellor should be by a committee of eminent scientists, who are known for their impeccable integrity. The recommendation of the selection committee should go directly to the Chancellor for action.

- An international review committee needs to be formed to put Indian higher agricultural education at par with world class universities. Eminent educators, scientists, and researchers from India and abroad should be included in the international review committee. The main task of such a committee would be to recommend specific and detailed action plan to modernise Indian agricultural education system.
- Higher decision making body in agricultural university is Board of Management or Board of Governors in collective form. Thus, the Board of Management/ Board of Governors should ensure good governance by prudent means and accept their collective and individual responsibilities. They must ensure and respect university's autonomy and accountability.
- Establishment of college level committees which include external experts to monitor and evaluate performance of teaching, research, and extension activities undertaken by faculty members.
- Each SAU should have their short and long term master plan for their human resource development and human resource planning.

13
Teacher Education

Teachers have a vital role to play in character building of the students and in preparing them to succeed in their lives. This aspect of education cannot be more relevant than in current times as the demand of knowledge economy needs to be driven by experimentation, innovation, and creativity, which in turn requires education systems to equip students with different skills. Thus, it is crucial for teachers to be well-rounded and equipped with necessary expertise so that they can build required knowledge and skills in the students to enable them to succeed in a world of tremendous opportunities and challenges. Teacher is a change agent and there is a dire need for change from narrow nationalism to universalism; from ethnic and cultural prejudice to tolerance, understanding and pluralism; from autocracy to democracy in its various manifestations. Further the teacher has to play wider role in bridging technologically divided world where high technology in the privilege of the few to a technologically united world. All these challenges place enormous responsibilities on teachers who participate in the molding of the minds and characters of the new generation. This proves that the role of teacher educators becomes even more important in future. Only a robust teacher education can produce robust teacher education. Teacher educators are key actors in the space of quality education. This is turn enforces the whole teacher education system to put up its best show for the development of the whole nation.

After independence the emerging socio-economic and political situations influenced the national scenario of teacher education. The Government of India set up different committees and commissions for addressing to the specific issues of education in general and teacher education (TE) in particular. A large number of teachers were found to be untrained and an attempt was made to clear the backlog. The main concerns of teacher education pertain to both quality and quantity. In 1948, the Central Institute of Education was established in Delhi and the Government Training College at Allahabad was developed into the Central Pedagogical Institute.

The University Education Commission (1948-49)

Just after independence the University Education Commission was appointed under the chairman of Dr. S. Radhakrishnan. The Commission submitted its report in 1949. The Commission observed that obviously there was no difference in the theory papers offered in the various teacher training colleges. But there was much difference in the practice followed by them. The number of supervised lessons varied from ten to sixty and the type of practice teaching and student teaching varies from one to another.

The Commission observed that training colleges had no basic orientation in the essentials. For improvement of teacher training, it suggested that the teacher educators must look at the whole course from a different angle—that the theory and practice should support each other; that there should be intelligent following of rule of thumb methods; trainees be recruited from people having a firsthand experience of school teaching; that courses in the theory of education must be flexible and adaptable to local circumstances; that original work by professors and lecturers in education should not suffer from isolation and lack of inter-university planning.

Many attempts have been made from time to time for restructuring teacher education with different and diverse aims of improving the status and arena of teacher education. Pioneer contributing agencies/commissions are tabulated here:

Timeline of Reforms for Teacher Education

S. No.	*Pioneer Committees/ Commissions*	*Year*	*Focal Area*
1.	Kothari Commission	1964-66	For effective professional preparation for teachers, teacher education must be brought into the mainstream of academic life of universities on the one hand, and the school life and education department on the other.
2.	NCTE Curriculum Framework	1978	Proposed first curriculum framework emphasising the need for developing task oriented M. Ed. curriculum with scope for practical work in education.
3.	Chattopadhyaya Committee	1983-85	For relevant teacher education, the minimum duration of training for a secondary teacher should be five years following the completion of Class XII.

(Contd.)

S. No.	*Pioneer Committees/ Commissions*	*Year*	*Focal Area*
4.	Yash Pal Committe	1985	Content of the programme should be restructured to ensure its relevance to the changing needs of school education focusing on self-learning and independent thinking.
5.	National Policy on Education (POA)	1993	Centrally sponsored scheme of restructuring and reorganisation of teacher education to create a sound institutional infrastructure for pre-service and in-service training of elementary and secondary school teachers.
		1995	Became as a statutory body to look into the teacher education programme in India to maintain quality.
		1998	Became an autonomous body through act of parliament and given independent charge to eliminate all the anomalies breeding in the teacher education programme.
6.	National Council for Teacher Education (NCTE)	2005	Released position paper declaring current teacher education practices inadequate in preparing teachers and teacher educators.
		2009	Recommended integration of study and observation of a teacher education in an institution, as a part of M.Ed. course practicum. Observation, study, instruction, and reflection conducted during internship were expected to fulfill this need.
		2010	Draft syllabus for the M.Ed. programme suggested a theory dominated course with 1000 marks in six core and four specialisation courses, 200 marks for dissertation and viva-voce.
9.	Justice J. S. Verma Committee	2012	Proposed a paradigm shift in the way pre-service teacher education is perceived in India by providing detailed lacunae in teacher education

Intake in Different Courses as per MHRD Guidelines, 2012

S.N.	Courses	Number of Government Institutions	Annual Admissions	Number of Private Institutions	Annual Admissions	Total Admissions
1.	D.Ed.	757	49089	4831	298278	347367
2.	B.Ed.	224	20031	5730	609486	629517
3.	M.Ed.	102	3672	790	25285	28957
4.	B.P.E.D.	19	1284	538	28150	29434
5.	Others	76	16760	800	51422	68182
6.	**Total**	**1178**	**90836**	**12689**	**1012621**	**1103457**

Teacher Education Curriculum: Issue and Concerns

A teacher functions within the broader framework of the school education system—its goals, curricula, materials, methods, and expectations from the teacher. A teacher education curriculum framework for school education needs to focus on how a teacher needs to be prepared in relation to the needs and demands arising in the school context. As such, it needs to engage with the questions of the learner, the learning process, and the content, and pedagogy of educating teachers. Moreover, the Right to Education (RTE) Act mandates that the teacher would be responsible for enrolling all children seeking admission, refraining from inflicting corporal punishment, complete the given curriculum in the given time, assess students, hold parent meetings to orient them on their ward's progress, and as part of the school management committee, organise the overall running of the school. Teacher education and school education have a symbiotic relationship. Developments in both these sectors mutually reinforce the concerns necessary for the qualitative improvement of the entire spectrum of education. NCTE undertook a major exercise by developing a new National Curriculum Framework for Teacher Education against this backdrop, which is both contextual and in tune with the emerging concerns and imperatives of the fast changing canvas of education both nationally and globally.

The National Curriculum Framework for Teacher Education, 2009

The National Curriculum for Teacher Education (NCFTE) broadly dealt with the foundations of educations, curriculum, pedagogy, and school internship. Considerable focus has been given in this Framework on continuing professional development strategies. This Framework is visualised to act as a catalyst to change the profile of teacher education so that the teacher education institutions become active centres, not only of research but also of practical experiments directed to the improvement of educational methods and curricula.

The Framework seriously deplores the status of training of teacher educators and remarks that the weakest aspect, perhaps, of teacher education is the absence of professional preparation of teacher educators.

National Curriculum Framework for Teachers, 2009 points to various facets of the teacher education programmes. The document also throws light on the insufficiency of various programmes for preparation of teacher educators, while arguing that the quality of pedagogical inputs in teacher education programmes, and the manner in which they are transacted to realise their intended objectives depend largely on the professional competence of teacher educators.

The layout of NCFTE, 2009 consist of three broad curricular areas—(A) Foundations of education which include courses under three broad rubrics, namely, child studies, contemporary studies, and educational studies (understanding oneself as a person and as a teacher and of theories related to child development and learning and the social and cultural context of education); (B) Curriculum and pedagogical theory which include courses under two broad rubrics, namely, curriculum studies, and pedagogic studies (understanding of the nature of subject disciplines in the social context of learning and ways of transacting knowledge with children in formal contexts); and (C) School internship leading to the development of a broad repertoire of perspective, professional capacities, and skills. Together, these areas constitute the common core curriculum for teacher education programmes across stages—pre-school, elementary, secondary, and higher secondary. The nature and form which these core components may take and the quantum, intensity, their relative importance, quality of learning experiences to be provided under them, and their relative importance may, however, vary with reference to the stage of teacher preparation, the school and learner context, and other factors (NCTE, 2009).

The Framework has been prepared in the background of the National Curriculum Framework (NCF), 2005 and the principles laid down in the Right of Children to Free and Compulsory Education Act, 2009, which necessitated an altered framework for teacher education which would be consistent with the changed philosophy of school curriculum recommended in the NCF, 2005. While articulating the vision of teacher education, the Framework has some important dimensions of the new approach to teacher education, as noted below:

- Reflective practices to be the central aim teacher education.
- Student-teachers should be provided opportunities for self-learning, reflection, assimilation, and articulation of new ideas.
- Developing capacities for self-directed learning and ability to

think, be critical, and to work in groups.

- Providing opportunities to student-teachers to observe and engage with children, communicate with, and relate to them. The Framework highlighted the focus, specific objectives, broad areas of study in terms of theoretical and practical learning, and curricular transaction and assessment strategies for the various initial teacher education programmes. The Framework made several recommendations on the approach and methodology of in-service teacher training programmes, and also outlined a strategy for implementation of the Framework. As a natural corollary to the NCFTE, the NCTE also developed 'model' syllabi for various teacher education courses.

National Council for Teacher Education Initiatives

The quality of teacher education not only depends on professionally sound and relevant curriculum, but also on the way curriculum is implemented in teacher education institutions. This, in turn, depends on the expertise of the faculty, its quality, and the infrastructural and instructional facilities provided in the institutions. It is in this background that the National Council for Teacher Education (NCTE) was established in 1995 as a statutory body under the provision of the NCTE Act, 1993 with the main objectives of planned and coordinated development of the teacher education system throughout the country, for the regulation and proper maintenance of norms and standards in the teacher education system, and for matters connected therewith. NCTE is working from its genesis till now with some achieved and some to-be-achieved aims. Thus, in order to make it able to achieve its vision of quality TE in India, it must undertake some reforms and modifications, which are listed below:

- The NCTE needs to periodically review the existing norms and standard for the various teacher education programmes (TEPs) and create a standing committee for periodic review of curricula, as well as the norms and standards of the programmes.
- It should develop comprehensive guidelines for innovative teacher education programmes for grant of recognition.
- It should develop a new framework for undertaking inspection of the recognised institutions, with enhanced focus on process parameters, to ascertain the quality of the institutions, and take appropriate action to improve the overall quality of the teacher education system.
- Set up a Teacher Education Assessment and Accreditation Centre (TEAAC), and constitute a Committee to prepare a

comprehensive framework of accreditation, as suggested in this report.

- The NCTE should set up an institutional platform in close coordination and collaboration with state governments, universities, UGC, Distance Education Council (DEC), etc., and take decisions on standards, procedures, and quality parameters concerning teacher education.
- It should notify regulations to govern inspections of teacher education institutions. These should include eligibility condition for empanelment as inspection team members, composition of an inspection team, time required for conducting inspection, format for obtaining the required information from the concerned institutions, and submission of the inspection report.
- In order to ensure accountability, it is essential to establish a Vigilance Cell in the NCTE, on priority, which would investigate into any act of misbehaviour and misconduct on part of the various functionaries associated with the NCTE.
- The tenure of the office of the Chairperson and Vice Chairperson of the NCTE should be raised from four years to five years, and the upper age limit should be raised from 60 years to 65 years.
- The central government should develop guidelines regarding the manner of appointment of members of the Council. Further, members of the regional committee should be appointed by the Council.
- The NCTE should appoint a Task Force to undertake organisational restructuring of the NCTE, and to work out its human resource requirement, as suggested in this Report.

Some of the factors that have contributed to malfunctioning of NCTE may be:

- Making an act for NCTE which does not cover the whole nation.
- Failure of the central government to provide adequate number of academicians, and not ensuring that chairpersons and members of regional committees have direct experience of school teaching and school teacher training, in additional to possessing a teacher training qualification.
- Inadequate study of regulatory bodies and their functions in developed systems outside India.
- Forcing states to follow national level norms and standards for teacher training programmes, which do not take into account the diversity that exists among state in respect of school education.

- Failure, even after 15 years, to make provision for additional remuneration for teachers having acquired two year B.Ed. degree from three Regional Institutes of Education of NCERT at Ajmer, Bhopal, and Bhubaneswar.
- Failing to take action against NCERT-managed Regional Institutes of Education of NCERT and other institutions of state government, which failed to abide by its norms and standards.
- Failure to check large scale corruption in NCTE recognition process involving not only visiting team members, but also NCTE officials, as reflected in large number of court cases for which, academicians humorously describe NCTE as "Network for Corruption in Teacher Education."

Ministry of Human Resource Development (MHRD)

MHRD (2015) mentioned some of major reforms to be made and followed by teacher education institutions. Some of the latest recommendations are listed below:

- Intensive revision and upgradation of B.Ed. Course for two years, with at least 20 weeks of classroom teaching experience.
- An integrated four-year course leading to BA and B.Ed. Degree after 12th class.
- No more isolation of teacher education by permitting BA/B.Sc. and B. Tech. students to join B.Ed. course.
- Increase in intake in teacher education institutions from a unit of 35 to 50 and increase in multiples of 50 in most programmes.
- Change in M.Ed. programme allowing for specialisation in elementary education/primary education.
- Change in administration of teacher education institutions to bring transparency in the application process of education courses, only online applications, and online fee payment will be accepted.

Justice Verma Commission (2012)

The Verma Commission made a total of 30 recommendations for teacher education institutions and strengthening NCTE. The major recommendations are as follows:

- Government should increase its investment for establishing teacher education institutions (TEIs), and increase the institutional capacity of teacher preparation, especially in the deficit states.

- Government may explore the possibility of instituting a transparent procedure of pre-entry testing of candidates to the pre-service teacher education programmes, keeping in view the variation in local conditions.
- Teacher education should be a part of the higher education system. The duration of programmes of teacher education needs to be enhanced.
- It is desirable that new teacher education institutions are located in multi and interdisciplinary environment. This will have a significant implication for the redesigning of norms and standards of various teacher education courses specified by the NCTE.
- Current teacher education programmes (TEPs) may be re-designed keeping in view the recommendations in the National Curriculum Framework for Teacher Education (NCFTE, 2009-10) and other relevant material.
- Every pre-service teacher education institution may have a dedicated school attached to it as a laboratory where student teachers get opportunities to experiment with new ideas, and hone their capacities and skill to become reflective practitioners.
- There is a need to establish a national level academic body for continual reflection and analysis of teacher education programmes, their norms and standards, development of reading material, and faculty development of teacher educators.
- As a matter of policy, the first professional degree/diploma in teacher education should be offered only in face-to-face mode. Distance learning programmes and the use of blended learning material may be developed and used for continuing professional development of school teachers and teacher educators.
- The institutions capacity should be increased for preparation of teacher educators. There is a need to make the Masters in Education programme of 2-year duration with the provision to branch out for specialisation in curriculum and pedagogic studies, foundation studies, management, policy and finance, and other areas of emerging concerns in educations.
- The idea of creating opportunities for teaching practitioners to teach in teacher education institutions, as visiting faculty, may be explored. Similarly, teacher educators could be considered as visiting faculty in schools.
- Faculty development programmes for teacher education should be institutionalised.
- There is need for enhanced investment in promotion of research in education in general, and in teacher education in particular,

in the universities. Creation of an inter-university centre in teacher education could play a significant role in this regard.

Arguments in favour of Two Year B.Ed. Programme

- One year is insufficient time to provide adequate knowledge and skills to the trainee teachers.
- Two year programme will help in shaping the outstanding teachers by inculcating conceptual understanding in philosophical, psychological, and social concepts.
- The specific objectives given by NCTE are very difficult to be achieved in the duration of one year. There needs to be more focus on ICT in B.Ed. curriculum, because in this age of technology, it has become an important part of the educational system.
- The increased duration of B.Ed. programme will provide sufficient time for achieving overall development of personality. Increase in duration will provide a strong base for M.Ed. programme too.
- Due to increased duration, both teachers and students will have more time available for the theory and practical components, more time for co-curricular activities,
- ICT, yoga education, gender education, and inclusive education constitute the integral parts of the teacher's education programmes, which are crucial as well as desirable aspects of the society.

Arguments against Two Year B.Ed. Programme

- One year is sufficient time duration for developing pedagogical skills and knowledge among trainee teachers.
- Bright students show interest towards the professional courses which are of minimum duration and provide job opportunities. Increased duration of B.Ed. programme may attract fewer number of bright students.
- Increased duration will also increase the cost of the course, due to which some students from low and average economic status may not be able to participate in the course.
- No special benefit will be given to the students who pass through two years B.Ed. programme. They will be treated in the same way as the students who have passed B.Ed. in one year.
- Increased duration of B.Ed. programme may adversely affect the students as they have to spend one more year for the same degree.

- In 1985, Chattopadhyaya Commission suggested that the two summer months may be added to the academic year of B.Ed. programme with 220 working days, and also increasing hours per day for the effective transaction of B.Ed. programme. This would allow sufficient time for practical work which will enhances the quality of teacher education.

Strengthening of Teacher Education in 12th Five Year Plan

With the vast and diverse landscape of Indian education system, significant progress has been made towards the achievement of the goals laid out in the Constitution and the national policy on education. These include higher levels of funding, access, enrolment, infrastructure, and RTE Act. Inspite of these developments, critical challenges continue to remain in areas like retention, quality, and equitable opportunities. On the whole, about 5-7 per cent of government schools provide high quality education to students which depend on pivotal leadership, motivation, and competence of teachers. Thus, if the quality of teachers in all schools needs to improve, then the following issues are of key importance:

- Holistic teacher development.
- Radical overhaul of pre-service teacher education.
- Teacher recruitment.
- Involvement of teacher education.
- Development of academic resources.

14
Legal Education

Legal education is a vital link in the creation of knowledge as well as in the application of such knowledge in society. The need for trained legal personnel in academic, litigation, corporate practice, government, and civil society has increased significantly over the last few years. It is estimated that the demands for such trained personnel will rise far more exponentially in the years to come. Today, law is not viewed merely as an instrument of social control, but also an instrument of social change. The aim of legal education should be not only to produce good lawyers, but also create cultured, law-abiding citizens who are inculcated with concepts of human values and human rights, who can serve humanity in various capacities such as administrations, law teachers, jurist, judges, and industrial entrepreneurs, etc.

When India gained its independence in 1947, its legal profession and legal teaching were not able to play the role they ought to have played. The politicians, the economists, and the engineers were expected to rebuild the society. The law was to assist in the form of public law and administrative law; but private law, and the legal profession claimed only a small and marginal role in social changes. Since independence, the situation has deteriorated further. India, with its mixed economy and its significant planning efforts, makes extensive use of law and regulation. Administration, however, is largely in the hands of bureaucrats in whose recruitment and training, legal training does not carry significant weight, except for specifically legal jobs. The role of the legal profession as a whole is ordinarily restricted to giving advice after trouble emerges. India's elaborate written constitution, as applied to a diverse society in time of rapid changes, would require a wise and effective legal profession, but the flow of talent into the profession had declined. Before independence, most of the lawyers in India were foreign educated, usually in England. They had a sense of self-determination and played a prominent role in the freedom movement.

Traditionally the degrees that were conferred carried the title of LL.B. (Bachelor of Law) or B.L. (Bachelor of Law). The eligibility requirement for these degrees was that the applicant should have a Bachelor's degree in any subject from a recognised institution. Thereafter, the LL. B/B.L. course was for three years, upon the successful completion of which the applicant was granted either of the two degrees as mentioned above.

Advent of National Law University in India

As discussed, legal education was traditionally offered as a three year graduate degree course. However, the structure was changed in 1987. Law degrees in India are granted and conferred in terms of the Advocates Act, 1961, which is a law passed by the parliament of India, both on the aspects of legal education and also regulation of conduct of legal profession. Under the Act, the Bar Council of India (BCI) is the supreme regulatory body to regulate the legal profession in India, ensure the compliance of the laws, and maintenance of professional standards by the legal profession in the country.

The BCI prescribes the minimum curriculum required to be taught in an institution offering law courses to make them eligible to grant law degrees. The Bar Council also carries out periodic supervision of the institutions conferring the degree, and evaluates their teaching methodology, curriculum, and infrastructure amongst other things. After having determined that the institution meets the required standards, BCI recognises the institutions, and the degrees conferred by them.

However, based upon the suggestion by the Law Commission of India and the prevailing cry for reform, the BCI initiated an experiment in terms of establishing specialised law universities solely devoted to legal education to raise the academic standards of legal profession in India. This decision was taken sometime in 1985. Thereafter, the first law university (University National Law School of India popularly known as NLIS) was established in. This law university was meant to offer a multi-disciplinary and integrated approach to legal education. NLIS offers a five year law course, upon the successful completion of which an integrated degree with the title of "B.A., LL.B. (Honours)" is awarded. Thus, for the first time a law degree other than LL.B. or B.L. was awarded in India.

Subsequently, other law universities were set up, each offering five-year integrated law degrees with different nomenclatures. The next was the National Law Institute University set up in Bhopal in 1997. It was followed by National Academy of Legal Studies and Research, Hyderabad NALSAR University of Law set up in 1998. The National Law University, Jodhpur offered for the first time in 2001 the integrated law degree of "B.B.A, LL.B. (Honours)" which was preceded by the West Bengal National University of Juridical Sciences offering the "B.Sc., LL.B. (Honours)" degree. KIIT Law School, Bhubaneswar became the first law school in India in 2007 to start integrated law in three different streams and honours specialization; i.e. BA/BBA/B.Sc. LL.B. (Honours). Thereafter, Gujarat National Law University, Gandhinagar; Hidayatulla Law University, Raipur; National University of Advanced Legal Studies, Kochi; Ram Manohar Lohia National Law University, Lucknow; Rajiv Gandhi, National University of Law, Patiala; Chanakya National Law University, Patna; and the National Law University, Delhi were established.

Committees and Commissions Concerned with Legal Education

- First Indian University Commission, 1902
- Recommendations of Chagal Committee, 1910
- Bills on Legal Education, 1936-49
- Bombay Legal Education Committee, 1949
- All India Bar Committee, 1951-52
- Rajasthan Legal Education Committee, 1955
- Law Commission of India, 1958
- Advocates Act, 1961
- Gajendra Gadkar Committee, 1964
- All India Seminar on Legal Education, 1972
- Establishment of Bar Council of India Trust, 1974
- Legal Education Seminar, Bombay, 1977
- First National Convention on Legal Education, Hyderabad, 1981
- All India Law Teachers Conference, 1981
- Report of Bar Council of India, 1982
- All India Council for Technical Education Act, 1987
- Report of the Curriculum Development Centre in Law, 1990
- Bar Council of India Training Rules, 1995
- Report of Professional Legal Education Reform Committee, 1996
- 184th Report of the Law Commission of India

In the year 2002, the Law Commission of India (LCI) undertook a comprehensive suo moto review of the structure and regulation of the professional legal education system in India. The Report prepared by LCI was entitled "184th Report on the Legal Education and Professional Training, and Proposals for Amendments to the Advocates Act, 1961 and the University Grants Commission act, 1956" analyses in detail the regulation of professional legal education.

Law Commission of India (LCI) in its Report analyzes at length the quality of consultation envisaged between BCI and the Universities under Section 7(1) (h) of the Advocates Act, 1961. The Report notes that the responsibility of BCI in ensuring '…standards of legal education…', and that of UGC in ensuring '…standards of education…' are, in fact, not in conflict with each other, but have to be harmoniously construed. Section 7(1) (h), in providing for consultation between BCI and UGC, advances the proposition that both the statutory bodies share common goals vis-à-vis regulation of professional legal education. The Report stipulates that the requirement of Section 7(1)(f) is, in fact, 'effective consultation' between BCI and the University, thereby increasing the involvement of the members of academia in regulating legal education.

There are obviously, practical and logistical difficulties in BCI consulting the huge number of universities and other institutions imparting legal education. The LCI Report, therefore, recommended that instead of requiring 'effective consultation' with each university, the Advocates Act should instead be suitably amended to enable BCI to consult a representative body, which in turn, should be constituted by UGC, thus ensuring that both BCI and UGC remain equal partners in regulating legal education.

LCI in its Report also considered the composition of the BCI Legal Education Committee provided for under Section 10 of the Advocates Act, 1961. Regarding the concerns raised by the academia over their perceived under-representation in the BCI Legal Education Committee, LCI rightly notes that the roles of the Bar, Bench, and the academia vis-à-vis the regulation of legal education should be balanced. The Report rejects the proposition that the Bar Council's role should be limited to regulating entry into the legal profession, and maintenance of professional standards.

To represent the academia, the Report recommended the constitution of a UGC Committee on legal education, comprising a total of ten members, with six members being law teachers in office, and two members being Vice-Chancellors/Directors of statutory law universities. The Report envisages three faculty members to be common to both the BCI Legal Education Committee and the UGC Committee on Legal Education, in order to ensure better coordination between the BCI and the UGC Committees.

Report of the National Knowledge Commission (2007)

In the year 2007, the National Knowledge Commission (NKC), chaired by noted entrepreneur and policymaker, Dr. Sam Pitroda, submitted its Report to the Prime Minister of India on reform of legal education. The Report crucially notes that the "…. Vision of legal education is to provide justice-oriented education essential to the realisation of values enshrined in the Constitution of India …" in discharge of its functions in the field of legal education in the country. The working group, through a consultative process with the stakeholders in the field of legal education, made a number of reformatory proposals vis-à-vis the structure of professional legal education in India, which were forwarded as part of NKC's report to the Prime Minister.

NKC recommended the establishment of a new regulatory body comprising eminent layers, BCI members, judges, academicians, representatives from trade, commerce and industry, economists, social workers, students, and others; for the purpose of revamping legal education to meet the needs and challenges of all sections of society. NKC envisaged that this new regulatory mechanism would function under the auspices of the Independent Regulatory Authority of Higher Education (IRAHE), and would be vested with powers to deal with all aspects of legal education. The decisions of this authority shall be binding on the institutions teaching law as well as the union and state governments.

NKC also recommended the development of an independent rating system based on a set of agreed criteria to assess the standard of all institutions teaching law, as a mechanism to ensure consistent academic quality throughout the country. The criteria for rating would be evolved by the Standing Committee for Legal Education, while the rating would be done by independent agencies licensed by IRAHE for that purpose. Recognition could be either granted or withdrawn on the basis of such ratings. The rating result should be reviewed annually, regularly updated, monitored, and made available in the public domain.

Further, in order to attract and retain talented faculty, the NKC Report recommended better incentives, including improved remuneration and service conditions. According to NKC, it may be necessary to think of salary differentials within and between universities and law schools, along with other means of attracting and retaining talented faculty members. Such salary differentials between and within universities and law schools could be effective without being large, and would retain talent in legal academia where the problem of inadequate remuneration is far more acute than in other disciplines. Salary differentials could be considered as a means to retain quality talent, and also promote a culture of excellence.

Importantly, the NKC Report recommended that to foster quality and create better incentives, there is also need to remove fetters on faculty that pertain to opportunities in legal practice (such as consultancy assignments and legal practice in courts). These reforms need to be introduced in a balanced, reasonable, and regulated manner to ensure adequate incentives for faculty without compromising on the maintenance of consistent academic quality. As a further incentive, it is necessary to create better opportunities for active involvement of academia in the shaping of national legal education policy.

The National Knowledge Commission, in the report presented to the Prime Minister, also lamented that institutions offering law courses in India are 'far from standard'. Coming out very strongly against the BCI, the NKC report declared that, "In the light of the changed scenario in the last fifty years and the existing gaps and deficiencies in overall quality, it is clear that the BCI has neither the power under the Advocates Act, 1961, nor the expertise to meet the new challenges both domestically and internationally."

In a recent development, the central government expressed its keenness to bring in a new legislation to set up a National Commission for Higher Legal education and Research. The Bill, which has been specifies the role of the Commission, and at a first glance conveys that BCI would no longer have anything to do with legal education. It says, the Commission shall specify:

i. Norms and standards of academic quality for accreditation, and benchmarking of higher legal education institutions, which means criteria for quality control.
ii. Norms and processes for declaration of a law university or higher legal education institutions empowered, by or under any law, to award any degree or diploma, to commence its academic operations. This is vital since no law college could commence operation without the Commission's approval.
iii. Norms of academic quality for a law university or law school.
iv. Regulate the entry and operation of foreign law education institutions.

The bill mandates the Commission to undertake research to identify future direction and processes in higher legal education, and to assess further knowledge manpower requirements in different fields of law to meet the needs of the bar and the Bench, courts, arbitration, and conciliation. It will advise and facilitate the states or a body of institutions in establishing a law university in accordance with the norms and standards specified by it. The government proposes to ask the proposed Commission to chalk out future of entire legal education.

The Commission is also expected to maintain the directory of academics for leadership position in law for appointment as vice-chancellor, director, or head of a legal educational and research institution.

Legal education is stated to be suffering from uncontrolled growth of law colleges, poor quality of teaching, poor organisation and management, lack of continuing legal education, old and traditional methods, stereotype question papers lacking imagination, faculty examination, lack of infrastructure, lack of adequate library facilities, poor attendance in class, mass copying in examination, absence of practical training, lack of finances, etc. Therefore, time has come to set right goals, revamp and modernise legal education, prepare students to adopt modern technologies, and comprehend the intricacies arising out of developments in cyber laws, forensic sciences, medical sciences, etc.

The present legal system has to meet the requirements of the society, which has entered the 21st century. Law has to deal with problems of diverse magnitudes. A student of law and an advocate has to be trained in professional skills to meet the challenges of globalization and universalisation of law. With the advent of multinationals in India, as anywhere else, the task of lawyers has become highly technical. There is an imperative need to have competent lawyers who are trained in the right principles of legal education. This makes a sound case for introducing reforms in legal education.

15
Women's Education

Promotion of gender equality in education is essential for human resource development. By educating a woman you educate the whole family. Given that a woman has the responsibility of the whole family on herself, an educated woman is better capable of taking care of the health, nutrition, and education of her children, and be more of an active agent in the social and economic development of the country. It is evident that economic success everywhere is based on educational success. Literacy is the basic building block of education. It is a basic component of social cohesion and national identity. It leads to an improvement in the depth and quality of public opinion. No society has ever liberated itself economically, politically, or socially without a sound base of educated women. Education has a direct impact on women empowerment as it creates in them awareness about their rights, their capabilities, and the choices and opportunities available to them. Studies have indicated that there is a strong correlation between female education and developmental indicators.

Importance of Women's Education

The importance of women's education is manifold:

- *Economic development and prosperity:* Education will empower women to come forward and contribute towards the development and prosperity of the country.
- *Economic empowerment:* As long as women remain backward and economically dependent on men, their helpless condition cannot be changed. Economic empowerment and independence will only come through proper education and employment of women.
- *Improved life:* Education helps us to live a good life. A properly educated woman's identity as an individual would never get lost. She can read and learn about her rights, ensuring that her rights are not trodden on. The life and condition of women would improve a lot, if we take a broad outlook in the field of female education.

- *Improved health:* Educated girls and women are aware of the importance of *health and hygiene.* Through health education, they are empowered to lead a healthy lifestyle. An educated mother can take better care of both herself and her baby.
- *Dignity and honour:* Educated women are now treated with dignity and honour. They become a source of inspiration for millions of young girls, who make them their role models.
- *Justice:* Educated women are better informed of their rights for justice. Such knowledge is likely to eventually lead to a decline in instances of violence and injustice against women such as dowry, forced-prostitution, child-marriage, female foeticide, etc.
- *Option to choose a profession of her choice:* Educated women can be highly successful in various professional fields. A girl-child should get equal opportunity for education, so that she can plan to become a successful doctor, engineer, nurse, air-hostess, cook, or choose a profession of her choice.
- *Alleviate poverty:* Women education is a pre-requisite to alleviate poverty. Women need to take equal burden of the massive task of eliminating poverty. This would demand massive contribution from educated women. There cannot be much social and economic change unless girls and women are given their rights for education.

Women in Decision Making

UNESCO found some strong barriers against participation of women in decision-making processes in a study entitled "Women in Higher Education Management." These barriers are:

- Limited access to education, especially higher education.
- Cultural stereotyping.
- Family attitudes.
- Career interruption.
- Alienation from the men, and continued resistance to women being career oriented.
- Discriminatory appointment and promotion practices.
- Absence of adequate policies and legislation to ensure the participation of women in higher education and professional engagements.

National Policy on Education

National Policy on Education (NPE), 1986 and its Programme of Action (POA) gave high priority to gender equality and committed the entire educational system to work for women's empowerment. The National Perspective Plan (1988-2000) reiterates this point of view and states that women themselves must overcome their handicaps. Thus, there has been a careful articulation of education for equality for women, which is reflected in the educational policy discourse. Central and state governments attached lot of significance to actually operationalising the NPE's Programme of Action. In a series of regional meetings with the state governments, consensus emerged that a special review of gender concerns must be built into all educational processes. Monitoring committees for women's/girls' education at the Ministry of Human Resource Development level, and also state level were formed to monitor the indicators of gender concerns in all policies and projects.

Women's Empowerment

The National Policy on Education (NPE) is a landmark in the approach to women's education when it proclaims: "The Education System will play a positive interventionist role in the empowerment of women. It will foster the development of new values through redesigned curricula, textbooks, training and orientation of teachers, decision makers, and administrators." The programme implementation document explains women's empowerment through collective reflection and decision-making. For this higher education needs to take responsibility for:

- Cultivation of positive self-image and self-confidence;
- Developing capacity for critical thinking;
- Achieving group cohesion and fostering decision-making and action;
- Providing women's centres in agricultural and home science colleges;
- Providing continuing education and correspondence centres for organising vocational and literacy skills;
- Revamping the Industrial Training Institutes (ITIs) in terms of diversification of trades and courses, keeping in view the job potential, facilities for vocational counseling, imparting information about credit, banking, entrepreneurial development, and access to women's technical education;
- Providing women's studies research centres direction to identify issues, areas of improvement, organise seminars and workshop to discuss and analyze women-related issues, disseminate information, and encourage interaction with students and the general public through the media;
- Providing classes on legal literacy, programmes for women's

socio-economic development delivered via media, adult education, information and training support;

- A more relevant and responsive curriculum catering to the cultural and occupational needs of women;
- Meeting the expenses of higher education for the rural, backward sections with incentives like scholarships and fee waivers;
- Meeting the requirement of achieving full integration of women within the democratic and developmental efforts of the country.

The concept of women empowerment was introduced at the women conference in 1985 at Nairobi. Empowerment is defined as the expansion in women's ability and freedom to make these strategic choices: a process that occurs over time and involves women as agents who have the ability to formulate choices, control resources, and take decisions affecting important life outcomes. The most common explanation of women's empowerment is the ability to exercise full control over one's action.

The Programme of Action, 1992 has comprehensively given the parameters of empowerment of women mentioned below.

- Enhance self-esteem and self-confidence in women.
- Build a positive image of women by recognising their contribution to the society, polity, and economy.
- Develop in them an ability to think critically.
- Foster decision making and action through collective process.
- Enable women to make informed choices in areas like education, employment, and health—especially reproductive health.
- Ensure equal participation in the developmental process.
- Provide information, knowledge, and skill for economic independence.
- Enhance access to legal literacy and information related to their rights and entitlements in society with a view to enhance their participation on an equal footing in all areas.

Fourth World Conference on Women, held in Beijing in 1995, recognised that women's literacy is a key to empowering women's participation in decision-making in society and to improving families' well-being. In addition, the United Nations has articulated the Millennium Development Goals (MDGs), which include goals for improved education, gender equality, and women's empowerment. The MDGs emphasise education's essential role in building democratic societies, and creating a foundation for sustained economic growth. Education is an important tool for promoting gender equality, and advancement of female youths in socio-economic and political development of the nation.

According to the International Conference of Population and Develoment Programme of Action paragraph 4.2 "Education is one of the most important means of empowering women with the knowledge, skills and self confidence necessary to participate fully in the development process." Therefore, young girls should be given opportunity to gain proper education. Girls who have adequate education are likely to marry later and to have smaller and healthier families. Educated women can recognise the importance of healthcare, and know how to seek it for themselves and their children. Higher education helps girls and women to know their rights and to gain confidence to claim them and achieve a better position in the society.

Education at all levels, but higher education especially, gives women options, empowers them to be independent thinkers and agents of change.

Women education in India plays a very important role in the overall development of the country. It not only helps in the development of half of the human resources, but in improving the quality of life at home and outside.

Women's Studies

Women studies in India as an academic discipline has a history of more than four decades. Other than the women's studies centres, we also have various non-academic forums for addressing women's rights/issues in academic institutions, and there has been a gradual process and change among these forums—from ladies' forums or women's cells to gender studies forums—addressing non-academic, academic, or political issues related to women's/gender/sexuality issues. There are women's studies centres established and funded by state governments, independent, autonomous academic institutions, and government institutions under the guidance of the University Grants Commission (UGC). There are around 160 women's studies centres in the country today under the UGC, divided into different phases (phases I, II, III, and advanced studies centres) running different academic programmes in women's/gender studies.

At present the UGC's attempt is to make the women's studies centres more academic oriented, to initiate more academic programmes, along with teaching and research, and a focus on the development of a new teaching curriculum (as envisioned in the Twelfth Five Year Plan). In 2009, the UGC with the help of its Standing Committee on Women's Studies, initiated a Curriculum Development Committee at the national level which worked towards a common model curriculum in women's/gender studies for the whole country. Research in women's/gender studies has come a long way from the 1970s, debating feminist research methodologies and its epistemological standpoints.

Present Status

Even after 69 years of independence, women's education has not achieved the desired results despite many efforts. The reasons for this failure are:

- A major section of Indian society does not give importance to girl education, because of their restricted mindset, conservative norms, and underdeveloped mentality.
- Girls are not allowed to take decisions for themselves or step out from their homes, because of social discrimination in a male-dominated society.
- Some girls are unable to go to school as they participate in agricultural and household chores.
- With education getting costlier day by day, people prefer to educate their boys rather than their girls, despite numerous facilities provided by the government.
- Most of the India's population lives in villages. The guardians are hesitant about sending their girls to school due to lack of basic facilities such as non-availability of hygienic water, no arrangement for separate sanitary facility for girls in schools.

Some of the areas of gender studies that need deliberation and have to be addressed are:

- Reduce gender disparities, and all forms of discrimination in education at all levels in rural, semi-urban, and urban contexts.
- Address gender bias and stereotypes in the content and process of education.
- Link knowledge, understanding, skills, and their application to real life situations so that metamorphic social changes are initiated in the society.
- Combat patriarchy by focusing on new and emerging roles taken up by women in different fields.
- Link development agenda with the girl child's life, education, and livelihood.
- Capacity building of girls and women with a judicious mix of new emerging technologies.
- Proactive approach in all sectors of the economy to ensure safety and security of women.
- Undertake regional research studies on barriers to girls' education and empowerment.

Distance Education

To overcome the rigidities, compulsions, and limitations of the formal system of education, new efforts to develop non-formal education (distance education) began five decades ago in Indian higher education system. Women, who mostly remained outside the formal system for a variety of reasons, are expected to be the major beneficiaries of distance education. Distance education is a home-based and learner-centred form of education, which is free from the constraints of time, place, and pace.

In order to assess the impact of distance education on women, their motivation, persistence, and the success rate of distance learners. Mother Teresa Women's University School of Distance education conducted a study, which revealed the following impact on women learners:

- Gained confidence.
- Improved their career opportunities.
- Achieved greater degree of satisfaction.
- Updated their skills.
- Provided second chance to dropouts.
- Acquired new knowledge.
- Changes occurred in the socialization pattern of children.
- Acquired better decision making capacity.
- Increased respect for family and community.
- Gave opportunities for networking and communication.
- Broadened vision.
- Gave freedom and flexibility to learners.
- Assisted in facing challenges in life.
- Increased literacy rate of state and country.

A review of research in distance education recommends the following for the women's wider utility of distance education:

1. Continuous efforts to reduce and eliminate barriers that prevent and restrict women's participation in learning activities.
2. Develop courses that build upon women's diverse experience, but do not impose rigid external expectations, and arbitrary requirements.
3. Recognise that student learning environments comprise the home and local centres from which women study, as well as the educational institutions. This means that "education like technology has to be adapted to local circumstances."
4. Create supportive and safe environments in distance education contexts. Educators need to be sensitive to women's personal and unique circumstances, and need to investigate ways to help students develop effective support systems.
5. Increase the number of women's studies courses available via

distance learning, and ensure that feminist perspectives are incorporated into curriculum in other disciplines.

6. De-emphasise the utility of prescribed materials to promote the assumption that course materials are not the course per se. Women students need opportunities to make real and significant choices regarding their learning goals and activities.
7. Conduct research into the types and levels of interaction essential to feminist learning in distance education contexts. Collect empirical data about actual interactions and breaks that student and tutors experience in distance learning. The nature and prevalence of the social aspects of learning essential to feminist learning also require specific investigation in distance settings.
8. Provide tutors employed for feminist distance courses with useful, appropriate training. Orientation activities need to include skills training in telephone and teleconference technologies, and their applications. Such training should have as its focus effective use of communication strategies and feminist processes for facilitating adult learning in distance settings.

Literacy Rate in India

Year	*Persons*	*Males*	*Females*
1901	5.3	9.8	0.7
1911	5.9	10.6	1.1
1921	7.2	12.2	1.8
1931	9.5	15.6	2.9
1941	16.1	24.9	7.3
1951	16.7	24.9	13.0
1961	24.0	34.4	18.7
1971	29.5	39.5	24.8
1981	36.2	46.9	39.2
1991	52.1	63.9	54.0
2001	65.38	76.0	65.46
2011	74.04	82.14	65.43

Girls' Enrolment and Number of Girls Colleges in Higher Education in India

Year	*Total (Boys + Girls)*	*Students Enrolment Girls only*	*% of Girls*	*No. of Girls Colleges*
2001-01	8399443	3306410	39.4	1578
2001-02	8964680	3571656	39.8	1756
2002-03	9516773	3811691	40.1	1824

2003-04	10011645	4026187	40.2	1871
2004-05	10542262	4259072	40.4	1977
2005-06	11137627	4510738	40.5	2071
2006-07	11887095	4820216	40.6	2208
2007-08	2727082	5167192	40.6	2360
2008-09	13641808	5649102	41.4	2565
2009-10	14624990	6080373	41.6	3612
2010-11	16974883	7048688	41.5	3982

Men and Women Students—Growth in Higher Education (1950-51 to 2012-13)

Year	*Men (Per 1000)*	*Women (Per 1000)*	*Total Enrolment (Per 1000)*	*Women as percent of all students*
1950-51	1857	17	174	10.00
1955-56	252	43	295	14.60
1960-61	468	89	557	16.00
1965-66	849	218	1067	20.40
1970-71	1563	391	1954	20.00
1975-76	2131	595	2426	24.50
1980-81	2003	749	2752	27.20
1985-86	2512	1059	3571	29.60
1990-91	2986	1439	4425	32.50
1995-96	4235	2191	6426	34.10
2000-01	4988	3012	8001	37.60
2005-06	6562	4466	11028	40.50
2012-2013	13468	10687	24180	44.20

Overall Enrolment in Higher Education in India

	Total	*Male*	*Female*	*Female % in Total*
Ph.D.	1,12,812	67,330	45,482	40.32
M.Phil.	32,371	13,676	18,695	57.75
Postgraduate	38,09,322	18,47,651	19,61,671	51.50
Undergraduate	2,65,76,140	1,40,88,649	1,24,87,491	46.99
PG Diploma	1,86,548	1,09,371	77,177	41.37
Diploma	22,47,430	16,18,329	6,29,101	27.99
Certificate	1,75,907	78,597	97,310	55.32
Integrated	1,32,192	83,101	49,091	37.14
Total	**3,32,72,722**	**1,79,06,704**	**1,53,66,018**	**46.18**

Source: Compiled from AISHE Report 2014-15.

16
Distance Education

Soon after independence the government realised the important role education plays in the overall national development. They visualised education as a major tool for the regeneration of India society, and consequently set before the nation the objectives of notion of democratization of education and "equal opportunities for access to education." The authors of the First Five Year Plan realised the need for the creation of educational opportunities outside the formal system.

They envisaged the provision for "facilities of private study through correspondence courses ... and allowing students to take various examinations privately." However, those in charge of implementation of the Plan did not formulate any policy to translate the idea into action. In 1961 the Central Advisory Board of Education suggested the Government of India to constitute an expert committee headed by D.S. Kothari to look into the suitability of correspondence courses for expanding educational opportunities.

The Committee recommended the introduction of correspondence courses to expand and equalise educational opportunities. Thus Open Distance Learning (ODL) in India was introduced by Delhi University in 1962 through the School of Correspondence Courses and Continuing Education to enable those who had the inclination, and the aptitude to acquire further knowledge and improve their qualifications. Subsequently, some other universities started correspondence courses. Rapid expansion of the ODL courses took place in the years to come.

In the eighties, the distance education system expanded further. Not only did more and more universities start opening correspondence course units, but the decade also saw the establishment of single mode distance education institutions (open universities). The Andhra Pradesh Open University, later designated Dr. B.R. Ambedkar Open University (BRAOU), was established in 1982 in Hyderabad by the state of Andhra Pradesh. It was followed by the setting up of the Indira Gandhi National Open University (IGNOU) by the Government of India in 1985 by an Act of Parliament. The establishment of IGNOU is considered to be a landmark development in the country. In our country the growth of distance education has been exponential over the last five decades beginning in 1962. As of 2016, in addition to IGNOU, 16 State Open University and about 200 distance education institutions offer diverse programmes in different disciplines.

The journey of distance education in India is through five decades:

- First Decade (1962-63 to 1971-72)
- Second Decade (1972-73 to 1981-82)
- Third Decade (1982-83 to 1991-92)
- Fourth Decade (1992-93 to 2001-02)
- Fifth Decade (2002-03 onwards)

Who Offer Distance Education

Today distance education in India is offered by the following institutions:

1. National open university
2. State open universities
3. National open school
4. State open schools
5. Correspondence courses/distance education institutions of formal universities
6. Educational radio and TV broadcasts
7. Distance education departments of technological universities
8. Extension education directorates of agricultural universities
9. Central/state government agencies
10. Public and private professional organisations
11. Public and private professional organisation recognised by centre/state governments

Benefits of Distance Education

Distance education provides benefits for major stakeholders:

For the Student/Learner

- Increased access and flexibility.
- Ability to combine work and education.
- Reduced travel time and costs.
- More learner-centric approach.
- Relevance to actual learning needs.
- Enrichment, higher quality of education, and use of newer ways of interaction.
- Acquisition of 21st century skills necessary for the workplace.

For Institutions

- Attracting global underserved populations of potential students.

- Improved teaching quality.
- Support for continuing education.
- Reduced need for bricks and mortar infrastructure.

For Employers

- High quality and usually cost effective professional development in the workplace.
- Reduced travel time and costs.
- Easy, regular upgrading of skills.
- Increased productivity.
- Development of a new learning culture.
- Sharing of costs and training time.
- Increased portability of training

For Governments, Potential to:

- Increase capacity and cost-effectiveness of education and training systems.
- Reach target groups with limited access to conventional education and training.
- Reduce gender inequality by allowing women to access higher education through distance learning, while staying at home with their families, and in their own countries and communities.
- Ensure the connection of educational institutions and curricula to the emerging networks and information resources.
- Support and enhance the quality and relevance of existing educational structures and programmes.
- Promote innovation and opportunities for lifelong and worldwide learning.

Aims and Objectives

The aims and objectives of distance education institutions are as follows:

- Provide an alternative cost effective non-formal channel for tertiary education.
- Supplement the conventional university system and to reduce the pressure on it.
- Provide 'second chance' education to those who have had to discontinue their formal education, or could not join regular or universities owing to social, economic and other constraints.
- Democratize higher education by providing access to large segments of the population, in particular the disadvantaged groups such as those living in remote and rural areas, working

people, women, and other adults who wish to acquire and upgrade their knowledge, and/or skills.

- Strengthen and diversify the degree, diploma, and certificate courses related to employment, which are necessary for building the economy of the country on the basis of its natural and human resources.
- Provide continuing and life-long education to enrich the lives of the people.
- Provide an innovative system of university level education, which is flexible and open in terms of methods and pace of learning, combination of courses, eligibility of enrolment, age of entry, conduct of examination, and operation of the programmes with a view to promoting learning, and encouraging excellence in new fields of knowledge.

From the charters of various distance teaching universities/open universities the following broad objectives can be identified:

- Expand opportunities for higher education.
- Provide higher education to those who cannot leave their homes and jobs.
- Improve academic and professional qualifications of people engaged in professions.
- Raise the general educational level of society.
- Provide training for teachers.
- Obtain reduction in education costs.
- Develop a more individualized and student centred system of teaching and learning.
- Support reforms in education.
- Democratize and revolutionize education.

Whom do the Distance Education Institutions Serve?

- School leavers who are qualified for traditional university entry, but cannot be admitted because of non-availability of seats in traditional universities and colleges.
- Adults who desire to acquire university level qualifications, but cannot choose to apply for entry to a traditional university because they:

a. lack of education qualifications required for entry;
b. have family commitments, especially to young children, which tie them to their homes;
c. prefer to study independently;

d. live in institutions (e.g. the handicapped) which they are unable to leave;
e. are in full-time jobs and cannot or choose not to give them up.

- Teachers, professional and manpower groups who require vocational training, professional updating, and increased knowledge levels, but cannot be released from their employment to attend a campus based university or training college.

Adults who wish to pursue lifelong learning opportunities (continuing education) unrelated to the pursuit of a degree level qualification.

Distance Courses

A distance education institution does not solely duplicate the courses run by other traditional institutions. It has to foster and promote the educational development of a community in which it is located. Different sections of community have different types of educational aspirations and needs. It has to educate people who remain uneducated due to a variety of reasons—economic, social, cultural, and historical.

Many distance education institutions offer academic, vocational, recreational, and literacy programmes. Courses can also be classified as training, awareness, updating, conversion, and academic courses.

A former Vice Chancellor of IGNOU classified the distance courses as: (a) non-conventional courses, (b) job oriented courses, (c) welfare oriented courses, (d) continuing education courses, (f) courses for conventional students. The first open university in India in 1982 (Dr. B.R. Ambedkar Open University) aimed:

- to provide educational opportunities to those students who could not take advantage of institutions of higher learning.
- to realise equality of educational opportunities for higher education for a large segment of population including those in employment, women including housewives, and adults, who wish to update their education or acquire knowledge and studies in various fields through distance education.
- to provide flexibility with regard to eligibility for enrolment, age of entry, choice of courses, methods of learning, conduct of exams, and operation of the programmes.
- to provide programmes complementary to those of the existing universities in the state in the field of higher learning, so as to maintain the highest standards on par with those of the best universities in the country.

- to promote integration within the state through its policies and programmes.
- to offer degree courses and non-degree certificate courses for the benefit of the working population in various fields, and for the benefit of those who wish to enrich their lives by studying subjects of cultural and aesthetic value.
- to make provision for research and for the advancement and dissemination of knowledge.

IGNOU offers more than 200 need based academic, professional, vocational, awareness generating, and skill-oriented courses, leading to certificates, diplomas, and degrees. These courses are prepared by 21 academic schools of the university. Significant among them are the School of Law, School of Computer and Information Sciences, School of Engineering and Technology, School of Vocational Education and Training.

Student Support Services

All institutes of distance education, whether they are divisions of traditional universities or open universities, provide student support services to their students either through their regional centres or through their study centres. They provide varied student support service such as:

- Information support
- Guidance support
- Counseling support
- Tutorial support
- Library support

Distance education divisions of conventional universities do not provide varied student support service in view of scarcity of funds. This is the major difference between the divisions of distance education of conventional universities and open universities.

Open universities have well prepared manuals along with a student support service. The manuals of IGNOU and BRAOU are well prepared and proved to be very useful to tutorial and counseling staff. The Handbook for Academic Counselors prepared by BRAOU can well be adopted by other state open universities.

The manual for academic counsellors of IGNOU is a well designed and highly useful document. It suggests several important tasks for academic counsellors in relation to students. The important tasks are: (a) helping students in mastering units of courses; (b) improving study skills in students; (c) expanding knowledge of students through group activities;

(d) encouraging student's academic progress; (e) developing in independence in students; and (f) improving basic study skills.

Use of Technology

Of all the distance education institutions in India, IGNOU is using technology to the maximum extent. Instructional system of IGNOU consists of multi-channel, multiple packages. The different components used for teaching-learning include self-instructional print and audio-video materials, radio and television broadcasts, face-to-face tutoring, counseling, laboratory, and hands-on experience, teleconferencing, video conferencing, interactive radio counselling, interactive multimedia CD-ROM, internet based learning, and the mobile phones for instant messaging for courses in sciences, computer sciences, nursing, medical sciences, education, engineering, and technology. Arrangements are made to enable students to undertake intensive practice classes/practice teaching at select study centres/work centres/programme centres. While the traditional distance education delivers through print, and study centre support is being strengthened, the university is strengthening the development of interactive multimedia content and learner support through video conferencing and web based platforms.

Promotion, Coordination, and Maintenance of Standards

Until recently, the ODL system in India was governed by the Distance Education Council (DEC) set up by IGNOU in 1991. DEC was primarily entrusted with the promotion, coordination, and maintenance of standards of ODL system in India, and was expected to create an effective mechanism to monitor implementation and enforcement of its norms. Institutions offering ODL programmes found the norms prescribed by DEC too rigid and unrealistic lacking the flexibility to meet the diversity of local contexts and emerging concerns.

In August, 2010, the HRD Ministry constituted a committee under the Chairmanship of N.R. Madhava Menon to suggest measures to regulate the standards of distance education. The committee questioned the authority of DEC as the apex regulator of ODL system, mainly on the basis of conflict of interest, lack of adequate manpower, and technological support. The committee observed that DEC, UGC, and AICTE do not have the wherewithal to enforce their norms in distance education space. The committee felt that the ODL system was practically unregulated, and recommended the dissolution of DEC, and the establishment of an independent and effective regulator authority to regulate ODL system. Following this recommendation, the MHRD and IGNOU dissolved DEC in May, 2013 and entrusted UGC and AICTE to perform the roles and responsibilities of DEC within their respective jurisdictions.

Research in Distance Education

A rapid review of research activity in distance education indicates the following:

- Research efforts have been fragmentary and isolated. From the point of view of theoretical value and design, the research activity leaves much to be desired.
- Most of the studies conducted so far have focused on issues at the micro-level.
- From the point of view of methodological aspects, most of the studies are of a descriptive type—highlighting the status and functioning of the system after exploring facts and figures related to its different dimensions.
- Maintaining quality in spread of distance education does not seem to be the concern of distance education. With the number of institutions offering distance courses growing day by day, the problem of quality assurance should demand immediate attention.

The research done so far is limited in quantity and quality. The following are some of the broad areas on which further research needs to be promoted intensively:

- Politico-socio-economic factors leading to the establishment of distance education institutions.
- Aims and objects—their fulfillment.
- Organisational structure—reasons for adopting a particular model.
- Role of regional and study centres.
- Course development—approaches—models—significance and problems in course streams.
- Identification of education needs—methods and mechanisms.
- Characteristics of students.
- Problems of drop out and persistence.
- Multi-media instructional system—nature and components.
- Role of communication and information technology.
- Offering science and technology courses—problems in providing lab facilities, practical works.
- Student support services—Why? What? How?
- Face to face tuition and correspondence tuition.

- Assessment procedures and methods.
- Evaluation of the system—organisation, methods, procedures results, modification of the system on the results of evaluation.

Reforms in Distance Education

Various research studies highlight the need for following changes:

- Increase in the number of courses.
- Development of need based and socially useful courses.
- Importance of computer education.
- Organisational accounting and extension education activities.
- Effective provision of student support services.
- Expansion and strengthening of study centres.
- Mobile counselling for the benefit of students in remote areas.
- Transformation of all course materials into self-instructional form.
- Change in timings of television broadcasts.
- More training for the teaching and non-teaching staff of the university.
- Careful selection and training of academic counsellors.
- Removal of regional imbalances in the provision of student support services.
- Improvement in the infrastructural facilities at study centres.
- Pre-admission counselling to learners.
- Career guidance to learners.
- Provision of special facilities for women learners.
- Collaboration and cooperation of the distance education units of conventional universities in the state in course development, and student support services to avoid duplication and wastage of resources.
- Application of new technologies in the delivery of courses.
- Institutionalization of research.
- Apex role for promoting and strengthening distance education in the states.
- Continuous research and development activities in all the units of the University.

Effective operation

The feasibility of distance education in any country depends on the circumstances in which it operates. Even countries within similar levels of economic development will differ according to geography, local infrastructure, educational structures, and levels of human resources.

However, there is a core set of activities which need to work, if a distance education system or institution is to be effective operationally. These activities include:

- Provide all learners (wherever they are) with specially designed learning materials (whatever the media) in time for learners to make use of them.
- Provide learner with opportunities for interaction with others in a variety of ways.
- Give learners feedback on their learning, in some way, as rapidly as possible.
- Keep accurate records, processed within a given time-scale, and used to manage the system.
- Monitor key aspects of the operation (whatever the scale), at the centre, and in the field on a regular basis, using the data to assist evaluation and improvement.
- Monitor student progress regularly, for individuals and groups, and modify the materials and the system in response to findings.
- Provide training and support to local support staff and centres, either directly or indirectly (through other agencies), monitor and evaluate their role.
- Evaluate the materials (both in development and in use) and the services offered, in a systematic way.
- Coordinate the functioning of the sub-systems in the whole operation (production of materials or programmes, support service, administrative functions, and assessment activities) so that conducive conditions for learning are created for the learners.
- Enable learners to complete courses successfully, with results comparable to effective conventional systems, or with demonstrable skills.

	Open Universities in India	*Year of Establishment*
1.	Dr. B.R. Ambedkar Open University, Hyderabad	1982
2.	Indira Gandhi National Open University, Delhi	1985
3.	Vardhman Mahaveer Open University, Kota, Rajasthan	1987
4.	Nalanda Open University, Patna, Bihar	1987
5.	Yashwant Chavan Maharashtra Open University, Nashik, Maharashtra	1989
6.	Mdhya Pradesh Bhoj Open University, Bhopal, Madhya Pradesh	1991

	Open Universities in India	*Year of Establishment*
7.	Dr Baba Saheb Ambedkar Open University, Ahmedabad, Gujarat	1994
8.	Karnataka State Open University, Mysore, Karnataka	1996
9.	Netaji Subhash Open University, Kolkata, West Bengal	1997
10.	Uttar Pradesh Raj Rishi Tandon Open University, Allahabad, Uttar Pradesh	1998
11.	Tamil Nadu Open University, Chennai, Tamil Nadu	2002
12.	Pandit Sundarlal Sharma Open University, Raipur	2005
13.	The Global Open University, Nagaland	2006
14.	K. K. Handique Open University, Guwahati, Assam	2007
15.	Uttaranchal Open University, Dehradun, Uttarakhand	2007
16.	Venkateshwara Open University, Lekhi, Arunachal Pradesh	2012
17.	Odisha State Open University, Sambalpur, Odisha	2016

Different Dimensions

17
Autonomy

Of late, there has been a lot of discussion on autonomy of higher education institutions in various forums and situations. Our Prime Minister, Narendra Modi, during his address at the 102nd Indian Science Congress gave a call for more autonomy and academic freedom to the universities. In simple terms, autonomy of an institution is the degree of freedom given to it to function to achieve its goals. In operational terms, it is the authority delegated to take decisions in functional areas. Autonomy is essential for the effective performance of an institution.

Concept of Autonomy

The concept of autonomy is a structural solution intended mainly to provide an enabling environment to improve and strengthen the teaching and learning process. Autonomy alone may not guarantee higher quality; just as non-autonomy need not preclude better performance. The essential factors for high quality education are the caliber and attitudes of students towards learning, the competence and commitment of teachers towards educational processes, the flexibility and foresightedness of the governance system and the social credibility of the educational outcome. Autonomy is expected to provide a better framework for fostering these factors than the affiliation system with all its constraining conditions hanging as a dead weight on the higher education system.

At the core of the concept of autonomy is the decentralised management culture. The delegation of responsibility with accountability for academic as well as associated management functions is essential for the success of autonomy. For understandable reasons, there has been a great deal of reluctance on the part of the higher echelons to delegate these responsibilities to decentralised units. At the same time there has been hesitation on the part of the functional units to undertake the decentralised responsibilities.

The successful implementation of the concept of autonomy requires willing and honest participation of the students, teachers and management in the education process. They should be willing to stand up to intense scrutiny of their role in autonomy. A system of academic audit at every step of the implementation of the concept of autonomy should be acceptable to all concerned parties.

Indicators of Autonomy

Dimensions of Autonomy	*Indicators of Autonomy*
Academic Autonomy	• Capacity to decide on overall student numbers • Capacity to select students • Capacity to introduce and terminate degree programmes — Capacity to introduce programmes (at B.A., M.A. level) — Capacity to introduce programmes (at doctoral level) • Capacity to choose the language of instruction (at B.A. and M.A. level) • Capacity to select quality assurance mechanisms and providers • Capacity to select quality assurance providers • Capacity to design content of degree programmes
Financial autonomy	• Length and type of public funding • Ability to keep surplus • Ability to borrow money • Ability to own buildings • Ability to charge tuition fees for students (B.A., M.A., Ph.D.)
Organisational autonomy	• Selection procedure for the executive head • Selection criteria for the executive head • Dismissal of the executive head • Term of office of the executive head • Inclusion of external members in university governing bodies • Selection of external members in university governing bodies • Capacity to decide on academic structures • Capacity to create legal entities
Staffing autonomy	• Capacity to decide on recruitment procedures (senior academic staff) • Capacity to decide on recruitment procedures (senior administrative staff) • Capacity to decide on salaries (senior academic staff) • Capacity to decide on salaries (senior administrative staff) • Capacity to decide on dismissals (senior academic staff) • Capacity to decide on dismissals (senior administrative staff) • Capacity to decide on promotions (senior academic staff) • Capacity to decide on promotions (senior administrative staff)

In the first half of the 19th century, prior to the establishment of the first set of Indian universities, several colleges came into existence with full autonomy such as:

- The Hindu College, Calcutta (1817)
- The Agra College (1827)
- The Poona College (1833)
- The Elphinstone College, Bombay (1834)
- The Hooghly College (1836)
- The Patna College (1840)
- The St. Joseph College, Nagapattinam (1844)
- The Hislop College, Nagpur (1844)
- The Bethune College for Women, Calcutta (1849)
- Madras Christian College (1852)

With the establishment of the first three universities in Calcutta, Bombay, and Madras, 27 existing autonomous colleges were affiliated in 1857 these three universities, when rules were adopted for common admission, courses, examination, and results.

In independent India, efforts towards autonomy were made to create autonomous colleges out of the deserving affiliated colleges.

One of the earliest committees on colleges under the chairmanship of G.S. Mahajan emphasised the need for introducing autonomy as follows: "In an affiliating system, the weak colleges tend to determine the policy of the university with regard to course of study, teaching requirements, examination, etc. The good colleges which are capable of rising to much higher standards are consequently not allowed to do so. Unless the colleges which can do better than the rest are permitted to go ahead with their plans for modern rising and improving their academic programmes, they will not be able to hold to the superior standards. They will not be able to hold to the superior standards indefinitely."

The first formal and specific recommendations on college autonomy appeared in the Report of the Education Commission (1964-66) under the chairmanship of D.S. Kothari. The relevant portion of the Report reads, "We should like to refer to the question of 'autonomous' colleges which has been under discussion for many years. Where there is an outstanding college (or there is a cluster of very good colleges) within a large university, which has shown the capacity to improve itself markedly, consideration should be given to granting it an autonomous status. This would involve the power to frame its own rules of admission, to prescribe its own courses of study, to conduct examinations, and so on. The parent university's role will be one of general supervision and actual conferment of the degree. The privilege cannot be conferred for once and for all. It will have to be continually earned and deserved and it should be open to the university after careful scrutiny of the position, to revoke the autonomous status if the college begins to deteriorate in its standards. We recommend that provision for the recognition of such autonomous colleges be made in the constitution of the universities. It should be possible in our opinion, by the end of the Fourth Five Year Plan, to bring about fifty of the best colleges under this category."

In October, 1966, the UGC appointed a high level committee consisting of D.S. Kothari P.B. Gajendragadkar, A.C. Joshi, A.L. Mudaliar, P.N. Kirpal, B. Malik, K.L. Shrimali, and R.K. Singh, to examine the feasibility and mechanism for implementing the recommendations of the Education Commission regarding autonomous colleges.

The suggestions of the Committee, in brief, were:

- In the first instance the possibility of establishing one or two autonomous colleges in each university within the framework of existing University Acts should be explored;
- The basic prerequisites are good students, good staff, good facilities, and good management. The Board of Governors and other academic bodies in an autonomous college should be properly constituted with suitable external representatives;
- The proposal for the conferment of autonomy on any institution should originate from the university and the college concerned. The UGC may be associated with the process of selection, but the primary responsibility has to be undertaken by the university.
- Autonomous colleges may be permitted to modify the syllabus in the light of the facilities and staff available, prescribe their own admission policy, and devise their own assessment procedures.
- The approach may be flexible, and there may be a graduated scale of autonomy for institutions depending on their performance and achievement in various fields.
- The parent university should award the degree, but the name of the autonomous college should be specifically mentioned.
- Development grants on a liberal basis should be provided for the development of autonomous college.

The National Policy on Education, (NPE) 1968, based on the Kothari Commission Report, suggested that autonomy should be available to the colleges in selection of students, in appointment and promotion of teachers, in determination of courses of study, methods of teaching, and in the choice of areas for research and their promotion. The Programme of Action for NPE-68 recommended developing a large number of autonomous colleges as well as creation of autonomous departments within universities on a selective basis.

Considering the absence of any headway in establishing autonomous colleges, due to the lack of provisions in the University Acts, the UGC Committee on the Governance of Universities and Colleges under the Chairmanship of P.B. Gajendragadkar (1971) proposed as a model the relevant provisions of the Himachal Pradesh University Act, 1970 as given below:

1. The university may grant in the manner, and after following the procedure prescribed in the relevant statutes, to a college, department or unit, which satisfies the conditions laid down in the statutes in this behalf, the privileges of modifying or changing for the students the course of study prescribed by the university, and of holding examination in the course so modified and such college, the department or unit shall be declared in the manner prescribed in the statutes to be autonomous college.
2. The extent to which the course may be varied and the manner of holding examinations conducted by such college or department as the case may be shall be determined by the University.

Based on these efforts the UGC sent a circular to all universities in October, 1973 entitled "Autonomous Colleges, Criteria, Guidelines and Pattern of Assistance," highlighting the distortions and consequences of the affiliation system while attributing the failure of all attempts to reform university education to the existing rigidity in the structure of university education, and the lack of academic autonomy. The UGC, on the recommendation of an expert committee, in consultation with the state government and the university concerned, confers the autonomous status on colleges to enable them to determine their own curricula, rules for admission, evolve methods of assessment of students' work, conduct of examination, use modern tools of educational technology, and promote healthy practices such as community service, and extension activities for the benefit of the society at large.

In spite of such eminent and tireless efforts to introduce college autonomy, the progress till 1978 was disappointing. Malcolm Adiseshiah, former Vice-Chancellor of Madras University and Former Chairman of the Madras Institute of Development Studies typically characterised this as follows: "Everybody is in favour of autonomous colleges. Yet they have been non-starters because everyone, including the colleges, is afraid of disturbing the dismal but demanding status quo." Due to his efforts, the Acts of Madras University and Madurai Kamaraj University were amended in 1978 providing for autonomous colleges. By June, 1978 eight colleges of Madras University and four colleges under the M.K. University started functioning as autonomous colleges after due process.

As of 2013, India has several autonomous colleges (441 in 2013) which conduct their own examinations and set their own curricula, but the degree is provided by the university to which they are affiliated. The autonomous colleges were also faster than the affiliated colleges in introducing choice based credit system, semester system, etc. There are efforts being made to amend the UGC Act, 1956 to give the autonomous colleges the degree-granting powers. In 2013 the government decided to convert 45 autonomous colleges into universities over the next three years. These are part of the efforts by the government to enhance the capacity of India's higher education institutions.

UGC Guidelines on the scheme of autonomous colleges spelt out the objectives of autonomy as:

- to determine their own courses of study and syllabi;
- to prescribe rules of admission, subject to the reservation policy of the state governments;
- to evolve methods of evaluation, and to conduct examination;
- to achieve higher standards, and greater creativity;
- to promote national integration; and
- to ensure accountability of the institution and its members.

The NEP (1986) and the POA (1992) formulated the following objectives for autonomous colleges—An autonomous college will have the freedom to:

(i) determine and prescribe its own course of study and syllabi, and restructure and redesign the courses to suit local needs; and prescribe rules for admission in consonance with the reservation policy of the state government;

(ii) evolve methods of assessment of students' performance, the conduct of examinations, and notification of results;

(iii) use modern tools of educational technology to achieve higher standards and greater creativity; and promote healthy practices such as community service, extension activities, projects for the benefit of the society at large, neighbourhood programmes, etc.

The status of Autonomous Colleges as on 01.08.2014

- Number of States: 24
- Number of Universities: 93
- Number of Colleges: 487

The weaknesses apparent in the system of autonomy are:

- Autonomy is directed mostly for colleges and not for all higher education institutions.
- Approval process is still time consuming.
- Universities presently do not have complete academic, administrative, and financial autonomy and are governed by the state agencies.
- Manpower deficits affect the efficiency of the system.
- Infrastructure shortcomings.
- Implementation obstacles; financial crunch faced by autonomous institutions.
- Systemic weakness where managements do not support autonomy.
- Apprehensions among teachers about salary and stability.
- Apprehensions among students.
- Insufficient powers, inherent or delegated, to the heads of higher education institutions.

The strengths of ideal autonomy are:

- Experimentation.
- Expansion and maximization of potential.
- Quality improvement.
- Societal relevance.
- Full involvement of teachers in the entire system.
- Confidence building between students and teachers.
- Transparency in teaching and evaluation.
- Increased scope for educational reforms.
- Speedy implementation of programmes.

The CABE Committee on Autonomy

The Central Advisory Board on Education (CABE) constituted a committee on the subject of "Autonomy of Higher Education Institutions" under the chairmanship of Kanti Biswas, then Hon'ble Minister for Education, Government of West Bengal. (MHRD 2005). The terms of reference of the Committee included:

- To suggest measures for enhancing the autonomy of higher education institutions, especially those with potential for excellence.
- To institutionalise regulatory provisions for promoting autonomy and accountability of higher education institutions.

Its salient recommendations relating to autonomy are as follows:

- There is a need to grant autonomy to individual institutions for designing curriculum. University may provide a broad framework within which individual faculty member both within the university and in the colleges should encouraged to innovate and experiment transform teaching and learning into a fascinating and rewarding experience.
- Each institution should have the autonomy design its own procedure for selection of research fellows with due regard to merit and also ensuring appropriate budgetary provisions for purposes.
- All universities and colleges should be given the autonomy to start self-financing courses, particularly in new and emerging areas where opportunities exist, subject to the overall framework provided by their funding and regulatory bodies.
- Acts, statues, and ordinances of the universities should be reviewed for their better management, as also for granting autonomous status to affiliating colleges. The new form of management in the university should encourage speedy decision making, networking, team effort, and collective responsibility to meet the challenges of the new millennium.
- The present system of assigning fixed number of positions of Professors, Readers, and Lecturers to each department should be replaced by a system wherein the head of the institution should have the autonomy to determine both the rank, and the number of these positions in accordance with the tasks envisaged in the development plan of the institution.
- Higher education institutions need to be given complete autonomy to undertake consultancy assignments and sponsored research projects.
- All higher education institutions need to be given full autonomy to establish linkages for academic and research collaboration with their counterpart academic and research institutions, industry and professional organisations both in India and abroad.
- Norms of accountability which must be open, participative, and data based should be developed by higher education institutions in consultation with the faculty.

The Yash Pal Committee (2009) pointed to importance of governance structures to ensure the preservation of such autonomy. According to the Committee there are interferences, very often, in the university functioning in the areas such as admission of students; pressures in selection of teachers; manipulation in appointment of senior functionaries like vice-chancellors, registrars, and deans; purchase of equipment, and allotment of construction contracts. It also observed that blaming private initiative, political interference, and other forces for the loss of autonomy of universities is not sufficient. There was no rigorous resistance from within the academic community to the role played by socio-political and market forces to manipulate and subvert the normative structures of the university system.

National Knowledge Commission (2009) also expressed similar views and underlined the importance of the structures of governance of universities to preserve autonomy and accountability. The appointments of Vice-Chancellor must be freed from direct or indirect interventions on the part of governments and should be based on search processes and peer judgement alone. The size and composition of academic councils and executive councils, which slow down decision-making processes and sometimes constitute an impediment to change, need to be recognised on a priority basis.

India has a variety of higher education institutions. There are multi-faculty universities established by the central and state governments; some are unitary while others have affiliating colleges. There are open universities established by the central and state governments; professional and technical institutions; deemed universities which are not established by central or state acts but charted by the UGC; private universities; institutions of national importance established by the Acts of parliament such as Indian Institutes of Technology (IITs), National Institutes of Technology (NITs), Indian Institutes of Management (IIMs), and Indian Institutes of Science, Education and Research (IISERs), etc.

Accreditation status of Autonomous Colleges

Sl. No.	*State*	*Autonomous colleges as per UGC data*	*Accreditation by NAAC*
1.	Andhra Pradesh	100	36
2.	Arunachal Pradesh	-	-
3.	Assam	1	-
4.	Bihar	1	1
5.	Chhattisgarh	10	10
6.	Goa	1	-
7.	Gujarat	3	-
8.	Haryana	1	0
9.	Himachal Pradesh	5	-
10.	Jammu and Kashmir	3	-
11.	Jharkhand	5	1
12.	Karnataka	49	11

(Contd.)

Sl. No.	State	Autonomous colleges as per UGC data	Accreditation by NAAC
13.	Kerala	9	1
14.	Madhya Pradesh	36	13
15.	Maharashtra	28	4
16.	Manipur	1	
17.	Meghalaya	-	-
18.	Mizoram	-	-
19.	Nagaland	2	
20.	New Delhi	-	-
21.	Odisha	39	19
22.	Punjab & Chandigarh	6	-
23.	Rajasthan	3	-
24.	Sikkim	-	-
25.	Tamil Nadu	157	76
26.	Tripura	-	-
27.	Uttar Pradesh	12	5
28.	Uttarakhand	4	1
29.	West Bengal	9	1
30.	Andaman & Nicobar Islands	-	-
31.	Puducherry	3	-
32.	Lakshadweep	-	-
33.	Daman	-	-
34.	Dadra, Nagar & Haveli	-	-
	Total	**488**	**179**

The UGC 12th Five Year Plan document states that considerable challenges still remain, which include grant of autonomy to colleges. Access to higher education is still less than the minimum international threshold levels, distribution of institutions is skewed, enrolment in public universities is largely concentrated in the conventional disciplines; whereas in the private self-financed institutions, the student enrolment is overwhelmingly in the market-driven disciplines. Much greater challenges continue to exist with respect to quality and the provision of relevant education. Curricular reforms leading to regular revision and upgrading of curricula, introduction of semester system, choice-based credit system, and examination reforms are yet to take place in all higher educational institutions across the country. Exceptions apart, the majority of our higher education institutions perform poorly in the area of quality on a relative global scale.

18 Accreditation

Higher education institutions internationally are facing the challenges of increasing student population, diversity within student groups, increasing workloads, and decreasing resources. The past six decades have witnessed the transformation of higher education in most of the countries from elite to a mass system. This expansion has come about through the mass-based higher education, which has been accompanied by the development of a set of much more intrusive quality assurance, and inspection arrangements. Quality assurance is the achievement of desired standards through application of agreed procedures. It requires continuous monitoring of performance. Accreditation is a formal recognition by an authorised agency of an institution having achieved agreed standards. It is based on quality assessment. The system of accreditation is seen by many as being a means of assuring the quality of a programme, or an institution.

International Initiatives in Quality Assessment

The reasons for the concern for quality in higher education vary from country to country. Factors like history, culture, state of economic development, awareness, and approach for growth of higher education play a significant role in the evolution of quality assurance and controlling system in a particular country. However, it is becoming clear that self-regulation coupled with peer review carried out by an independent agency could bring in an era of quality in higher education. But in the changing context of globalization of economic activities, education has become an international service, and there's a need to withstand the pressure of this changing context. Countries have been pressurized to ensure and assure quality at an international level. Consequently, many countries have initiated quality assurance mechanisms.

In recent years, the creation of national system for the assessment of quality in higher education has been a major feature of development in many countries. There are now over 70 quality assessment agencies around the world which have responsibility of undertaking a review of the quality of higher education provision in their respective countries. Concern for quality in higher education has become the prime agenda of the countries world over. In countries like India though, the explicit focus on quality assurance in higher education is relatively new.

Within Europe, both the European Commission and the Association of European Rectors have initiated development work in the field. The Organisation for Economic Cooperation and Development, through its programme on Institutional Management in Higher Education, has a project which extends from Europe to America and Australasia. In addition, UNESCO has supported activity in this field at its European Centre for Higher Education, and various national quality agencies have formed an international body, the International Network for Quality Assurance in Higher Education.

The United States has had a diverse system of mass higher education for many decades. This new economic and social reality has brought fresh attention to its quality assurance practices by both state and federal policy makers. At the state level, growing concerns about the quality of college graduates entering the work force first led to policies in the 1980s on student assessment designed to improve the quality of undergraduate education.

Accreditation

Accreditation is a type of quality assurance process under which academic programmes, and student and staff related services offered by a higher education institution are evaluated by an external body, known as accreditation body or accreditation agency which determines whether the higher education institution meets applicable standards. Accredited status is granted to the institution by the accreditation body or agency.

During the last fifteen years there has been a sharp increase in awareness, amongst all connected with higher education regarding the need to maintain quality in university-level institutions, and the desirability of adopting formalized quality assurance procedures. Concern for quality of education is being expressed by society (represented by the government and the tax-payers); the institutions of higher learning (represented by its management and faculty); and their clients (students, and prospective employers).

It is true that higher education in India is heavily dependent on government support and as such as it can hardly generate private funds to maintain its independent status and expansion. Governmental funding on such a large scale also has resulted in lowering of the quality, getting higher degrees and diplomas easily, thereby compromising the academic merit and competence. A change in this pattern is needed. The University Grants Commission has been given the primary mandate to monitor and maintain the standard of teaching examination and research. According to the UGC, the objectives of assessment and accreditation are:

- To accord recognition to the quality and excellence of education imparted by higher educational institutions, and thereby to advance academic quality;
- To enable students and other stakeholders to make informed choice with regard to higher educational institutions;
- To enable students, teachers, and other stakeholders to provide inputs concerning the quality of education imparted by the higher educational institutions;
- To facilitate higher educational institutions to gain international recognition, cross-border and trans-national collaborations; and
- To facilitate effective teaching-learning processes, and access to quality teaching-learning material in all the languages permitted by the higher educational institution as medium of instruction or examination.

The National Policy on Education (NPE, 1986) and the Programme of Action (PoA, 1992) that spelt out strategic plans for the policies, advocated the establishment of an independent national accreditation agency. Consequently, the National Assessment and Accreditation Council (NAAC) was established in 1994 as an autonomous institution of the University Grants Commission (UGC). The mandate of NAAC as reflected in its vision statement is in making quality assurance an integral part of the functioning of higher education institutions (HEIs).

Vision and Mission

The Vision of NAAC is:

To make quality the defining element of higher education in India through a combination of self and external quality evaluation, promotion, and sustenance initiatives.

The mission statement of the NAAC aims at translating the NAAC's vision into action plans, and define specific tasks of NAAC engagement and endeavour as given below:

- To arrange for periodic assessment and accreditation of institutions of higher education or units thereof, of specific academic programmes or projects;
- To stimulate the academic environment for promotion of quality in teaching-learning, and research in higher education institutions;
- To encourage self-evaluation, accountability, autonomy, and innovations in higher education;

- To undertake quality-related research studies, consultancy, and training programmes, and
- To collaborate with other stakeholders of higher education for quality evaluation, promotion, and sustenance.

Striving to achieve its goals as guided by its vision and mission statements, NAAC primarily focuses on assessment of the quality of higher education institutions in the country. The NAAC methodology for assessment and accreditation is very similar to that followed by quality assurance (QA) agencies across the world, and consists of self-assessment by the institution, and external peer assessment by NAAC.

Core Values

The accreditation framework of NAAC is based on the following core values:

i. Contributing to national development;
ii. Fostering global competencies among students;
iii. Inculcating a value system among students;
iv. Quest for excellence.

The Process of Accreditation followed by NAAC at Present

Once an institution is ready for accreditation, the process involves completion of a self-study report followed by a NAAC peer team visit to the institution in order to validate the self-study report. These factors form the basis of the final grade assigned to the institution as well as its certification and accreditation status. As of now, NAAC functions in a voluntary manner, meaning that the institutions who are interested in getting their systems validated by accreditation are accredited and the rest are left alone. While this defines the highest order of quality assessed by a government body that has experts in the panel, the voluntary nature of the process does not satisfy the very idea of uniform quality set throughout the country. In order to correct this lacuna, the process needs to be made compulsory for recognised institutions.

Benefits of NAAC Accreditation

- Grading of higher education institutions (HEIs) and their programmes. Further, promote and enhance the academic environment and quality of teaching and research in these institutions. Help the institutions through workshops about the academic objectives, and how to achieve the standards set.
- Expected to promote needed changes, innovations, and changes that need to be attained in all aspects of the institution that is being accredited.

- Encourage innovations, self-evaluation, accountability in higher education, overall assessment of the quality aspects of the departments and programmes, and ensure the quality is sustained over period of time. Help establish internal quality assurance cell (IQAC) to ensure that the quality attained is continued and sustained.
- The grade clearly shows the quality level of the institute, but at the same time informs the various quality measures that need to be put in place, and thus improve the system. The improved quality helps teachers to work towards raising teaching and learning capabilities and be on a par with the quality standards laid by regulatory bodies.

Presently, accreditation is not mandatory, and there is no law to govern the process of accreditation. Some of the states have made it compulsory, particularly for their government colleges, while UGC has made it compulsory for all universities.

Milestones in the Journey of NAAC

The following are a few milestones of the past decade in the NAAC's journey of promoting quality-related initiatives in higher education:

- A significant achievement of the NAAC is the partnership with stakeholders for proactive measures to promote assessment and accreditation.
- Many states have established quality cells to promote assessment. The NAAC's efforts to promote usage of the assessment outcome as reliable information for decision making have been very successful.
- The NAAC accreditation has been made a prerequisite for the granting, and continuation of autonomous status, and deemed-to-be university status for institutions.
- The level of funding under the UGC scheme for "Colleges with potential for excellence," consideration for expansion in terms of courses and student intake in teacher education institutions by NCTE, granting of permanent affiliation, etc. are now linked to the accreditation status.
- Due to stakeholder usage of assessment outcome, a large number of institutions are volunteering for assessment. The training programmes of the NAAC for the peers who are involved in the assessment-related activities have ensured the professionalism of the NAAC's process for the large volume of assessment. In fact, NAAC is building a collegium of assessors.

- Action plans for quality evaluation, quality sustenance, and quality upgradation have been developed by the NAAC with the participation of a cross-section of academics in the country.
- The Ministry of Human Resource Development (MHRD) has accepted the NAAC's action plans. In September, 2001, during the meeting of State Higher Education Secretaries organised by the MHRD, the year 2002 was declared as the year of "Quality in Higher Education."
- In 2002, about 300 institutions got accredited, and in 2003 about 600 institutions have been accredited by the NAAC. This is a remarkable achievement in the history of assessment and accreditation all over the world.
- Moving beyond accreditation, the NAAC has expanded its scope by strengthening its advisory role. State-wise analysis of accreditation reports has been initiated for policy initiatives—this exercise is for states where at least 15 percent of higher education institutions have been accredited
- Collaboration with other national professional bodies for accreditation of specialised subjects have been initiated. The NAAC and Distance Education Council have jointly laid down the guidelines for accreditation of open universities and distance education units.
- The National Council for Teacher Education has an MoU with the NAAC for assessment and accreditation of teacher education institutions.
- The NAAC is active in international forum too. As a member of the International Network for Quality Assurance Agencies in Higher Education (INQAAHE), which is the largest such network in the world, the NAAC organised the sixth biennial meet of the member agencies in 2001 at Bangalore.
- The NAAC is actively collaborating on many quality assurance initiatives of other countries, especially in the Asia-Pacific region. In 2002, with the support of the UNESCO, it organised the Expert Meet on Indicators of Quality and Facilitating Academic Mobility in the Asia-Pacific Region.

Recent Failed Attempts of Government to Enhance the Strength of Accreditation

The Government of India through National Accreditation Authority Bill, 2010, attempted to enhance the strength of accreditation through mandatory accreditation. The bill envisaged the establishment of National Accreditation Authority. The Authority will grant license to accreditation agencies in India to accredit higher education institutions. It was intended to create competitiveness among accreditation agencies in India. The National Accreditation Authority Bill was an attempt to make a complete paradigm shift with respect to the accreditation regime in India.

The following points were raised against the bill: (1) With the regime of mandatory accreditation, the government, central and state, need to assure that in their own institutions the institutional infrastructure and teachers' positions are well in place. Otherwise, for no fault on the part of institution, they will be penalized. For example, many rural colleges will necessarily have lower grades. The assumption that accreditation may lead to competition through level playing field may not hold. In fact, level playing field should be the precondition for accreditation; (2) Accreditation, as defined in the bill, is the process of certification of minimum standard. If affiliating system continues, and there is no check on mushrooming of colleges, then accreditation system will find it difficult to control quality which is the important aim of accreditation; (3) In Indian higher education system there has been regulated growth. This was required historically. Nowadays, it is felt that control regime has not been working well as it controls too much, allowing little space for creativity and autonomy. Unless government institutions have autonomy, they cannot do too much for the growth of institutions as the strings will always will be in the hands of the government, as long as it is funding the institution. Will that then mean that government will allow autonomy, and ask institutions to raise resources to respond to the calls for accreditation? This will mean that accreditation will lead to withdrawal of governmental funding, and this will be harmful for the growth of the Indian higher educational system; (4) With different accreditation agencies, an important challenge for the regulatory authority will be to ensure uniformity in accreditation standards; (5) If there are multiple accreditation agencies, it will lead to improvement in accreditation standards through competition. That is only possible when there is no uniform accreditation process. However, authority would like to impose uniform accreditation process to achieve standardisation in accreditation. This will defeat the purpose of multiple accreditation agencies; (6) The national accreditation system that exists today will be endangered with the independent multiple accreditation agencies; (7) Since the practice of accreditation is new to India, not many will be qualified to accredit, except NAAC, NBA, or few others. Many new accreditors with foreign accreditors' collaboration will be tempted to do so. The motive may be profit through the backdoor system. How is that to be prevented? Examples of private institutions reaping profit inspite of education being non-profit is not uncommon, and government has not been able to prevent that. The bill remains as it is till today.

19
Financing

Higher education is recognised as a critical input in human development and social development of any society. The tertiary level of education provides not only the high level skills necessary for every labour market, but also the training essential for teachers, doctors, nurses, civil servants, engineers, humanists, entrepreneurs, scientists, social scientists, and myriad personnel. It is these trained individuals who develop the capacity and analytical skills that drive local economics, support civil society, teach children, lead effective governments, and make important decisions which affect entire societies (World Bank, 2002). Development of education became an important agenda after Theodore Schultz published an article in *American Economic Review* in 1961 entitled "Investment in Human Capital." Higher education is regarded crucial to the development of developing countries, and their ability to compete in the global economy.

After independence, the most significant action of the Government of India in the field education was the appointment of the University Education Commission (UEC) under the chairmanship of Dr. S. Radhakrishnan in 1948. The Commission was appointed to report on Indian university education, and suggest improvements and extensions that may be desirable to suit present and future requirement of the country. The UEC has submitted its report in 1949. The Commission laid stress on the finances of University colleges and affiliated colleges. One of the major recommendations of the commission was that the state should recognise its responsibility for financing higher education. The Government of India took the recommendations of the Commission seriously, and central financial assistance to Universities was revived from 1951 onwards. The University Grants Commission (UGC) was set up in 1953, and statutory status was accorded to it in 1956 when parliament adopted the UGC Act (Model Act). The commission also recommended that income tax laws be amended to encourage donations for educational purposes, and the Government should contribute an additional annual amount of Rs. 10 crores during the next five years for the development of university education.

The Government of India appointed the Education Commission in July, 1964 to advise on the national pattern of education, and on the general principles and policies of development of education at all stages, and in all aspects. The Commission was headed by Prof. D.S. Kothari, Chairman of the University Grants Commission, and hence the report of the Commission is also called the Kothari Commission Report. The Commission submitted its report in 1966. The Report of the Education Commission made a survey of the growth of educational expenditure in the post-independent period, and the source of educational finances. The Commission recommended allocation of six percent of the GDP for education. The Commission was of the view that education should continue to be basically a state responsibility as provided in the Constitution. While it was not in favour of including education in the concurrent list, it was also opposed to state absolutism in education. As the Constitution vests the central government with large and growing resources, it should provide adequate financial support to education. This should be done by increasing the Central and Centrally-sponsored sectors in a very substantial way. The Commission stated in its report that the funds of the central and state governments would have to bear about 90 percent (or even more) of the total educational expenditure. Contributions of voluntary organisations must be stimulated and utilised for the purpose of development through appropriate policies of grant-in-aid. The Commission found that a national system of education would need a much higher level of financial support. The Commission found that ultimately the total expenditure would have to be divided almost equally among the different sectors—one-third for elementary education, one third for secondary education, and one third for higher education.

The University Grants Commission appointed in January, 1987 a Committee to make a detailed study of the observations and recommendations made by various Education Commissions and Committees on the various issues related to educational management. A. Gnanam, Vice Chancellor of Bharatidasan University, Thiruchirapally was the Convener. So the Committee is popularly known as the Gnanam Committee. The Committee took note of the National Policy on Education (NPE) 1986, the Programme of Action (POA), and also made an extensive study of the Acts of Indian Universities. It submitted its report in 1990. With regard to finance, the Committee made some recommendations like: (a) The universities in India are funded either by the central or state governments, hence they have control in their functioning. Too much control of finance by these governments is affecting the administration of the universities. The Vice-Chancellors must have some freedom to re-allocate some of the funds for different purposes, and to create new posts, or change the level of posts; (b) Specific norms regarding the basic grants ought to be evolved which may be made obligatory for the state government to adopt; (c) The grants provided by the central and state governments should be reviewed every year. In addition, there should be a regular increase in allocation of ten percent every year; (d) The state government should also provide a matching grant to the development expenditure provided by the UGC; (e) Steps should be taken to mobilise resources from trade, industry, and development agencies for undertaking research, which would be useful to these agencies; (f) Permission be given to universities to raise their own funds through fees, funds from private industries, corporations, individuals, and trusts.

Ramamurti Review Committee, 1990

Government of India appointed a Committee on May 7, 1990 to review the National Policy on Education, 1986. The National Policy on Education Review Committee (NPERC) was headed by Acharya Ramamurti. Hence, the Committee is known as Ramamurti Review Committee. The NPERC submitted its report titled "Towards an Enlightened and Humane Society" on December 26, 1990. The commission maintained that it was justifiable to increase the fees of students in higher education. The increase must be related to the cost of higher education and the income level of the parents. The rich should, therefore, pay more and less privileged pay less. The Committee has recommended that at least six percent of the GDP should be provided for education. All technical and professional education should be made self-financing. It has suggested alternate methods of funding higher education like graduate taxes, increase in fees, and student loans. According to the Committee, an appropriate increase in the fees payable by students going in for higher education is a justifiable strategy, and this increase should be appropriately linked to at least the cost of recurring expenditure, and levels of income of the parents of the beneficiaries.

Ramamurti Reviews Committee opined that besides tuition fees, fees charged for specific purposes in the higher educational institutions like laboratory fees, library fees, building fees, magazine, and games fees, etc., also have to be increased on a rational basis with reference to the cost of providing the relevant facilities/services. Examination fees can also be an important means of raising internal resources to meet the cost of higher education.

CABE Committee Report on Policy, 1992

The Central Advisor Board of Education (CABE) in its meeting held on 8th and 9th March, 1991 decided that a CABE committee be constituted by the Chairman, viz., the HRD Minister, to consider the recommendations of the National Policy on Education Review Committee (NPERC). On 31st July, 1991 the Chairman of the CABE, appointed a Committee to review the implementation of various parameters of NPE, taking into consideration the report of NPERC. Shri N. Janardhan Reddy, chief minister, and education minister of Andhra Pradesh was appointed its Chairman with 15 members.

With regard to resources for education, the Committee made these recommendations: (a) In the matter of allocation of governmental resources there should be prioritization within the education sector; (b) Higher education, technical, and management education must be made largely self-financed by revising fee structure. At the same time, the needy students must be given appropriate support by the way of student loans; (c) Education infrastructure should be developed through institutional finance; (d) Academic institutions must be given incentives to increase their income through consultancy and other studies; and (e) Community and the cooperative sectors must be encouraged to come forward to extend financial support to education.

Policy Perspective of Financing Higher Education in Post-Economic Reforms Period

As the national and international agencies began expressing their commitment to education and faith in human capital for development, the countries like India has introduced many new economic policies, familiarly known as adjustment polices in the early part of 1990s. This structural adjustment programme includes the curtailment of government expenditure by way of withdrawal of subsidies and price support programmes; reduction in investment of socio-economic overheads; disinvestment in the state owned enterprises; reduction in import duties for capital goods and raw materials; increased incentives for inflow of foreign capital and technology, etc. The state began to gradually withdraw from those sectors that were seen as non-profit making, and a burden on its treasury. As a result, the social sector became the obvious target. In the field of higher education these policies had a direct impact. This resulted in drastic reduction in public subsidies accompanied with shifting the burden of financing, and delivery of educational service from government to parents, communities, NGOs, and the private sector.

In the post-economic reform period (i.e. from 1992 to till now), different commissions/committee have been constituted by government or its agencies on education. The review of important commissions and their recommendations with regard to financial aspects of higher education are as follows:

Programme of Action (1992) for the National Policy on Education (1986)

Programme of Action (1992) for the National Policy on Education provided that, "All institutions will be encouraged to achieve maximum self-reliance by generating resources through measures like enhancement of fees coupled with provisions of soft loans to needy students; consultancy; testing; sponsored projects; community contributions; institution chairs; raising donations for infrastructural development with a provision for tax exemption; establishment of industrial foundation; charging fees for specific facilities such as laboratories; library, games, magazines, etc. The grant-in-aid institutions will be allowed to utilise additional income generated from infrastructural and other developmental activities without linking it with government grants. As with higher education, a high powered committee would be set up to consider steps for mobilisation of additional resources for technical education, to bring about a better balance in the funding of institutions for technical and management and research and to improve cost efficiency of the technical education system. Efforts will also be made to streamline the scheme of educational loans with a view to making it more customer friendly."

In pursuance of the provision in the POA two committees were set up by the Government of India in the year 1992 to make recommendations regarding the mobilisation of additional funds for universities and technical institutions. Both these committees and various other policy documents, committees and commissions made significant recommendations regarding the funding of higher education.

Committee on UGC Funding of Institutions of Higher Education (Punnaya Committee, 1993)

The Committee on UGC funding of institutions of higher education, popularly known as Punnayya Committee, while recognising that the state must continue to accept the major responsibility for funding the essential maintenance and development requirements of the universities, recommended that universities should be encouraged to augment their resources for covering a large proportion of cost of education than what prevails. It further recommended that for generating internal resources fees for library, laboratory, and sports should be revised upwards to recover a significant part of recurring cost. Hostel fees should be revised to meet the actual recurring cost, and in due course of time a part of capital cost as well. The committee emphasised that for generating income, universities should let out their infrastructure facilities like playgrounds, auditoria etc., and also organise short term courses for which there is demand. It also opined that resources generated by the universities should constitute at least 15 percent of the total recurring expenditure at the end of the first five years, and at least 25 percent at the end of ten years. The Punnayya Committee made it clear that increased burden of fees and charges must be borne mainly by those who can afford. Besides, UGC may explore the possibilities of introducing soft loan scheme in collaboration with nationalized banks.

High Power Committee for Mobilisation of Additional Resources for Technical Education (Swaminadhan Committee, 1994)

The recommendations of the High Power Committee for Mobilisation of Additional Resources for Technical Education (Swaminadhan Committee, 1994) was also similarly in tune with those of Punnayya Committee. It stated that over-dependence on government support has led to both inadequacy and rigidity in resource allocation to various sectors of academic activity. It is essential that institutions should reduce this dependence through training, raising internal and external resources like contribution from industry alumni and charitable trusts, etc. For enhancing internal resources, the committee recommended that the tuition fees in all government funded and aided institutions in all the states should be revised to a rational level of at least 20 percent of annual recurring cost per student. Besides, the institutions should generate revenue through such activities as consultancy, testing, and certification, sponsored research projects, part-time courses, development of software, etc.

Another significant recommendation of this committee was regarding the establishment of an Education Development Bank of India (EDBI). It also opined that a National Loan Scholarship Scheme may be introduced under EDBI, and the needy students should be provided soft loans through this scheme,

From the above observations we can very well say that both committees emphasised the need for reducing reliance or public financing in higher education sector, and advocated exploring and mobilising alternative resources. The government found it very convenient to accept these recommendations and to act upon them as these recommendations are also in conformity with some of the important components of the macro-economic policies of structural adjustment, that were adopted by the government at the same time with recommendations of the World Bank outlined in its policy paper.

Discussion Paper on Public Subsidies (1997)

Another significant development having implications for policy making pertaining to financing of higher education was a discussion paper entitled "Government Subsidies in India" issued by the Ministry of Finance, GoI in

May, 1997. This paper sought to differentiate between merit goods and non-merit goods on basis of their externalities or social returns. This paper suggested that cutting down subsidies on non-merit goods could reduce fiscal deficits. Education beyond elementary level was classified as non-merit goods because here the benefit of subsidies accrues primarily to the recipients. On the contrary, the benefits of providing elementary education spreads well beyond the immediate recipients. Therefore, it was argued that the subsidy on higher education should be reduced from the existing 90 percent to 25 percent over a period of five years. In justification of the stand, it was also pointed out that the rich often appropriate subsidies in higher education, and the target population is not actually benefited by the subsidies. Since public spending is financed by public tax, subsidizing higher education would actually amount to subsidizing the rich by the poor.

Report on Policy Framework for Reforms in Education (Ambani-Birla Report, 2000)

The policies adopted by GoI regarding higher education are a boon to private sector which is ready to enter the field of higher education as they view it as an industry like steel, petroleum, or automobile manufacturing industry without realizing that in education inputs are human beings, process is on human being, and outputs are also human beings who cannot be managed by business principles alone. But the government was keen to privatize higher education. So, through the Prime Minister Council on Trade and Industry (PMCTI), it constituted a 'special subject group on policy framework for private investment in education, health and rural development.' The Prime Minister found no experts in the concerned areas, but the noted industrialists Mukesh Ambani (Convener) and Kumaramanglam Birla (member) to constitute this special subject group. The report was submitted to PMCTI in April, 2000 and it proved to be another significant development in education policy making in India.

As far as the perspective for financing of higher education is concerned, the report also echoed the World Bank's version by suggesting that "given the sustained fiscal deficits the government must focus strongly on primary and secondary education and leave higher and professional education to the private sector." Such privatisation of higher and professional education can relieve government funding from these areas, which can be used for primary education and improving literacy. It also sought to convert the entire system of higher education in the country to a market where profit making will be the only consideration. That is why it recommended that the government legislate a private university bill to encourage establishment of new private universities in the field of science and technology, management, and finance areas.

The report suggested two methods in order to overcome the problem of financing higher education. It stated: "Subsidies for higher education should be gradually withdrawn through higher fees and changes in fee structure" and "user pay principle to be enforced strictly for higher education supported by loan schemes as well as financial grants for economically and socially backward sections of the society." In this regard, the report proposed that the financial institutions should be encouraged to offer assistance in the form of loans to students in higher education and professional streams.

Thus the Ambani-Birla report outlined the contours of educational development in the country as commensurate with the needs of emerging global economy on one hand, and those of the local corporate sector on the other.

Report on Central Government Subsidies in India, 2004

The Government of India revised its earlier position of defining higher education as a non-merit good, probably by taking into consideration the revised version of the World Bank's conception regarding the nature of higher education, and also in response to strong criticism to its earlier stand. In its report on Central Government Subsidies in India, 2004, the Ministry of Finance, reclassified higher education as 'Merit-IP good' while school education was termed as, 'Merit-P good.' It was recognised that Merit-II goods also need to be subsidized, but the extent of subsidy could be much less than that in case of Merit-I goods.

Report of the CABE Committee on Financing of Higher and Technical Education, 2005

The CABE committee took a comprehensive view of the problems related to financing of higher and technical education in the country. It recommended that generous state funding of higher education was critically required for quantitative expansion, for improvement in quality and excellence, and for preserving and promoting equity in higher education. The total allocation to education sector should be raised to the level of six percent of GNP from the current level of about four percent. Twenty-five percent of the total budget should be allocated to higher and technical education together. This would mean that higher and technical education would together get about 1.5 percent of GNP approximately one percent for higher education and 0.5 percent for technical education (CABE, 2005).

While dealing with the issue of cost-recovery in higher education, the committee categorically stated that the rates of cost recovery in higher education were already fairly high in many universities, and the scope for any further increase in cost recovery is extremely limited. The committee observed that revenue generation through student fees beyond twenty percent may seriously affect access to higher education.

The committee emphasised the need for developing careful monitoring mechanisms so that loans are available mainly to economically needy, and educationally deserving students to pursue higher education. It also suggested setting up of a body like Higher Education Finance Corporation (HEFC) with contributions from the government and corporate sector, to coordinate the student loan schemes being operated by several banks, and to provide on its own scholarships and soft loans to students.

Regarding mobilisation of additional resources, the committee proposed that universities might to be encouraged to generate additional revenue from non-governmental sources, without affecting equity, and other academic aspects of institutions.

Overall, CABE committee was of the opinion that state funding of higher education out of tax and non-tax revenues should remain as the best and only sustainable way of financing higher education.

So, this report exhibited some points of departure from the earlier policy stances in the post-economic reforms period. These may be the reflections of the shift in the notion of higher education at the international level, especially with the publication of the World Bank reports i.e. *Higher Education in Developing Countries: Peril and Promise*, 2000 and *Constructing Knowledge Societies: New Challenges for Tertiary Education*, 2002. These reports highlighted the importance of state funding of higher education, and argued for an almost U-turn in the policies on higher education in developing countries.

CABE Committee on Autonomy of Higher Education Institutions (2005)

Central Advisory Board of Education (CABE) Committee on Autonomy of Higher Education Institutions was set up by Ministry of Human Resource Development, Government of India, to suggest measures for enhancing the autonomy and accountability of institutions of higher education. The Committee, headed by Shri Kanti Biswas, submitted its report in 2005. It made many recommendations related to academic, administrative, financial, and general aspects on autonomy of higher education institutions. With regard to financial aspects, the Committee made the following recommendations:

- One-third of entire investment in education sector should be made on higher education.
- Since full public financing of higher education to manage growth

and diversity within the context of overall funds constraints is no longer possible; universities and colleges have to search for alternate funding sources.

- Funding of individual institutions should be provided on block grant pattern so that they have greater degree of freedom to set up their own priority.
- Higher education institutions should be encouraged and facilitated to generate internal resources. The scheme for promoting internal resource generation should be broader based and be redesigned, so as to provide financial incentives for overall performance of the institution against objectively defined parameters that may be captured through the performance radar mechanism. The internal resources generated should not be adjusted with any other grants by an institution under any circumstances, and institutions should be allowed to use it exclusively for developmental purpose.
- The Central Government and the State Government or their authorised agencies as the case may be, will be empowered to set a ceiling on fee levels. All institutions should be required to adopt certain disclosure standards with a view to containing malpractice in relation to fees.
- All institutions should have the provision to provide free-studentships and scholarships to meritorious and deserving students coming from lower socio-economic strata of the society.
- The practice of financial disclosure standards should be introduced in self-financing institutions with a view to bringing greater level of transparency in their financial management.
- The audit systems, including system of internal audit, should be strengthened with a view to ensuring proper expenditure management and compliance of financial rules and regulations.
- Higher education institutions should be given complete autonomy to undertake consultancy assignments and sponsored research projects.
- The recommendations made by the CABE Committee, some of which question the present policies, will go a long way in moulding public policy towards higher education.

National Knowledge Commission, 2007

In National Knowledge Commission's view, the expansion of the system of higher education in India is not possible without enhanced levels of financing, which must necessarily come from both public and private sources.

The commission recommended that the government support for higher education should be at least 1.5 percent of GDP from a total of six percent of GDP for education (NKC, 2007). But at the same time, the commission also argued in favour of raising the fee levels in higher education institutions. In its view, on an average fees constitute less than ten percent of total expenditure in our universities. So, it stressed the need for rationalising fees in universities and other higher educational institutions. It suggested that as a norm, fees should meet at least 20 percent of the total expenditure in our universities. In addition, fees need to be adjusted every two years through price indexing.

Furthermore, the commission recommended tapping such sources as alumni contributions, licensing fees, or user charges (for facilities in universities used by people from outside), and creating supportive institutional mechanisms that allows universities to engage professional firms for mobilising resources. It also recommended stimulating private investment and public private partnerships where the government provides the land, and the private sector provides finances.

Thus, it is clear from the report that the commission strongly favoured autonomy for universities to set up fee levels, tap other sources, and also make commercial use of university facilities. Noting that college education in engineering, medicine, and management is de facto privatized, the commission favoured similar privatisation of university education by setting up private universities and enabling public private partnerships.

Report of the Committee to Advise on Renovation and Rejuvenation of Higher Education (Yash Pal Committee Report, 2009)

The Yash Pal Committee viewed higher education from a different perspective. It stated that higher education is a means to overcome caste and class hierarchy, patriarchy, and other cultural prejudices. It is also a source of acquiring new knowledge and skills, a space for creativity and innovations. Higher education, therefore, was and continues to be considered a national responsibility, and the state has to make necessary provisions to realise its potential (YCR, 2009).

The committee also argued that the absence of differential fee has led to the subsidisation of a segment of student body that can afford to pay for its education, and there is no reason why both of these two categories of students be placed on same level when it comes to financing their education.

Thus, following the popular discourse. the Yash Pal Committee also opined guaranteed student loans at low interest for those who can take loans. However, it also recommended free education for those who cannot afford it.

20
Regulatory Framework

When we talk of governance reforms for quality in higher education, we need to examine the problems associated with the regulatory regime of the UGC and the professional councils. Various commissions and committees have examined the regulatory character of the higher education and arguments were presented for reform. We need to assess those arguments for some future direction to be incorporated in the new education policy for higher education. We also need to understand the reasons for the lack of proper attention by the state government to maintain the standards. What institutional processes need to be established by the state government so that quality becomes an integral aspect of the responsibility of the state government? Lastly, universities need not be the examining body alone. We need to understand the failure of universities to have adequate control, such that the affiliated colleges are required to maintain the standards.

After the lawful establishment of institutions, various apex institutions have been entrusted, either by an Act of Parliament, or by an Act of Legislative Assembly, or by central or state governments with the responsibility to regulate the standards of education. For example, UGC was established by UGC Act, 1956 to coordinate and maintain standards of university education. NAAC was established in 1994 under 12cc of UGC Act to assess the standards of quality. It assesses and accredits universities along with their constituent and affiliated colleges. Similarly, AICTE was established under AICTE Act, 1987 for planned and coordinated development of technical education system in the country. Under Section 10 (U) of AICTE Act, National Board of Accreditation was set up to assess and accredit the technical institutions in the country, and to make recommendation to the concerned authorities for recognition and derecognition of qualifications. Further, National Council of Teacher Education, Medical Council of India, Dental Council of India (DCI), Council of Architecture, Bar Council of India (BCI), Pharmaceutical Council of India (PCI), Indian Council for Agriculture Research (ICAR), Rehabilitation Council of India (RCI), Central Council of Homeopathy (CCH), Central Council of Indian Medicine (CCIM), Distance Education

Council, etc., are some of the apex statutory bodies which regulate the standards of education in various professional fields.

An important point to note is that the standards of education in various fields cannot be expected to be uniform throughout the country, although some minimum standards of education must be maintained by all means. The term standard is as dynamic as the term development. Hence, there is bound to be differences in standards depending upon the mission and goal of universities/institutions, availability of resources, geographical location of institutions, management, etc. However, the most worrying fact is that many institutions established within the framework of domestic regulation do not maintain the minimum standards of education. Various reasons are cited for such a situation, including non-availability of qualified teachers, lack of financial resources, administrative procedures, continuous pressure to increase the intake without augmenting physical and academic facilities, etc. The argument of malpractices and falling ethical standards are only secondary arguments to the falling standards of higher education. The fact of the matter is that there exists domestic regulation for regulating standards. However, apex regulation bodies have not been fully successful in ensuring maintenance of minimum standards in higher education system.

National Knowledge Commission (2009)

It would be interesting to note the observations and the recommendations of the NKC (2009) on the regulatory regime as far as governance of quality is concerned. It observes that the regulatory system is flawed in three important aspects: (i) The barriers to entry are high, presumably because the universities are established by an Act, except deemed universities; (ii) There is a multiplicity of regulatory agencies where mandates are both confusing and overlapping; (iii) The system, as a whole, is over-regulated but under-governed. From the above observations, the conclusion follows that there is a clear need to establish an Independent Regulatory Authority for Higher Education (IRAHE). The IRAHE must be at an arm's length from the government, and independent of all stakeholders, including the concerned ministries of the government. IRAHE would be a body responsible for setting the criteria on entry of institutions, and it would authorise the degree granting power to institutions of higher education.

A review of the existing structure of regulatory system in India, and the way it regulates various aspects of higher education show that the existing regulatory procedures are extremely burdensome and counter-productive. They often control supply limiting choice by erecting formidable entry barriers for new institutions to be set up through private enterprise. Time consuming, non-transparent, and complex procedures applied arbitrarily, create conducive environment for rent seeking and patronage. It makes higher education institutions less accountable. The system is strait-jacketed and inhibits innovation. Overall, the system works towards standardisation in higher education, and not for maintenance of standards. There is a widespread feeling that regulatory bodies in India have miserably failed to discharge their responsibility towards maintenance of standards. Summing up the situation, Mehta and Kapur (2004) conclude that the existing laws regulating higher education in India tend to promote adverse selection. It deters genuine investment in education, but encourages those who are adept at manipulating in the system.

In a recent survey of the degree of regulatory control of the major higher education system in the world, *The Economist* noted that whereas, most nations in the world (including China) are working towards loosening of statutory control over their higher education systems, India is moving in reserve direction and tightening government control in institutions of higher education. It is also clear from the mapping of the regulatory system in India that there is a diarchy in higher education in India. While UGC is expected to oversee it; the state governments regulate it in practice. In addition, the higher education institutions are subjected to a multi-layered regulatory and control process involving a number of agencies and bodies. Despite all this, higher education in India has virtually remained an unbridled horse (Pinto, 1984).

In view of the above, it is no surprise that many of the better known institutions of higher education in India such as—the Indian Institutes of Technology (IITs), the Indian Institutes of Management (IIMs), National Institute of Fashion Technology (NIFT), National Institute of Design (NID), Indian Institute of Science (I.I.Sc.), Tata Institute of Social Science (TISS) and Birla Institute of Technology and Science (BITS) Pilani—are all outside the conventional university system in India. IIMs, NIFT, and NID offer only diplomas.

Complex and dysfunctional regulatory arrangements for higher education in India have raised serious concerns about the credibility of the Indian higher education system. There is a need to safeguard its integrity, and enhance its credibility. Loss of credibility would have serious repercussions. Our competitive advantage as a nation with huge reserve of highly qualified and trained manpower may be lost. Many countries are shying away in signing mutual recognition agreements with us because of horror stories that they hear about deteriorating standards of higher education in India. This would become more difficult in the years to come, if we allow any further compromise on the standards of higher education in the country.

Since regulation is blamed for all the ills besetting higher education, it is often argued that total deregulation of higher education in India would serve the public interest best. This argument is based on the simple principle of economics, that if the market regulates institutions more efficiently and effectively than the state, then the task of regulation should be left to the market; facilitating oversupply would be the best way to subject market sensitive institutions to the regulations of the market. The manner in which clearing of demand and supply takes place in higher education suggests that leaving higher education to market forces may not be most viable option. Though, academics would normally object to the concept of regulation, especially as it relates to academic quality. However, it needs to be understood that due to its very nature, academic standards need to be determined and coordinated across universities requiring some kind of external scrutiny. This makes regulation important; though equally important is the nature of regulation, who is responsible for developing them, and who would implement these regulations.

The Eleventh FYP laid a good deal of emphasis on the reforms agenda in higher education. Guided by the recommendations of the NKC, and later as suggested by the Yash Pal Committee, it prescribed a series of measures for reforming the higher education system. Some of the key focus points in this regard has been the reforms in the regulatory system in higher education. Aimed at reviewing the regulatory mechanism for higher education at the national as well as state level, the major initiative was to address the issue of multiplicity of regulatory bodies; thereby making higher education better governed and regulated. Driven by that consideration, the following five legislative proposals have been developed.

(i) The Educational Tribunals Bill, 2010;
(ii) The Foreign Education Institution (Regulation Entry and Operations) Bill, 2010;
(iii) The National Accreditation Regulatory Authority for Higher Educational Institutions Bill, 2010;
(iv) The Prohibition of Unfair Practices in Technical Educational Institutions, Medical Educational Institutions, and Universities Bill, 2010;
(v) Higher Education and Research Bill, 2010.

These proposals have been before the parliament for a long time.

21
Academia-Industry Interaction

In an era of globalization industry-academia linkages have become significant to generate industrially relevant knowledge at affordable cost. The current level of linkages between industry-university/academia/R&D institutions in India has to go a long way to work in tandem. There are several institutional bottlenecks in forging such relationships. These obstacles need to be overcome in the larger interest of the nation, and competitiveness of the Indian industry in the global arena.

The need for institution-industry collaboration was foreseen in various policy statements of the Government of India. During the preparation of the National Policy on Education, a document entitled "*Challenges of Education—A Policy Perspective*" was prepared by the Ministry of Education which noted that, "the collaboration between industry and technical institutions, which is so crucial for ensuring relevant quality and cost-effectiveness, remains weak despite exhortations for closer cooperation." Subsequently, the National Policy on Education adopted by the Parliament in 1986 emphasised the need for the collaboration by stating that:

> "The curricula of technical and management programmes will be targeted on current as well as the projected needs of the industry or user systems. Active collaboration between technical or management institutions and industry will be promoted in programme planning and implementation, exchange of personnel, training facilities and recourses, research and consultancy and other areas of mutual interest... Networking will have to be established between technical education and industry. R&D organisations, programmes of rural and community development, and with other sectors of education with complementary characteristics."

The technology policy statement, prepared by the Department of Science and Technology in 1993 (DST, 1993), for widespread dissemination emphasised the collaboration between engineering educational institutions and industry through statements such as:

> "Attention will be directed to further enlarge the base of

> polytechnics, technical, and vocational institutes, and engineering institutions and launch programmes for training and retraining and technical personnel in numbers significantly more than what has been attempted hitherto. Industrial [cooperation] will be involved in this process of upgrading the human skills ... Pursuit of R&D as a career prospect will de deliberately encouraged through further concrete measures so as to attract scientists and technologists to the challenges of creative science and innovative development with a target of doubling their number in R&D by 2000 AD."

The Technology Policy Statement, (DST, 1993), further stated that:

> "In view of such a predominant role being envisaged for Research, Design and Engineering (R&DE) in the coming years, continual examination and reorienting the work programmes of the R&D institutions are necessary, based upon the emerging needs of the country and the areas where large foreign investments are taking place or substantial foreign technological inputs are needed. The linkages with industry, markets, customers, and feedback and feed-forward research would become important and mechanisms to achieve these would be provided for".

The DST Policy Statement, 1993, further suggested various steps for encouraging collaboration:

- Funding national laboratories and academic institutions through linked projects.
- Promoting university-industry linkages by diverse means, including adjunct positions for necessary personnel.
- Encouraging the use of national laboratory facilities and their expertise by industrial units by way of contract research projects appropriately paid for by the industry.
- Developing the consortium approach involving academic institution, national laboratories, including those of the mission agencies namely, Department of Atomic Energy, Space, and Defense Research and Development, wherever feasible, and the user industry, for goal oriented programmes, and new product development.
- Facilitating easy mobility of personnel among universities, laboratories, industry (including R&D institutions connected with industry), and the ministries.
- Assigning multi-dimensional responsibility to the existing technological institutions.

State governments have been assigned a special role in encouraging R&D and in providing linkages at the local levels. The DST Policy Statement, 1993, further stated, "R&D institutions including academic institutions would be encouraged to interact with industry and other agencies for contract projects. Income arising out of such initiatives will become additional resources for furthering their infrastructure and other R&D activities ... All measures will be taken to accelerate the process of transforming of a laboratory technology to an industrial operation through strengthening and involvement of design, consultancy, and project implementation groups."

The lack of strong linkages between universities and the industry has led to the present situation where:

- The faculty, in general, have no industrial experience or exposure.
- There is not much provision for continuing education in the universities and institutions for practicing engineers to update their technological competence.
- State of art research in the industry prevents flow between organised research in the universities and institutions and evolution of industrial R&D.
- There is no suitable mechanisms available for collaboration in most of the departments of the universities and institutions.
- Some of the universities and institutions feel constrained to accept contracts with time bound results.
- There is chronic dependence of our industry on foreign collaboration.

The universities and professional institutions should come out of their ivory towers and interact with the outside world. Similarly, the industries should build confidence in the capabilities of the universities and the institutions, and interact with them for mutual benefit. It should be recognised that the academic world, industries, and R&D organisations together hold the key to the technological development in many of the core sectors of our country. This requires insight into the problems of industry, and it provides a base for research and education. Survival of industry largely depends on improved, innovative, and new technologies and for this purpose it needs the support of the academic institutions. Unfortunately, in our country universities, including technological institutions, and the industry have been run on parallel lines without interaction.

World Bank and Overseas Development Agencies of Britain have extended support to polytechnics and regional engineering colleges, respectively, for improving the collaboration between the two sectors.

The universities have, for the first time, been asked to generate, at least in part, their own resources, and find that they must assist business to ensure survival. It is evident that, in the coming years, industry, universities, and research institutions will, out of necessity, have to assist each other. In order to do so they will, however, have to first overcome attitudinal differences, and remove some obvious impediments. With the policy of liberalization, globalization, and privatisation, Indian industries have to face stiff competition with large multi-national giants. To meet the challenges, the Indian higher technical education system needs revamping and restructuring. Not only has the science and technology base to be strong, but also our human resource have to rise to the occasion and meet the emerging challenges. This calls for major emphasis on close-industry-institute-partnership, resource generation, and faculty exposure by the technical education institutes.

Benefits of Industry-Academia Interaction

It goes without saying that the training of technical manpower in the country must be consistent with the needs of the country, both in terms of numbers, and the nature of the training. Naturally, therefore, the curricula and course structures have to be designed keeping in mind the nature of work that the graduating students are expected to undertake. The vast majority of the graduates of engineering colleges and diploma polytechnics are employed by industry, both in the private sector and the public sector. Relatively smaller numbers go into entrepreneurship. Some find employment in government organisations. Only a few go in for higher education with the ultimate objective of taking up a career in the academic institutions. Thus, the needs of the industry, which is the major employer of our graduates, should constitute an important factor in the design of our curricula.

With an aim to strengthen the industry-academia linkage, the MHRD has taken steps for setting up of an "incubation fund." To have an industry incubation fund is worth considering, though the operational and logistics details need to be worked out. The All India Council for Technical Education (AICTE) also has initiated a scheme where one crore rupees will be provided for starting an incubation centre on the campus, if there are matching grants available from the industry. The institute will need to provide about 2500-3000 sq. ft. on the campus for this to happen. Cluster colleges can also participate in this.

MHRD is in the process of enabling institutions to have collaborations with other institutions globally, so as to help them evolve as 'centres of excellence.' The MHRD is also establishing 50 centres of excellence in frontier areas of science. There is a need for greater private sector involvement. The industry should engage itself more in terms of not only funding, but also skill development, innovation, and entrepreneurship. The target of enhancing access to higher education by creating ten million additional seats aligned to the skill needs of the economy, calls for more innovative and viable models of funding higher education. The National Vocational Qualification Framework (NVEQF) offers students an alternate path that can offer employment, and provides an opportunity to acquire a degree or diploma. Skill building can only be imparted by the industry or its associates. The same needs a greater involvement of the industry not only in providing skills, but also in promotion of innovation and encouragement of entrepreneurship among our youth.

The MHRD will also launch the National Employability Enhancement Mission (NEEM) through AICTE. The objective of NEEM is to offer on-the-job practical training to enhance the employability of a person either pursuing his/her graduation/diploma in any technical or non-technical stream, or someone who has discontinued his/her degree or diploma course to increase employability. Any society/trust/company registered under section 25 of the Companies Act, 1956 shall be eligible to apply for registration as a NEEM agent. It is expected that when the educational institutes and industry will work together for training, internships, and consequently better employability of students. The framework will provide a vehicle for companies and entrepreneurs to provide employability skills and internship as value added proposition to students of all fields.

The Ministry of Human Resources Development (MHRD) announced key initiatives to promote industries-academia collaborations in the country for greater national productivity, (Pallam Raju, 2013) including the setting up of an incubation fund for 100 institutions. MHRD will set up an Academia-Industry Interface Council with representatives of industry and academia. The Council will promote collaboration between the two and create a culture of innovation. MHRD will identify ten institutes with the potential to have research parks at tier one, two, or three, depending on the optimum size of industry presence required and current level of academia-industry engagement in the institute. As in the case of IIT Madras Research Park, while the initial funding would come from government, the research park would be expected to raise resources from the market, and generate its own revenues later on.

MHRD will explore the possibility of funding for research on competitive basis for national priorities where industries and academia collaborate. It has begun documenting case studies as an MHRD-CII collaboration initiative. MHRD will recognise good works of collaboration between industry and academia through annual awards. In coordination with industry, MHRD will put in place a mechanism to invite applications for best outcomes of industry-academia partnerships. The gap between industry and academia has to be bridged to enhance the employability of our people.

Recent Initiatives of CII in Industry-Academia Linkages

Indian industry is keen to work with academia, (Forbes, 2013), for its own benefit as the quality of manpower in industry cannot be improved without focusing on quality in academic institutions. The Confederation of Indian Industries (CII) has taken several steps in this direction, including increasing the number of Ph.D. fellowships from one hundred to one thousand and funding of global innovation alliance. However, the scale of collaboration is low between these two sectors.

Suggested Modes of Industry-Academia Linkages

There are various ways in which academia and industry can help each other. It is believed that the Swaminadhan Model for University, Industry, R&D Organisation Symbiosis, if implemented, will result in pooling, sharing, and optimization of the use of resources in terms of men, materials, and finance in these sectors and help towards national development through industrial growth. Teaching and research activities in universities get enriched. There would be better and relevant industrial R&D output and the industries will thus be well prepared to face the global competition.

Academia and industry are increasingly seeing greater value in collaboration. The academic world is eager to bring in cutting edge knowledge that practicing industry professionals can provide to bring curricula abreast of contemporary developments and make it relevant. In turn industry is also realising the value of collaboration, especially by exposing the faculty and students to the latest industry and technology trends, and ways to improve employability of students

India is steadily shifting to a fast track of economic and industrial development, which has led to mounting demands on education, and calls for a highly diversified human resource. Already India is witnessing several paradigm shifts in the social, business, and industrial environment. The shift from low tech to high tech, national to global, production to service economy, state to private sector, and the changing occupational patterns create demand for a new work force with a different skills profile than was demanded in the yester years. The onus of making available this resource lies on our system of higher education. This supply of competent human resource is vital for our economic restructuring and achieving global competitiveness.

22
Internationalisation

Internationalisation is not an altogether unknown phenomenon in higher education in India and other developing countries. Students have for many decades gone aboard for higher studies, and professionals have gone out to teach or do research. Foreign faculty have come to our shores for teaching and managing institutions. Foreign books and journals have been an indispensable source of knowledge for our university students and teachers. Thus, teaching and learning, research, and institution building have all been influenced by some form of internationalisation or the other.

Internationalisation of higher education (IHE) is a process of integrating an international, intercultural and global dimension into the purpose, functions (teaching, service, research), and delivery of higher education. International higher education means a series of international activities such as academic mobility for students and teachers, international linkages, partnerships and projects, new international academic programmes, and international initiatives. IHE is the delivery of education to other countries through new types of arrangements such as branch campuses and franchises, and using a variety of face-to-face and distance learning techniques. To many it means the integration of an international, intercultural, and global dimension into the curriculum and teaching-learning process. Traditionally, higher education has been considered to be a social responsibility, and government and society have both contributed to its development. However, with the expansion of higher education to make it easily available to the masses, there has been a continuously increasing demand for professional programmes, first at the national level, and then increasingly at the international level.

The governments of various countries support higher education programmes by providing scholarships, fellowships, exchange programme support, and chairs. A number of ways exist for collaborating with the international higher education system:

- By promoting international student mobility through exchange and scholarship programmes.
- Promoting faculty mobility.

- Promoting cultural understanding by way of scholarships, fellowships, and chairs.
- Offering offshore distance education programmes.
- Establishing academic partnerships with foreign institutions related to teaching.
- Promoting research collaboration at individual and institutional levels.
- Setting up international branch campuses abroad.
- Developing linkages in sports and cultural activities.

International organisations, associations, and the governments of a number of countries support several international programmes/schemes/ scholarships, and fellowships for international higher education.

Favourable Effects of Internationalisation

- Quality of higher education will improve following the close cooperation of universities at a worldwide level.
- Students would have greater choices in selecting courses as per their aptitude and interest.
- Economies of scale could bring down the cost of education.
- International standards of education can be ensured.
- ICTs would benefit students, irrespective of their nationality.
- Research and development may scale new heights.
- Mobility of teachers is likely to enhance homogeneity in teaching quality.
- Cultural, specific, and technological integration may lead to more multifaceted development.
- Modern system of examination, education, and testing would develop and spread.

Possible Adverse Effects of Internationalisation

- Global education may adversely affect national sovereignty, and lead to domination by the west.
- Indigenous arts and culture of a country may face a threat of loss or extinction.

Earlier Efforts in India: The Mysore Statement

Perhaps, for the first time the issue of internationalisation was deliberated as a desirable change by the Association of Indian Universities in 2001. The AIU organised a Roundtable of Vice Chancellors on Internationalisation of Indian Higher Education in February, 2001 at the University of Mysore under the leadership and guidance of Prof. K.B.

Pawar, the then Secretary General, AIU and an expert in the field of internationalisation of higher education. The Roundtable was attended by senior Indian educationists and planners, international educators, and representatives of developed as well as developing countries. After an in-depth discussion on the global scenario related to the internationalisation of higher education, several recommendations were made for the government, academic institutions, and the AIU to act upon.

Some of the recommendations were:

- Urgent action should be taken in the matter of finalisation of government policies relating to the promotion of Indian education abroad. They proposed that a Committee for the Promotion of Indian Education Abroad (CoPIE) be constituted at an early date and its functioning activated.
- The University Grants Commission Act, 1956, and the Acts of other statutory councils, need to be amended to include a specific provision allowing universities to open offshore campuses, and export Indian education through the distance mode. These is also a need to enact legislation that would regulate the operation of foreign institutions, and thereby prevent the gross commercialization of education. It is also necessary to frame legislation that would regulate the operation of Indian partners of foreign institutions to allow only genuine academic institutions to participate in twinning activities.
- Urgent steps should be taken to strengthen the data and information base so that prospective international students can obtain information related to academic programmes available at different universities, eligibility criteria, admission procedures, and tuition fees.
- Government, statutory bodies, and the University Grants Commission should grant greater autonomy and flexibility to universities in dealing with the process of admission of foreign students and in entering into collaborative arrangements with foreign institutions, especially in the establishment of offshore campuses and centres.
- The government should set up a mechanism for monitoring the standard of education that is imparted by foreign universities. here is also a need to establish a National Quality Framework that would provide for lateral transfer as well as vertical progression both nationally and internationally
- International education is a two-way process and it is essential that Indian academic institutions, and especially the universities,

should establish partnerships and develop networks with foreign universities in both the developed and the developing countries.

- In order to facilitate the internationalisation of Indian higher education, AIU should assume the role of coordinator. It should serve as the nodal agency within the university system, to be responsible for the coordination of activities of universities in the area of international education.

Amritsar Declaration

In the backdrop of the Mysore Statement, the Association of Indian Universities organised the second Roundtable on Internationalisation of Indian Higher Education in February, 2002. It was attended by representatives of the higher education system of the United States of America, Australia, Germany, France, and India. The Roundtable discussed the issues related to government policies, student mobility, building institutional links, and marketing of education. Along with other recommendations, it was suggested that AIU should assume the role of coordinator. Some of the recommendations were:

- The Indian government needs to play a pro-active role in order to promote the internationalisation of Indian higher education. The Indian embassies and high commissions should take the initiative in providing informationon the Indian higher education system, and about the facilities for higher education available in the country. The formalities related to registration, entry test requirements, issue of 'No Objection Certificate,' and issue (and extension) of visa need to be simplified. There is a need to adopt an 'open door' policy as regards self-financing students. A single-window clearance mechanism should be set up for admitting students to different professional programmes. It is also desirable that a mechanism to monitor the quality of education imparted to foreign students by the Indian institutions be formulated.
- As stated in the World Declaration on Higher Education for the Twenty-first Century, partnership and alliances based on mutual respect and credibility will be a prime matrix for renewal in higher education in the twenty-first century. Indian academic institutions should establish links with foreign institutions (twinning programmes), and if possible, be a part of an international consortium. This will help the institutions to develop and maintain international standards in both teaching and research.
- There is a need to establish a nodal agency that will be

responsible for maintenance of databases, networking with other international agencies, coordinating student exchange programmes, developing institutional links for both teaching and research, and possible marketing Indian higher education abroad. The Association of Indian Universities has already taken the initiative as regards internationalisation of higher education and could be assigned this role by the government, with adequate financial support.

AIU Task Force (2004)

The general body of the Association of Indian Universities in its 78th Annual Meeting held at Sri Venkateshwara University, Tirupati on November 21, 2003 resolved to constitute a Task Force to examine various issues involved in internationalisation of higher education. Following the resolution, a Task force was constituted. The recommendations of the Task Force were:

- Before plunging into any agreement related to higher education with the trade partners of the country, the following measures should urgently be taken: (a) All 'requests' and 'offers' regarding higher education received by the government from the WTO members should be made publicly available with full details, to the public at large; (b) An impact assessment of these proposal should be carried out by several groups of experts having different ideological backgrounds; (c) This impact assessment should particularly focus on the following issues: (i) What will be the impact of GATS, policy of 'progressive liberalization' and its rule of 'non-discrimination' on Indian higher education? (ii) What kind of short-term and long-term restructuring of higher education would be required as a result of this? (iii) Will it result in reduction or complete elimination of public funding/subsidy of higher education? If so, what will be its effect on the quality of opportunity to access higher education, quality of education, on various types of 'profitable' and 'non-profitable' courses/ activities, and on cross-subsidization? (iv) Will it make international cooperation in the field of higher education more difficult, expensive, and less meaningful? (v) What will be the impact on society of the reduction in the regulatory capability of government, and elimination of policy options available to it in future? (vi) How will it affect the academics? How will it affect their academic freedom? What will be the effect on their employment/service conditions, bargaining capacity etc.? Will it make their life more 'miserable' and less creative/exciting through contractual/ad-hoc/temporary/casual appointments? (vii) What will be its impact on the students? Will the reduction or complete elimination of public funding, fee deregulation along with increased self-financed courses become the norm? Will it affect the access to higher education and make it more dependent on their financial capability, rather than their intellectual worth? Will it lead to widespread indebtedness of students? If so, what will be its effect on the students, their education, and the society at large?

- These impact assessments should be made publicly available, and an exhaustive and widespread public debate based on these impact assessments should be promoted among all the stakeholders of higher education. Moreover, all relevant government departments and ministries such as NGOs, UGC, AIU, MHRD, Commerce Ministry, Finance Ministry, Home Ministry, Youth Welfare Ministry, Foreign Ministry, Defense Ministry, Planning Commission, etc. should be actively and jointly involved in this nationwide debate.
- The Task Force noted a few points which are positively in favour of the liberalization policy of the GATS are mentioned here: (a) Innovation development in higher education; (b) Entry to new service providers; (c) Greater student access; (d) Increased economic gains; (e) New hybridization; and (f) Fusion of culture through mobility of people.
- At the same time the Task Force desired to put forth the lurking dangers awaiting us if we jump into the plans laid down by the GATS. These dangers are enumerated below: (a) Sovereignty of the country will be at stake; (b) Government will be forced to reduce subsidies; (c) Only professional courses will find place in the education system; (d) Depriving the poor of developing countries the benefits of higher education and benefiting mainly the upper middle and the rich classes; (e) Development of unrest in students at large; (f) Threat to linguistic diversity, especially through dominance of English; (g) Commoditization of higher education will erode the autonomy of the universities and the academic freedom of the university teachers; (h) Higher education under GATS may not be in congruence with national policy of education, which will lead to larger socio-political turbulence; and (i) GATS could undermine cooperative internationalisation.

- After having thoroughly examined the strengths and weaknesses of Indian higher education, and also the opportunities and threats to the Indian higher education under the GATS, the Task Force thus came to the conclusion that it is not in the interest of the country at this stage to open up its higher education system for global competition under GATS. It suggested an all pervasive and exhaustive national debate, involving all the stakeholders in the country on the issue of liberalizing higher education, to arrive at a final decision for its acceptance or otherwise.

Initiatives by the University Grants Commission

The recommendations of both the Roundtables organised at Mysore and Amritsar by the Association of Indian Universities culminated in the formation of a Standing Committee of University Grants Commission on Promotion of Indian Higher Education Abroad (PIHEAD). In the tenth Five Year Plan, UGC recognised internationalisation as a thrust area. Hence, it formed an expert committee to encourage free flow of students from other nations to India and vice versa. The PIHEAD committee submitted its report in 2004. PIHEAD has been engaged to ensure speedy implementation of various proposal initiated by the UGC. A provision has been made to obtain the required information from the universities/ institutions with regard to their programmes, course content, admission criteria, fee structure, transaction of curricula, evaluation procedures, etc. which would provide support to PIHEAD to promote higher education abroad.

In 2006, UGC formed a study group which came out with the report '*Modalities to Provide Educational Opportunities to Foreign Students and to Generate Resource for Higher Education*' suggesting setting up of 'Consortium for International Education' either at UGC, AIU, or at any university in Delhi. Further, in 2009 a panel of UGC prepared a plan on 'Internationalisation of Higher Education,' but a decision on it is pending for want of further action.

Initiatives by Ministry of Human Resource Development

The Government of India made a legislative attempt to regulate the educational system better by putting forth in the parliament the Foreign Education Institutions (Regulation of Entry and Operation, Maintenance of Quality and Prevention of Commercialization) Bill in 2007. The objective of the bill was to provide an ideal regulatory framework in which reputed institutions are able to enter and operate in terms of India's National Policy, while at the same time check and control substandard operators. However, the bill could not be enacted.

Recently, the Union Cabinet approved a new programme titled Global Initiative of Academic Network (GIAN) in Higher Education aimed at tapping the international talent pool of scientists and entrepreneurs, to encourage their engagement with the institutes of higher education in India, so as to augment the country's existing academic resources, accelerate the pace of quality reform, and elevate India's scientific and technological capacity to global excellence.

Further, an innovative scheme—Connect to India—was launched by the Ministry of HRD on the assumption that this initiative will be a value added programme, under which around 200 U.S. students would be provided opportunities to visit India every year to attend a 4-6-week study programme in one of the 15 select Indian universities. It is expected that the Connect to India programme would be beneficial to both Indian and American students.

Stand of the National University of Educational Planning and Administration

The National University of Educational Planning and Administration (NUEPA), the then NIEPA, has been engaged in taking up a few programmes on internationalisation of higher education in the form of research studies, seminars, conferences. The NUEPA organised a conference on "Internationalisation of Higher Education: Issues and Concerns" in 2004. The issues having implications on domestic regulation, improving competitiveness of higher education, and the issue of foreign direct investment (FDI) in higher education were deliberated. In 2009, NUEPA organised a "Consultation of Foreign Providers in Indian Higher Education: Issues of Entry, Regulation and Models of Engagement." The major recommendations were as follows:

- For degree and non-degree programmes, accredited and reputed foreign universities may be permitted to collaborate for the delivery of joint programmes.
- Such collaboration may take place with government, and government-aided universities and colleges for joint degree provision.
- Such collaboration may also take place with private universities and colleges under strict guidelines from the UGC to prevent commercialization.
- UGC may allow the grant of a joint degree for such collaborative partnerships.
- For non-degree programmes in vocational disciplines, all registered private institutions not included in higher education,

may be allowed to collaborate with foreign universities/ institutions after registration and regulation by appropriate vocation agencies of the government.

- The branch campus of a foreign university through the trust, and under 2f of UGC Act, with degree conferring right without university status may at present be deferred till the experiment gain from collaboration partnership warrants the need for more liberalization.

From the above analysis of India's response to the process of internationalisation of higher education it appears that the process of internationalisation has not yet taken off. If India has to benefit from the process of internationalisation, major policy initiatives and concrete programme activities in the area of student and scholar exchanges, as well as educational institutional tie ups for collaboration in teaching and research, will have to be put in place. Indian universities must increase the entry of international students with whom the local students can interact. Reforms in the higher education system of India are long overdue, and the emphasis on internationalisation must be given a high priority.

In formulating the Twelfth Five Year Plan 2012-17, India has projected a scheme for setting up an India International Education Centre for promoting internationalisation of Indian higher education. Unfortunately, there does not seem to be any political commitment towards going ahead with such a Centre that could help enhancing India's political standing through international education activities. In short, India has so far not shown its political willingness to use the international education route to play a leading role in a world of globalised education players.

The globalised economic scenario offers us a unique opportunity to establish India as an educational destination for international students as we can offer certain unique advantages, including affordable, quality education in supportive atmosphere strengthened by historic, cultural, and political ties. The provisos necessary for internationalisation of higher education are:

- Enhancing capacity and efficiency.
- Improving standards and quality.
- Competing in the global arena.
- Influencing international relations.
- Establishing a regional identity.
- Enhancing India's international reputation.
- Alleviation of faculty-crunch.

It is unfortunate that the Indian universities, barring only a few, have not been able to capitalize on the opportunities of offering their educational programmes to the world population in any significant manner. The reasons are manifold. The universities in India may not have realised the importance of offering their products and services to foreign clientele. The inherent limitations of the system may also be holding the universities back, or making their attempts to reach out the foreign clientele less successful. Quite often the restriction of territorial jurisdiction of individual universities is seen as a barrier in their effort to go international. Sometimes the limitations could be the lack of appropriate information about the Indian campuses to the foreign students. Paucity of suitable infrastructure and physical facilities are indeed a deterrent, but more importantly it is the self-imposed rigidity in the teaching, learning, admission, and evaluation processes that discourage foreign students.

Indian higher educational institutions should urgently start marketing their programmes abroad with the twin objectives of generating additional resources, and developing strong relationships with other countries of the world. It is high time that the universities develop international orientation to their working and operation, and the agencies responsible for the management of higher education institutions must ensure that the systemic hurdles in the way of internationalisation of Indian higher education are removed without any further delay.

23
Information and Communication Technology (ICT)

The most evident advantages of ICT are the following:

- increased productivity
- increased efficiency
- innovation and product leadership
- better quality of service
- better management and coordination
- better staff development and training

ICT has been used mainly for three educational purposes:

- to widen access to education;
- to raise its quality;
- to reform it.

UNESCO (2002) highlights how the application of ICT to education could benefit the students, employers, and the government.

Benefits of ICT in Education

Student	Increased access, flexibility of content delivery, combination of work and education, learner-centred approach, higher quality of education and new ways of interaction.
Employer	High quality, cost effective professional development in workplace, upgrading of employee skills, increased productivity, development of a new learning culture, sharing of costs and training time with the employees, increased portability of training.
Government	Increased capacity and cost effectiveness of education and training systems, reach target groups with limited access to conventional education and training, support and enhance the quality and relevance of existing educational structures, ensure the connection of educational institutions and curricula to the emerging networks and information resources, promote innovation and opportunities for life long learning.

Development of New Technologies in Education since 1980

- Audio cassettes
- Audio-conferencing
- Audio-graphic systems
- Video cassettes
- View data/Teletext/Telecom
- Computer based learning
- Laser video discs
- Cable TV
- Satellite TV
- Expert systems
- LCD Projectors
- Search engines
- Portals
- Wireless networks
- Compact discs
- E-portfolios
- Video cassettes
- Video conferencing
- Electronic mail
- Computer conference
- Internet
- World Wide Web
- Digital video discs
- Fiber optics
- Learning objects
- Mobile Phones
- Simulations
- Virtual reality

The increasing use of information and communication technologies has brought changes to teaching and learning at all levels of higher education systems (HES) leading to quality enhancements. Traditional forms of teaching and learning are increasingly being converted to online and virtual environments. There are endless possibilities with the integration of ICT in the educational system. The use of ICT in education not only improves classroom teaching learning process; but also provides the facility of e-learning. ICT has enhanced distance learning. The teaching community is able to reach remote areas, and learners are able to access qualitative learning environment from anywhere and at any time. It is important that teachers or trainers should be made to adopt technology in their teaching styles to provide pedagogical and educational gains to the learners. Successful implementation of ICT to lead change is more about influencing and empowering teachers and supporting them in their engagement with students in learning, rather than acquiring computer skills and obtaining software and equipment. ICT enabled education will ultimately lead to the democratization of education.

From the perspective of ICT, education can be classified in three main categories:

- E-learning
- Blended Learning
- Distance Learning

E-Learning or Electronic learning is a general term used to refer to computer-enhanced learning. It is commonly associated with the field of advanced learning technology (ALT), which deals with both the technologies, and the associated methodologies in learning using networked and/or multimedia technologies. It is also known as online learning. Distance education provided the base for e-learning's development. E-learning can be 'on-demand'. It overcomes timing, physical attendance, and travel difficulties. E-learning allows delivery, dialogue, and feedback over the internet. It allows mass customization in terms of content and exams. E-education can provide access to the best gurus and the best practices or knowledge available (UNESCO, 2002). It is possible to leverage the online environment to facilitate teaching techniques like role-play across time and distance. It can also facilitate the development of scenarios, which can be rarely witnessed in practice. ICT can play a valuable role in monitoring and logging the progress of the students across time, place, and varied activities.

E-learning allows higher participation and greater interaction. It challenges the concept that face-to-face traditional education is superior to it. The web and the internet are the core ICTs to spread education through e-learning. The components include e-portfolios, cyber infrastructures, digital libraries, and online learning object repositories. All the above components create a digital identity of the student, and connect all the stakeholders in education.

E-learning has the following advantages:

- Eliminating time and geographic barriers in educations for learners as well as teachers.
- Enhanced group collaboration made possible via ICT.
- New educational approaches can be used.
- It can provide speedy dissemination of education to target disadvantaged groups.
- It offers the combination of education, while balancing family and work life.
- It enhances the international dimension of educational services.

Blended Learning is the combination of multiple approaches to learning. It is usually used to define a situation where different delivery methods are combined together to deliver a particular course. These methods may include a mixture of face-to-face learning and online classrooms.

Face to Face Learning refers to learning that occurs in a traditional classroom setting, where a faculty member delivers instruction to a group of learners. This includes lectures, workshops, presentation, tutoring, conferences, and much more.

Self-paced learning provides the flexibility to learn according to the availability of learners' own time and pace, it occurs in a variety of ways such as reading a specific chapter from text book, studying course material presented through web-based or CD-based course, attending pre-recorded classes or sessions, reading articles referred by faculty member, working on assignments and projects, and searching and browsing the internet.

Online collaborative learning involves interaction between learners and faculty members through the web. This interaction can occur in one of the following modes:

- Synchronous interaction.
- Asynchronous interaction.

Synchronous, means 'at the same time.' It involves interacting with a faculty member and other learners via the web in real time using technologies such as virtual classrooms and/or chat rooms. On the other hand, asynchronous means 'not at the same time'. It enables learners to interact at their own convenience, such as interacting through email.

Distance Learning

It is a type of education, where students work on their own at home or at the office, and communicate with faculty and other students via e-mail, electronic forums, videoconferencing, chat rooms, instant messaging, and other forms of computer-based communication. It is also known as open learning. Most distance learning programmes include a computer based training (CBT) system, and communications tools to produce a vital classroom. Because the internet and world wide web are accessible from virtually all computer platforms, they serve as the foundation for many distance learning systems.

ICTs also allow for the creation of digital resources like digital libraries where the students, teachers, and professionals can access research material, and course material from any place at any time. Such facilities allow the networking of academics and researchers; hence the sharing of scholarly materials, and leads to quality enhancement in teaching and learning.

Factors Affecting Adoption of ICT in Education

There is a need felt worldwide for integrating ICT into education in order to reflect the societal change and improve pedagogy. The main goals of ICT adoption in the educational field are reducing costs per student, making education more affordable and accessible, increasing enrollments, improving course quality, and meeting the needs of local employers. Low overheads and cost efficiency are attracting many private players to the field of internet enabled education. This is also being driven by technologies advances, competitive pressure, and the positive experiences of many early adopters. The main factors that affect the adoption of ICT in education are the mission or goal of a particular system, programmes and curricula, teaching/learning strategies and techniques, learning material and resources, communication and interaction, support and delivery systems, students, tutors, staff and other experts, management, housing and equipment, and evaluation (UNESCO, 2002). National vision, support by coherent strategies and actions is the most important factor in integrating ICT in education. Successful implementation of ICT requires strong national support from government and local support from relevant institutions and education authorities. Sharma (2003) explains that the political powers of any nations affect the introduction of any new technology. Sharma (2003) and Amutabi and Oktech (2003) explain that cost is an important issue that decides and guides the adoption and growth of information and communication technology.

Evolution of ICT in Indian Education

Involvement of ICTs in different dimensions of the Indian education system is taking place at a fast pace. Use of audio visual aids, radio, and TV to support education and dissemination of information for national development is not new. The use of satellite in education started as Satellite Instructional Television Experiment (SITE) in 1975-76. This led to the establishment of CIET-SIET studios for production and transmission of school-oriented programmes, initiation of the countrywide classroom of the UGC with Consortium for Educational Communication (CEC) as the nodal agency by creating educational media resource centres (EMRCs) and audio-visual resource centres (AVRCs) in several universities. Presently, these programmes are counted as Vyas Channel supported by the CEC and various EMRCs, Gyandarshan II of the IGNOU, Open School and NCERT broadcast channels. Educational Satellite (EDUSAT) was conceptualized to meet the communications requirements of the education sector. The Eleventh Five Year Plan gave impetus to the use of ICTs in education by setting up a National Mission in Education through ICT. In this regard, use of ICTs would contribute significantly to enhance the access and quality of education, but at the same time it may generate situations, which warrant attention. For instance, to promote technology driven education and open and distance learning the country launched a dedicated satellite EDUSAT on September 20, 2004. It was expected that EDUSAT would bring both quantitative and qualitative revolution in education. However, the quantitative expansion appears to have been achieved in being able to reach out to large numbers, yet the qualitative revolution envisioned due to introduction of new services and better quality teaching with learning materials, has not been quite visible (Bhatia, 2009). In higher education sector also, a National Mission in Education through ICTs was launched to increase ICT coverage in all the 378 universities and 18,064 colleges. The Mission will focus on digitization and networking of all educational institutions, developing low cost and low power consuming access devices, and making available bandwidth for educational purposes. These initiatives would provide significant opportunities and pose new challenges as well for effective use of ICT in programme delivery (Eleventh FYP). Notable initiatives like various universities' and colleges' use of ICT in education in India include Indira Gandhi National Open University (IGNOU) which uses radio, television, and internet technologies. National Programme on Technology Enhanced Learning is a concept similar to the open courseware initiative of MIT. It uses internet and television technologies. An Eklavya initiative uses internet and television to promote distance learning. IIT-Kanpur has developed 'Brihaspati,' an open source e-learning platform.

Premier institutions like IIM-Calcutta have entered into a strategic alliance with NIIT for providing programmes through virtual classrooms. Jadavpur University is using a mobile-learning centre. IIT-Bombay has started the programme of CDEEP (Centre for Distance Engineering Education Programme) as emulated classroom interaction through the use of real time interactive satellite technology. Educational Research Network (ERNET) and EDUSAT (GSAT-3) systems provide support to tele-education system of distance learning to reach the people who have stayed outside the ambit of distance learning in every nook and corner of India. INFONET and CEC services of University Grants Commission supporting e-content, e-learning, and e-course systems. Information and Library Network (INFLIBNET) Centre is an autonomous inter-university centre (IUC) of the UGC involved in creating infrastructure for sharing of library, information resources and services among academic and research institutions.

Issues and Challenges Affecting Utilisation of ICT in Higher Education

While we glorify the role of ICT in the higher education sector, we also need to assess the problems and prospects in its implementation. Literature on ICT in education continues to project that it can help improve India's higher education system by providing greater equity better access and improved quality. There is a growing apprehension that though information and communication technology can transform India towards becoming a knowledge society, but can technology alone enhance the quality of higher education in the country? The penetration of ICT systems in higher education institutions is extremely poor, according to a survey of accredited colleges carried out by UGC in 2008. The survey report revealed the shortcomings in IT infrastructure. As the majority of Indians living in rural areas have poor access to internet, it is necessary that they are exposed and trained in basic computing skills and ICT utilisation.

Moreover, the low awareness on IT literacy is also a major challenge India faces in realising ICT implementation in higher education. According to the International Telecommunication Union: The Internet and Mobile Association of India (IAMAI) report, a majority of government institutions do not have sufficient IT systems.

India's linguistic diversity necessitates the development of content in multiple languages to increase ICT applications. According to the 2011 Census, the rural-urban distribution is 68.84 percent and 31.16 percent in terms of population, where majority of the rural people do not speak English. Therefore, the need to develop content in all the official languages of India becomes all the more important. In a multi-lingual country like India, this standardization becomes even more difficult. However, this needs to be addressed immediately. As ambitious ICT-based initiatives in higher education are envisioned, it is necessary to embark on a well-articulated 'Action Plan.'

Criteria for the Use of Technology

A.W. Bates, who has rich and varied experience in the use of technology in distance education, and has written extensively on the role of technology in open and distance learning, suggested that in distance teaching institutions decision making on the use of technology should depend on the analysis of the following seven criteria:

A. *Access*: How accessible is a particular technology for learners? How flexible is it for a particular garget group?

C. *Costs*: What is the cost structure of each technology? What is the unit cost per learner?

T. *Teaching and learning*: What kinds of learning are needed? What instructional approaches will best meet these needs? What are the best technologies for supporting this teaching and learning?

I. *Interactivity and user-friendliness*: What kind of interaction does this technology enable? How easy is to use?

O. *Organisational issues*: What are the organisational requirements, and the barriers to be removed before this technology can be used successfully? What changes in organisation need to be made?

N. *Novelty*: How new is this technology?

S. *Speed*: How quickly can courses be mounted with this technology? How quickly can materials be changed?

Twelve Golden Rules of Use of ICT

Bates (2005) proposed twelve golden rules of using technology in education and training that apply whatever technologies are being used:

1. *Good teaching matters*: Clear objectives, good structuring of learning materials, and relevance to learners needs—all apply to the use of any technology for teaching. If these principles are ignored, then the teaching will fail, even if the unique features of the medium are exploited. Good teaching may overcome a poor choice in the use of technology, but technology will never save bad teaching.
2. *Good design is essential*: Proper instructional design is essential for proper courses.
3. *Each medium has its own aesthetic*: Each medium and technology has a different range of production skills necessary to exploit its unique features.
4. *Education technologies are flexible*: Technologies are flexible, and hence interchangeable in education and training. The absence of a particular technology does not necessarily prevent learning from being achieved.
5. *There is no super technology*: All technologies have their strengths and weakness. Therefore, they need to be combined.
6. *Make all five media available*: Ensure that face-to-face, print, audio, video, and digital multimedia are all available for teaching purposes in one form or the other.
7. *Interaction is essential*: High quality interaction with learning materials, interaction between teachers and learners, and interaction among learners are all essential for effective learning.
8. *Student numbers are critical*: The total number of learners to be served over the life of a course is a critical factor in technology selection.
9. *New technologies are not necessarily better than old one*: There is no law that says new technologies will automatically be better for teaching than old ones.
10. *Teamwork is essential*: No one can know everything there is to know about the educational use and design of every technology now available.
11. *Teachers need training to use technology effectively*: Teachers and instructors need training not only in the choice and use of technologies, but also in how people learn and how to teach with technology.
12. *Technology is not the issue*: The issue is: how and what do I want students to learn? There is more than enough technology around now to allow you to teach in whatever way you choose.

24
Privatisation

The pressure of expansion of the higher education (HE) system has led to compromising the norms of standards set by the UGC. Till the 1970s, somehow the system held on to UGC's standards. However, from 1980s and 90s, in the face of decline government funding for HE, the universities and colleges found a way to make up for the resource gap to meet their maintenance cost, and also satisfy the increase social demands for HE without compromising UGC norms in respect of standards. That was by way of starting self-financing courses in public universities and colleges, as well as self-financing colleges by the government by offering the same courses approved by the UGC. Very soon, the state governments also allowed private agencies—charitable trust or societies—to establish self-financing colleges and offer UGC approved courses by charging high tuition fees as well as various kinds of fees and charges, not only to recover the cost but also to make profit.

The increased privatisation of HE through the self-financing institutions that accompanied the economic reforms and liberalization from 1991, came with an argument for autonomy. In the wake of liberalization, HE was seen as commodity, a tangible benefit and service that needed to be purchased, offered by the private institutions of HE for a price.

Almost a decade before the NPE, 1986 and its POA were formulated and adopted by the Parliament, many states like Andhra Pradesh (AP) decided to raise the fees in aided and unaided colleges for professional courses in engineering and medicine. Professional education in private sector was ardently promoted in AP from late 1970s, and was soon emulated by Tamil Nadu, Karnataka, Kerala, and Maharashtra. Trends such as these forced the NPE, 1986 and its POA to declare that: (i) State cannot legislate creation of colleges without UGC's consent and sanction; and (ii) statutory bodies like UGC would regulate admission on the basis of physical facilities, etc.

The government was conscious of the declining trend in the state allocations to higher and technical education. The NPE, 1986 and Revised POA, 1992 openly admitted the need for some alternative way out, like raising tuition fees and other charges, subject to an elaborate and effective system for providing free studentships, scholarships, and loans to students belonging to the weaker section of society. The POA declared that a high powered committee would be set up to consider steps for mobilisation of additional resources for HE, both general and technical, to bring about a better balance in the funding, and improve the cost-efficiency.

The Gnanam Committee was appointed in 1990 against the backdrop of state governments bypassing the UGC, and establishing self-financing public and unaided private colleges. In states like Andhra Pradesh, private professional colleges in engineering and medicine were charging between Rs. 2 lakh to Rs. 8 lakh fees per annum. The Gnanam Committee was requested to review the existing management system and structures in the HE system, and suggest alternative models. It recommended that: (i) The central government should make a legislation mandating incorporation in the Acts of all Universities that they must follow and adhere to the regulations issued by UGC from time to time; (ii) No new university should be established without the prior approval of the UGC, and with reference to the special needs, size of population, size of an existing university etc.; and (iii) New legislation (including amendments to existing ones) in respect to state universities should be referred to UGC prior to their enactment.

In pursuance of the announcement made by the Revised POA, the UGC set up a high powered committee in 1992 under the chairmanship of Justice Dr. K. Punnayya to consider steps for mobilisation of additional resources for HE. It was meant to examine the present financial situation of central universities, deemed universities, and colleges affiliated to Delhi and Banaras Hindu University, to make necessary recommendations about their financial needs, and to suggest changes which could be introduced in the system of grants to these institutions. The Punnayya Committee recommended that: any additional resources generated by universities/ institutions should be kept in a separate fund and should be used to further its objectives; UGC may give a matching grant as incentive to universities generating additional resources; cent per cent income tax concessions be given for all endowments and contributions made to universities/ institutions; and additional concessions be provided to donors sponsoring research projects. While universities should be encouraged to augment their resources for covering larger proportion of cost of education than what prevails now, the increased burden must be borne only by those who can afford it. State or government funding must continue to be an essential maintenance and developmental requirement of universities.

The high powered committee on technical education (1992), headed by Dr. D. Swaminathan, was to suggest ways for technical education institutions to become self-reliant in resources. Given the dwindling state of financial support, the Swaminathan Committee felt that the time was appropriate to take new initiatives, such as raising internal and external resources through contributions from industry, alumni, and charitable trust, etc. It recommended, among other things, raising internal resources, rationalization of fee structures, including fixing the fee at a fairly high level, and revising it from time to time, as done by private unaided institutions; besides attracting foreign students, enhancing consultancy work and sponsored research, and offering revenue-generating courses for the industry.

The NPEs' POA took note of the fees raised in aided and unaided colleges, and reiterated that statutory bodies' sanction is a must for their affiliation, which went unheeded. But it was also true that the policies, formulated for different sectors of HE at different times caused considerable confusion and harassment to competent agencies, and discouraged them while incompetent and unethical groups exploited HE. Perceptive observers cautioned that this anomaly needed correction.

The Ambani-Birla Report (2000) advocated: (i) establishment of world-class HE facilities in every district capital; (ii) fostering a healthy mix of state-supported education with private initiatives within affordable cost, and (iii) enforcing strictly the "user pays" principle for HE supported by loan schemes and financial grants for economically and socially backward section of society. The Ambani-Birla Committee wanted a clear policy outlined, with complete freedom to establish private universities, colleges, and other HEIs without any reference to the exiting statutory bodies like UGC, and price their programmes and courses as the private agencies/institutions deemed appropriate. It also wanted that all political parties should come to an understanding that they will keep away from universities and educations institutions, and ban any form of political activity on campuses of universities and educational institutions.

The National Knowledge Commission's take on the scope for private institutions in the provision of HE was one of implicit approval of their widespread presence and an explicit plea for their role—coexistence—as a matter of policy. The NKC advocated private investment in education by offering land grants, and other facilities, if need be, because "even with the best will in the world, government financing cannot be enough to support the massive expansion in opportunities for HE on a scale that is now essential."

The Review Committee on Deemed to be Universities (also known as Tandon Committee), constituted by the MHRD in 2009, observed that after "interacting with representatives of 126 deemed universities; we are struck by the aberrations and some unacceptable practices." It said that the deemed universities fall into three categories: (i) Those that justify their deemed university status eminently, numbering 38; (ii) Those deficient in some respects, which need to be rectified in three years, numbering 44; and (iii) Those which neither on past performance nor on future potential hold hopes and deserve their status, numbering 44. Continuation of the third category by allowing them to grant degrees is injurious to the cause of maintaining the quality of higher education, and, without doubt, would imperil the future of millions of our youth, and a committee at the national level is needed to salvage the future of the affected students is necessary (Tandon Committee, 2009).

With respect to the future of deemed universities, the Committee said: (i) The highest governing body of deemed university such as Board of Management, Executive Council or Governing Council, must always be headed by the vice-chancellor as in all conventional universities. Its membership should invariably include at least 50 percent of distinguished academics and professionals, and with not more than one or two representatives of the "Trust, Society, or President" in the case of private deemed universities, and government representatives, in the case of publicly sponsored deemed universities; (ii) The president of the deemed university should not be automatically designated as the Chancellor. President's role should only be ceremonial; (iii) The president or the Chancellor nominating close relatives to the Board or as Vice-Chancellor/ Pro-Vice Chancellor is undesirable and against the UGC rules, and must be discontinued; (iv) Admissions to all institutions of higher education, public or private, should be based on centralised examination. This will obviate the scope of malpractices now widely prevalent; (v) The fees charged for courses offered in deemed universities should be responsible in relation to the cost of running the courses and comparable to the fee levels in other institutions for similar courses. There should be a national committee to bring about a rational fee structure for deemed universities which can be reviewed periodically; (vi) There should be a more intensive and exhaustive external review of every deemed university once in every five years; (vii) While private participation in higher education is probably needed, it must be ensured that it does not lead to crass commercialization of education at the cost of equity and access to all deserving students and to the sacrifice of merit (Tandon Committee, 2009).

The Committee on Renovation and Rejuvenation of HE headed by Prof. Yash Pal was convinced that in order to reach the goals of doubling the present HE capacity, private sector participation should be encouraged. At the same time, government cannot afford to abandon its role and leave that task entirely to the private sector. In fact, all the different models are needed viz., state run, private, and Public Private Partnership PPPs with rational and consistent ground rules, overseen by a transparent regulator mechanism. But, the purely private initiatives require a credible corrective mechanism to do away with the ills associated with it currently.

The Yash Pal Committee was firm that private initiatives in HE should be not driven by the sole motive of profit, and confine themselves only to commercially viable sectors of education, such as management, accountancy, and medicine, etc., but should also establish institutions that will offer social and natural sciences. Otherwise, such institutions should be allowed to confer only diplomas and certificates, and not university degrees.

The Yash Pal Committee noted the sudden mushrooming of deemed universities as "another area of concern." It found that some of the private institutions took the deemed-to-be university route to get degree-granting powers. While the number of private-sponsored institutions that got the deemed university status was 26 during 2000-2005, it shot up to 108 by 2009. By a notification of the UGC, it was no longer necessary for them to use the adjective "deemed" and they all started calling themselves simply universities. It strongly recommended that in view of the considerable misuse of the provision for deemed university status, the granting of such status should be put on hold till unambiguous and rational guidelines are evolved. Institutions wishing to get deemed university status should demonstrate special capabilities as was originally intended, and should be rigorously evaluated to see if they fulfill the holistic and universal concept of university."

The Committee on Corporate Participation in HE, headed by N.R. Narayana Murthy, referred to the Working Group on higher and technical education for the Twelfth plan that projected a resource requirement of Rs. 4,13,368 crore. It felt that this large amount is unlikely to be made available, and the government has to find innovative and newer avenues of funding. It suggested that the corporate sector, as a key stakeholder in HE can collaborate with the academia in several ways, with varying funding commitments. This would lead to: (i) Creating enabling conditions to make the HE system robust and useful to attract investments; (ii) Improve the quality of HE … with corporate sector participation; and (iii) Engaging the corporate sector to invest in existing institutions, set up new institutions, and develop new knowledge clusters.

It was the Planning Commission that appointed this committee to suggest measures for corporate participation in HE. Having seen the report, and as a measure of the government's intention to give effect to its recommendation, the Twelfth Plan (2012-2017) said that, "private HE now accounts for 58.5 percent of enrolments. Private sector will be encouraged in the establishment of larger [number] and better quality

HEIs in Twelfth Plan." It said that the current no entry provision of for-profit private institutions needs a rethink to allow their entry in select areas where acute shortage persists. There should be "innovative ways to encourage private institutions in HE," like granting legal status to allow all types of private institutions under Section 25 of the Companies Act, including conversion of trusts and societies to do so, and giving priority recognition to it while providing infrastructure improvements with financial and tax benefits.

The FICCI Education Summit, 2013 came almost immediately after the Twelfth Five Year Plan legitimising and valuing private participation in HE. The FICCI Summit foresaw the situation in 2030, and described the progress as would have happened along the lines it recommended in 2013. It starts as: "2030. This year marks 80 years of constitutional democracy, 40 years of economic liberalisation, and 20 years of accelerated educational reform... The Indian HE system has undergone rapid expansion. In less than 20 years, the country has created additional capacity for a mammoth 40 million students ... aggressive expansion as a deliberate strategy and an organised design."

FICCI Vision 2030, looking back, states that the keys to this "revolution" and "transformation" in HE leading to the "50 percent GER and 40 million enrolment" and "massive online courses enrolling 60 percent of world's entire student population" are: (i) "diminishing government in governance," with government withdrawing from direct management through multiple regulators to a single independent regulatory body for entire gamut of HE; (ii) "enabling environment," with "less barriers for private and foreign participation"; and (iii) a change from government as single provider of funds to a position where institutions, and individuals—students, faculty and researchers—no longer have to rely on government, but could start sourcing funding, from other sources "to assure autonomy".

In sum, the space for private involvement in HE in India not just in actual practice but, more importantly, at the policy level as seen in policy discourses, moved from the margin to the centre, and began to clamour for the HE system to be handed over to the private sector. This was a plea for the government to shift from the field of HE, and confine its attention to primary education and literacy as its principal obligation. It was an expression of HE as not a public good, but a private good whose returns go to individuals and their families, and for which they have to pay to the provider—the private institutions. Private involvement in HE has to be legitimised and ensured by legislation both at the central and state level, and such legislation should also stipulate their autonomy and freedom in administration, academic, and governance matters, including the cost.

This argument for a legally-ensured dominant space for private involvement in HE also marks a metamorphosis. It is not as if the public institutions and the role of government involvement in HE has disappeared. It still retains substantial number of HEIs—universities, colleges, and diploma institutions. But, in the policy milieu as seen in the discourses of the commissions and committees, there is an increasing stridency in the argument for the government to leave the field, as well as policy justification in favour of private involvement in HE.

25
Under-Represented Groups

Our country suffered from several inequalities in education and employment based on caste, ethnicity, and even gender. Since the beginning of Indian history, its society has been plagued by the caste system, and to date precious little has been achieved against any movement towards its elimination. Although strongly identified with Hinduism, the caste system has been carried over to other religions on the Indian subcontinent, including small groups of Muslims, Buddhists, and Christians. The upper castes historically look down upon the lower castes involving them only in base jobs and this divide continues even now. The lower castes have always been under-represented across all sectors, forcing successive governments to take initiatives to bridge the divide in the form of reservations in education and employment to help them overcome their socially perceived backwardness.

The primary objective of the Indian reservation system is to increase the opportunities for enhanced social and educational status of the underprivileged communities, and thus enable them to take their place in the mainstream of Indian society. This has resulted in the categorisation of Scheduled Castes, Scheduled Tribes, and Other Backwards Classes, (ST/ST/OBCs). The central government stipulates a total reservation of 49.5 percent reservations for these communities which, however varies from state to state with some states such as Tamil Nadu having as much as 69 percent reservations.

On a close scrutiny of general statistics of employment in India, one cannot fail to observed that in most instances the higher level positions which contain fewer numbers continue to be held by upper castes; whereas at the lower end of the hierarchy where the numbers are large, it is inevitably filled with members of the lower castes. In central government services, reservations for SCs and STs have been operational for a few decades, and this has resulted in a rise in SC representation in all four categories of central services. However, upper castes continue to disproportionately occupy the more prestigious Class 1 services, while SCs/STs/OBs have been relegated to jobs lower in the hierarchy.

Furthermore, the cumulative percentage of SC/ST employees in central government services continues to be below their percentage in the general population.

In the context of representation in higher education, enrolment from Muslims has not demonstrated a proportionate rise beyond under graduate levels, while they remain 14 percent of the Indian population. As a point of reference, West Bengal which has a sizeable Muslim populace has only 10 out of 1,000 opting for post graduate education in males, and only two out of 1,000 in females. This is in stark contrast to Hindus with 30 in 1,000 males opting for postgraduate studies, whereas it is 32 in 1,000 females.

Women from all communities in urban India have shown remarkable participation in higher education, while those from rural areas still remain at a pitiable distance. Members who hail from physically handicapped sections, the socially destitute, and certain nomadic communities also are poorly represented in higher education in India

As far as the percentage representation of SCs and STs in higher education is concerned, the enrolment of SCs has shown an increase of approximately one percent from 2010-11 to 20011-12. However, the provisional figures for 2012-13 do not show any major increase in the enrolment. The enrolment of STs has remained constant over the span of years considered. The representation of ST and SC in higher educational institutions is four percent and 12 percent respectively, while the earmarked value in reservation of admissions is 7.5 percent and 15 percent respectively. This indicates that there is still scope for an increase in representation of each of them in higher educational institutions.

Again the figures for the GER also represent the same trend. There is a slight increase in the GER of the SCs from 2010-11 to 2012-13, but the GER of the STs remain the same over the span of years taken into consideration. Most importantly, despite the several measures already undertaken for SCs and STs and the weaker sections of the society, the social and the gender gap exists. In case of SCs, the social gap and the gender gap has not fluctuated much, but remained constant over this period of time. However, the STs show a completely different picture. The social gap and gender gap in case of STs has increased marginally over the years.

Due to the presence of these obstacles in the socio-economic growth of the SCs and STs, the Twelfth Five Year Plan came up with a new approach to deal with the issue of inequality of educational opportunities. The main focus of the Twelfth Five Year Plan is to enhance funding for the measures aimed at reducing inequality, and to bring all the equity related schemes in higher education under one umbrella. Various activities in the areas of legislations and resolutions, access, skill development, student support programmes, and equity promotion were undertaken to overcome the mentioned obstacles.

According to the Central Education Institutions (Retention in Admission) Act, 2006, 15 percent and 7.5 percent reservation in admissions is reserved for SCs and STs, which encourage SC and ST students to continue higher education, and make it mandatory on the part of the institutions to enroll a certain percentage of SC and ST students in their intake. Efforts are being made for continued implementation of the Act. The UGC formulated necessary regulations to promote equity in higher education institutions, as well as to address grievances in 2012. The AICTE has also undertaken measures for grievance redressal. These regulations help the organisations to promote equity in higher education and to deal with grievances of non-compliance with the established equity standards for the same. Moreover, these regulations and legislations will play a direct role in improving the rate of enrolment of the weaker sections of the society in higher education.

To improve access to the higher education institutions, centrally funded higher educational institutions have been established in the under-served areas. The Rashtriya Ucchattar Shiksha Abhiyan, and other schemes such as community college, submission on polytechnics, development assistance to universities/colleges by UGC, and opening of IGNOU's study centres in educationally backward districts all are creating an impact on the socio-economic development of the weaker section of the society. A provision to establish approximately 874 new higher educational institutions has been made for improving access.

Apart from these, several other programmes/schemes have also been launched which also equally lay emphasis on educational development of students belonging to SCs/STs and PwDs, which includes various student support initiatives, such as scholarships, remedial coaching classes, opening of equal opportunity cells in the universities, Rajiv Gandhi Fellowships, postgraduate scholarships for professional courses, postdoctoral fellowships, remedial coaching for NET/SLET, preparatory classes for IITs, interest subsidy on education loan, hostel facilities for students especially for girls, etc. The number of beneficiaries for the remedial coaching, including the NET/SET coaching, amount to around 19 lakhs. Also 250 universities and 2252 colleges have now established equal opportunities cell.

Despite already existing student support programmes, several new schemes have also been launched to meet the requirements of these categories, which inter-alia includes UGC's Ishan Uday Scholarship (1000) and Ishan Vikas Scheme, AICTE's SAKSHAM scholarship (1000), etc.

Several schemes for skill development have also been formulated to directly to address the problem of unemployment. The National Skill Qualification Framework was set up to enable easy movement of the students between technical education, vocational courses, and the job field. Other schemes such as National Scheme for Apprenticeship Training, Scheme of Community Colleges, and Scheme for Community Development focus through polytechnics on practical training, and create a synergy between community, colleges, and the job field.

With the urban and the rural divide having significantly narrowed due to the onset of technology, communication, and better infrastructure over the last two decades, there has been an appreciable improvement in the reach of better higher education to several under-represented groups across the country. However, the need of the hour is a provision of high quality education across all sectors to match the requirements of a growing Indian economy. The suffering of the under-represented communities has not been appreciably alleviated as unemployment, inflation, low income, and lack of adequate access to quality education continue to plague them.

Reasons for inadequate access to quality education, especially quality higher education include the following:

- *Poor Infrastructure:* This shortcoming is perhaps the chief of all in delivery of quality education. While focus on the urban segment has been heavy, the same is not replicated in most of the rural areas. Establishment of quality higher education institutions in the rural sector has not been significant, which is a serious deterrent for the rural community in general.
- *Inadequate faculty:* The student teacher ratio on the whole is in a lamentable state. While it is still lower in the urban areas, the rural areas take the brunt of the scene with the ratio being at very high rate.
- *Unqualified or untrained faculty:* Even as the woes of inadequate faculty remain, a major part of the ones who are present to impart higher education are woefully ill-equipped in terms of either qualifications, or experience, or proper training.
- *Inappropriate or overload in curriculum:* The curriculum of most higher education courses is very infrequently updated, even as the world sees a continuously changing scenario in industry manpower requirements. This has caused a huge divide between the industry expectations, and the graduates or postgraduates, who are poorly equipped with the right technical, business, or social skills to be employed.
- *Lack of financial resources:* Most under-represented

communities face a lack of financial strength to pursue any reasonably high quality education. While successive governments have declared financial aid for many economically weaker sections for higher education, many communities are denied the advantage due to complex processes.

- *Ineffective monitoring:* Higher education requires constant monitoring from the regulatory bodies through periodic inspections and performance measurement methodologies. There are no appropriate parameters to measure performance indexes once faculty are employed, and this has given rise to severe inconsistency in the delivery of quality education.
- *Social differences between classes:* This constraint has been historically a damaging element in healthy social relationships. While the upper classes look down upon the lower classes, the lower classes are de-motivated from continuing their higher education. This divide is more rampant in the northern states of India in comparison with the south.
- *Poor government funding:* With government funding in higher education receding over the years, many institutions themselves have suffered, barely managing to survive. In such a scenario employees are more focused on sustaining themselves rather than delivering quality education.

For many years it has been researched and found that one of the key causes of fewer enrolments in higher education is a shortcoming of financial strength across under-represented masses. To overcome this overwhelming challenge, the government has enabled several financial schemes through easy student loans, scholarships, and financial schemes. A few states have embarked on fee reimbursement schemes at certain lower income levels. Over the last decade these schemes have vastly helped in improving enrolments significantly.

The Twelfth Five Year Plan (2012-2017) confronts the challenges facing India's higher education system, and has proposed several initiatives to resolve them. These include increased funding for disadvantaged groups, imbibing cutting-edge technologies, faculty improvement programmes, improved governance, and provision of incentives for advanced research. The government has laid out plans to achieve enrollment of 35.9 million students in higher education institutions, targeting a GER of 25.2 percent through these initiatives towards the end of the Plan period. It also intends to improve the quality of the system significantly, while encouraging the co-existence of multifarious, research-centric, teaching, and vocation-focused institutions.

The overwhelming participation of the private sector in higher education has given a fillip to the under-represented communities who now have better access to education. While the role of the private sector in Indian higher education is undeniable, it is also a painful trend with more and more venturing into the stream with the sole intention of profiteering by disregarding stipulated norms, and severely compromising on quality on several fronts. This has adversely affected the delivery and substance of quality with the end result that most students are no better after their higher education than they were before. While the role of private participation in delivering higher education is quite appreciable, it behooves both the government and the individual players to comprehensively understand the responsibility they carry in shaping the direction of the country.

The Indian government has made ambitious plans to achieve a threefold increase in terms of number of institutions and enrolments by the end of the current Five Year Plan. While this does seem achievable, there are issues which must be retrospectively and holistically measured, and handled diligently, so that the results may fall within the projected framework. In addition, the government must put in place an effective monitoring system to ensure foolproof results in its endeavour to make quality higher education within the reach of all, and more so to the under-represented communities.

The action plan needs to have these elements:

- *Making a realistic financial plan:* This is imperative for the government before setting any unrealistic goals as financial planning becomes the key factor in achievement of all objectives. Any mismatch between budgets and targets will lead to unsuccessful results.
- *Infrastructure development:* While urban infrastructure has definitely seen progress, the rural sector still largely lies in dismal neglect. The government must ensure proper physical access to these communities, and insist on construction of higher education institutions in closer proximately to villages. Further, ample focus must be given to the development of appropriate technology to enable education through information technology.
- *Provision of adequate trained and qualified faculty:* Student-teacher ratio must be brought up to an ideal level, and all faculty must possess adequate qualifications and training before taking up education. Periodic refresher training is an indubitable necessity to ensure adherence to performance standards. While updating curricula, the faculty must be acquainted with the newer

studies and keep abreast of latest technologies to ensure proper delivery.

- *Eliminate ethnic inequalities:* Caste references must be removed from focus and only economic backwardness should be the main criterion for extending government support to any community. Several individuals from the traditionally downtrodden groups, even after having richly benefited from government support, continue to exploit the opportunities provided, preventing the real oppressed groups from any significant benefits.
- *Promote use of internet and communication technology:* Adequate emphasis must be placed on improvement of internet and communication technology, as it enables easier access to information and educational content, and facilitates better education than traditional methods.
- *Enable better funding for institutions:* Government must provide sufficient autonomy and funding for all institutions with an effective monitoring mechanism to ensure appropriate infrastructure, facilities, and aids to impart quality education.
- *Improve financial schemes' reach:* This can be a shot in the arm for the weaker sections as the promise of higher education comes closer to realisation. Traditionally backward sections have shirked away from higher education owing to their inability to bear the costs of higher education. But with genuine and easily available government financial aid, education becomes much more accessible across communities. Though there is ample funding on the government agenda, the complexities involved in obtaining finances makes them inaccessible to most lower groups.
- *Remove overlapping of authority:* Regulatory bodies function across parameters often with overlapping authority, affecting the delivery of quality education. Since education is a subject of both the central and the state governments, there are frequent conflicts in several areas of education. The government must resolve such complexities, and ensure proper delegation of authority for smoother functioning.
- *Make curriculum industry oriented:* The higher education system must provide for updating of curriculum with regularity to help learning match industry requirement. This way employability skills would improve, and so would their prospects.
- *Other measures:* In addition to these, governments must encourage public private partnerships in higher education, and also involve the industry actively through comprehensive

corporate social responsibility (CSR) activities. The role of civil society in widening access to higher education may also be an area of thrust. A comprehensive study on access to under-represented communities may be conducted every alternate year, and progress recorded for comparative references. Exhaustive studies on higher education programmes of developed countries are also required, and their systems replicated with reference to the Indian context.

India has historically been a nation divided on social, ethnic, and economic fronts. Successive governments have attempted to analyze and overcome the divide, but have not made much headway chiefly owing to political compulsions. With the onset of higher technology, easier access to communication and information technology, the divide has shown definite signs of narrowing down, even though only to a marginal extent. The government and the private sector will continue to play a key role in improving the reach of good quality education to all the corners of the country.

Most of the under-represented communities today are able to access better education at elementary and higher levels. However, the ancient system of social divide as a whole remains unshakably strong, and continues to resist change howsoever economy or technology attempts to. Still, it is appreciable that several policy initiatives undertaken by the government are continuing to demonstrate better efficacy and gradual success. The advent of the twenty-first century has brought about a revolution in technology and with it tremendous changes have been made across the educational system of the country. Though the community divide exists still and perhaps will continue to do so, it is shown that equity in higher education and a healthy economy is not at too far a distance.

26
Research

Research refers to the activities related to the acquisition of knowledge or information. It is an activity seeking to gain greater understanding of a phenomenon and is directed towards the solution or elucidation of a problem. Research in the field of higher education is the demand of the day because it is directly linked with social and economic development, skills, and knowledge generation of various subjects. It has been felt that without proper research, it will be difficult for any country to become self-reliant and be competitive in the arena of globalization and internationalisation. Changes in every aspect of human life have posed serious questions on the relevance of research in higher education, and its ability to cater to the multifaceted needs of the society. Problems and difficulties in the field of higher education necessitate purposeful and sustained research efforts. Reforms, progress, and excellence in research require competent and dedicated team of researchers. In addition to that, proper and systematic planning, actions according to the plan, review and feedback time to time for minimising the errors are some of the important aspects to ensure quality research in the field of higher education.

Council of Scientific and Industrial Research

Council of Scientific and Industrial Research (CSIR), established in 1942, is an autonomous body and India's largest research and development (R&D) organisation, with 37 laboratories and 39 field stations or extension centres spread across the nation, with a collective staff of over 17,000 people. Although CSIR is mainly funded by the Ministry of Science and Technology, it operates as an autonomous body registered under the Registration of Societies Act of 1860.

The research and development activities of CSIR include various fields such as aerospace engineering, structural engineering, ocean sciences, life sciences, metallurgy, chemicals, mining, food, petroleum, leather, and environment.

CSIR Achievements

- Developed first Indian tractor Swaraj in 1967 completely based on indigenous know-how.
- Achieved the first breakthrough of flowering of bamboo within weeks as against 20 years in nature.
- First to analyze genetic diversity of the indigenous Andamanese tribes, and to establish their origin out of Africa 60,000 years ago.
- Developed the first transgenic Drosophila model for drug screening for cancer in humans.
- First to introduce DNA fingerprinting in India.
- Helped India to be the pioneer investor under the United Nations Convention on the Law of the Sea.
- Invented once a week non-steroidal family planning pill Saheli, and non-steroidal herbal pill for asthma called Asmon.
- Designed India's first ever parallel processing computer Flosolver
- Partnered more than 50,000 companies with turnover ranging from Rs. 5 lakhs to Rs. 500,000 crore.
- Rejuvenated India's 100-year old refinery at Digboi using the most modern molecular distillation technology.
- Provided the critical technology for the NMP Lube Extraction Plant of capacity of 2,50,000 tonnes per year.
- With TCS, developed versatile portable PC-based software 'Bio-Suite' for bioinformatics.
- Designed 14-seater plane 'SARAS.'
- Established the traditional knowledge digital library—the first of its kind in the world—accessible in five international languages, English, German, French, Japanese, and Spanish.
- Remained in top three in the list of PCT patent applications amongst all developing countries.
- Topped list of holders of U.S. patents.
- Successfully challenged the grant of patent in the USA for use of haldi (turmeric) for wound healing, and neem as insecticide.
- In 2009, completed the sequencing of the Human Genome.
- In 2011, successfully tested India's First indigenous civilian aircraft, NAL NM5 made in association with National Aerospace Laboratories and Mahindra Aerospace.

Shanti Swarup Bhatnagar Prize for Science and Technology

The Shanti Swarup Bhatnagar (SSB) Prizes are awarded annually by the Council of Scientific and Industrial Research (CSIR) for notable and outstanding research, applied or fundamental, in biological, chemical, earth, atmosphere, ocean and planetary, engineering, mathematical, medical, and physical sciences. The prize comprises a citation, a plaque, and a cash award of Rs. 500,000. In addition, recipients also get Rs. 15,000 per month up to the age of 65 years.

Research Funding Agencies in India

India has various funding agencies that strive to promote research in emerging areas like humanities, social sciences, languages, literature, pure sciences, engineering and technology, pharmacy, medical, agricultural sciences, and defence studies etc. They fall under the different ministries of the government. Some of the funding agencies at the national level include the University Grants Commission (UGC), Indian Council of Social Science Research (ICSSR), National Council for Educational Research and Training (NCERT), All India Council for Technical Education (AICTE), Department of Science and Technology (DST), Department of Biotechnology (DBT), Council of Scientific and Industrial Research (CSIR), Defence Research and Development Organisation (DRDO), Aeronautics Research and Development Board, Department of Atomic Energy (DAE), Department of Biotechnology (DBT), Department of Coal (DOC), Department of Ocean Development (DOD), Department of Science and Technology (DST), Department of Scientific and Industrial Research (DSIR), Indian Council of Medical Research (ICMR), India Meteorological Department (IMD), Indian Space Research Organisation (ISRO)—Department of Space, Ministry of Communications and Information Technology (MOCIT), Ministry of Environment and Forests (MOEF), Ministry of Food Processing Industries (MFPI), Ministry of Non-Conventional Energy Sources (MNES), Ministry of Water Resources (MOWR), Ministry of Power, Central Power Research Institute (CPRI), Indian National Science Academy (INSA), Science and Technology for Weaker Sections (STAWS), Science and Technology Application for Rural Development (STARD).

Indian Council of Social Science Research

The Indian Council of Social Science Research (ICSSR) was established in 1969 by the Government of India to promote research in social sciences in the country. It supports a network of 27 ICSSR research institutions.

The Council is meant to:

- Review the progress of social science research and give advice to its users;
- Sponsor social science research programmes and projects, and

administer grants to institutions and individuals for research in social sciences;
- Institute and administer scholarships and fellowships for research in social sciences;
- Indicate areas in which social science research is to be promoted, and adopt special measures for development of research in neglected or new areas;
- Give financial support to institutions, associations, and journals engaged in social science research;
- Arrange technical training in research methodology and provide guidance for research;
- Coordinate research activities and encourage programmes for interdisciplinary research;
- Develop and support centres for documentation service and supply of data;
- Organise, sponsor, and finance seminars, workshops, and study groups;
- Undertake publication, and assist publication of journals and books in social sciences;
- Advise the Government of India on all matters pertaining to social science research as may be referred to it from time to time; and take such measures generally as may be necessary from time to time to promote social science research and its utilisation.

National Social Science Documentation Centre (NASSDOC)

India's National Social Science Documentation Centre (NASSDOC) was established in 1969 as a Division of the ICSSR with the objective to provide library and information support services to researchers in social sciences, those working in academic institutions, autonomous research organisations, policy making, planning and research units of government departments, business, and industry etc. NASSDOC also provides guidance to libraries of ICSSR Regional Centres and ICSSR supported research institutions.

Facilities Available at NASSDOC

1. Documentation, library, and reference services;
2. Collection of unpublished doctoral dissertations, research project reports, current and old volumes of social science journals of Indian and foreign origin;
3. Literature search service from printed and digital databases, i.e. CD-ROMS, floppies, online database etc.;

4. Compilation of short bibliographies on request;
5. Study grant to doctoral students for collection of research material from various libraries located in different parts of India;
6. Financial assistance is provided for taking up bibliographical and documentation projects;
7. Document delivery service is provided by procuring books and journals through inter-library loans, or by photocopying the documents;
8. Short-term training courses are organised for research scholars, social scientists, librarians, and IT professionals to acquaint them with the latest information and communication technology; and
9. Cyber café to facilitate access to internet resources on social sciences.

Do's and Don'ts of Social Research

There has been a continuous debate over social research, its results, its objectivity, validity, and human interference, which still prevails among scholars. Why do people have problems with conducting social research?

In a broader sense, social researchers claim that they study social realities. Their units of study are people, their interests, protests, notions, opinions, and subjective experiences. There is great need of such researches because of rampant inequalities and discriminations within and between social groups, based on a wider range of purposes.

But some unresolved questions remain like, what is reality? How can it be checked? How is it to be measured? Reality is not static; it's dynamic and changing in nature. Then, how does a social researcher study a unit of society which is continuously changing? The real problem people have in social research is with operational definition of variables, and measuring such variables. Social researchers are trying and struggling to do it. On many occasions they have succeeded by creating matrixes, indices, scales, and established indicators etc. We must appreciate that.

Doctoral Research Programme

Some observations on doctoral research programmes.

- Research is not the prime focus in majority of the institutions of higher education till date. Orientation and creation of awareness towards research in these institutions is very rare. Rather they are busy in generating educated young unemployed workers who run after governmental jobs, and the public services like postal, railway, land surveys, etc.
- Though research has been a part of mandate of any university, a

critical look reveals that most of the Indian universities are not paying adequate attention to it.

- Very few students engage themselves in the pursuit of quality research, where as many of them are trying to get a degree.
- Not only the researchers, but also very few research supervisors pay adequate attention, or give sufficient time to their research scholars.
- Lack of research minded students in the campus undermines the quality of research as it is a collaborative, cooperative activity which requires rigorous discussion, interactions, etc.
- The traditional mindset of senior faculty members seldom allow a student to seek inter-faculty interaction, or undertake inter-disciplinary research.
- Misconceptions about information and communication technology and its utility undermine its usage in research.
- Lack of autonomy, and accountability are primarily responsible for poor research.
- Time and freedom to the researcher is another important factor.

It is a common observation that the demand and production for Ph.D. degree has exponentially increased over the last few decades, because Ph.D. degree is now linked with appointment and promotion (CAS) in the institutions of higher education. In response to the general demand, many universities increased their Ph.D. production without being sufficiently ambitious about the quality benchmarks. There was a time when rarest of the rare used to pursue a Ph.D. Degree even if the procedure for getting admissions was not as complicated as it is now. In the meantime, UGC regulation made either NET/SLET/SET or Ph.D. as the minimum eligibility condition for appointment as teachers/lecturers, especially in the colleges and universities. Again, a new resolution was passed by UGC in 2009 wherein those who pursue Ph.D. as per UGC Ph.D. regulation-2009 are exempt from the said examination.

Kakodkar Committee Fixed a Target of 10,000 Ph.D. Scholars a Year

The Kakodkar Committee, set up by the MHRD to suggest ways of enhancing the contribution of the IITs to the nation, recommended that the number of engineering Ph.D. scholars being produced per year should be increased to 10,000 over the course of the next decade.

The IITs are presently producing around 1,000 Ph.D. scholars per year in engineering and technology. "This figure is not adequate for a country of our size. The USA and China are producing around 8,000 to 9,000 Ph.D. scholars each in engineering and technology, each year.

Without sufficient numbers of persons trained in research, we will not have a firm foothold in the higher technologies that are key to our future development," observed Union Minister for HRD.

The Committee observed that as Ph.D. scholars would have first completed a master's degree, it is imperative that the intake in the M. Tech., M.Sc., and M. Phil. programmes in the IITs also be increased proportionally.

The Committee suggested that over the next decade, India should add another five IITs. India should also scale the IIT system to 16,000 faculty members, and 1,60,000 total student strength, with 40,000 at the Ph.D. level, 40,000 at the Masters level and 80,000 UG students.

The steps needed to make this a reality are given below.

1. Rejuvenate doctoral programmes across disciplines: While the above recommendations are aimed at attracting potential doctoral students and enabling a research environment, it is vital that prospective doctoral students are chosen with sufficient care. The following measures are proposed with this objective in mind:

- A review of the whole selection procedure and monitoring process for graduate students.
- Multiple pathways for entry to a Ph.D. programme, while maintaining entry standards.
- Support for quality research in arts, humanities, and other areas.
- Support and promotion of cross-disciplinary teaching and research programmes.
- Greater exposure of undergraduate and postgraduate students to cutting edge research.

2. Ensure quality of doctoral work and academic research in institutions: At the same time while striving for greater influx of people to a research career, institutions must ensure that the research undertaken matches global quality in the relevant field. In addition, the graduate programmes should be continually reviewed so as to make them vibrant, challenging, and internationally relevant. Here are some steps to be taken in this regard:

- A preliminary vetting of the synopses of the thesis followed by rigorous external examination of doctoral thesis.
- Broad funding for the organisation of and participation in workshops, seminars, and symposia in India and overseas.
- Encouraging doctoral students to teach, with remuneration provided via teaching assistantships.

- Wider dissemination of research work, especially through current digital media in universities and research institutions.

3. Enable vigorous industry-academic interaction: In the modern context, there is a crying need for a healthy and enlightened cooperation between private industry and academia, which replaces the existing feeling of doubt and mistrust. While industry should recognise that support for education is beneficial; universities should take cognizance of the changing needs of private enterprise in planning new courses. This could be achieved by taking the following measures:

- A policy framework for meaningful public private partnership in universities, and concerted efforts to nurture industry-academic interaction.
- Encouraging private investment in education, research, and innovation, backed by appropriate taxation measures.
- Promoting collaboration between research and development units within industry and universities.

4. Foster global outlook in research: Research is increasingly becoming a collective global endeavour. It is thus necessary to harness global talent and expertise to develop capacity within the country. This is also essential if the nation is to remain a participant in global cutting edge research. With this in view, the NKC recommended the following:

- Encouraging NR/PIO scientists to establish meaningful links with Indian institutions, and participate in the academic development of the nation.
- Creating joint Ph.D. programmes between universities, both within and outside the country.
- Financial and administrative support for international research collaboration.
- Identifying important areas of research where national expertise needs to be developed, and initiating steps for funding and capacity building by way of collaborations, guest faculty, pro-active hiring, etc.

In conclusion, it must be recognised that investment in education and research produces a broad range of dividends, both tangible and intangible. Our existing base in research needs to be urgently strengthened to arrest any further erosion. While the NKC welcomed the augmented allocation for education in the Eleventh Five Year Plan, it is important that these funds are effectively utilised to make a visible difference to our academic landscape. As a first step, we urge the government to set itself a target of tripling the existing research base within the next dozen years, and meaningfully work towards it. We strongly feel that a mission oriented approach is necessary for creating the required research ecosystem in the country.

Theses in Social Sciences

Sl.No	Year	No. of Theses in Social Sciences
1.	2000	926
2.	2001	793
3.	2002	1267
4.	2003	1519
5.	2004	1269
6.	2005	1239
7.	2006	1632
8.	2007	1501
9.	2008	1922
10.	2009	1319
11.	2010	1639
12.	2011	1349
13.	2012	1428
14.	2013	827
15.	2014	938
16.	2015	703
	Total	**20271**

Faculty-wise Number of Doctorate Degrees (Ph.D.) Awarded during 2007-2011

Sl. No.	Faculty	2007-08	2008-09	2009-10	2010-2011
1.	Arts	4405	3496	4862	5037
2.	Science	4514	3603	4619	5232
3.	Commerce/Management	873	724	980	1259
4.	Education	425	403	588	645
5.	Engineering/Technology	1427	1141	1449	1682
6.	Medicine	277	298	386	601
7.	Agriculture	664	427	652	586
8.	Veterinary/Science	123	93	162	165
9.	Law	127	152	146	220
10.	Others	402	444	633	666
	Total	**13237**	**10781**	**14477**	**16093**

Improving Quality of Research

In order to improve the quality of research, the following points need to be considered.

- Higher education institutions should generate adequate infrastructure which can meet the needs of researchers in emerging disciplines.
- Higher education institutions should create Information Resource Centre (IRC), which facilitates the researchers to give various information regarding ongoing researches.
- Higher education institutions should have a central instrumentation centre, as a result of which researchers of various departments can avail the opportunities to carry out their researches.
- Individual computers with high speed internet facilities should be provided to each researcher.
- Research scholars should be encouraged for carrying out independent, collaborative and inter disciplinary researches.
- There should be a research committee and concrete research policy for guiding the research scholars of various disciplines.
- Seminars/training programmes/workshops on research methodology in general, and concerned areas in particular, should be organised in order motivate and enhance the knowledge of researchers.
- Extension lectures should be organised at regular intervals.
- There should be proper budget allocation to carry out/promote the research.
- Incentives, and rewards/awards should be given for quality research papers.
- Higher education institutions should publish high quality research papers in appropriate journals.
- Each institution should publish a research bulletin mentioning the research work being carried out in various fields, the number of research papers published in online and offline journals etc., as well as research awards received by the research scholars.
- Library should be digitalized, and ongoing research work should be uploaded for dissemination of knowledge in the specific field.
- Higher education institutions should promote the participation of research scholars in research and extension activities.
- Higher education institutions should move ahead to strengthen the research culture by signing MOUs with national/international institutions of higher learning, and generating institution-industry linkages.
- More focus should be given to research aptitude tests at the time of selection of research scholars.
- Transparency should be maintained in research by disseminating of information on a regular basis.

27
Rashtriya Uchchatar Shiksha Abhiyan (RUSA)

Keeping in view the recommendations of the Planning Commission, the need for reforms in the state higher education sector, using central funds in a strategic manner to ensure holistic planning at the state level, and enhancement of allocations for the state institutions, a new centrally sponsored scheme is proposed. The scheme would be spread over two plan periods (12 and 13), and would be an overarching scheme for funding state universities and colleges in order to achieve equity, access, and excellence. This scheme is called the Rashtriya Uchchatar Shiksha Abhiyan (RUSA). The scheme has the following salient features:

- It is an umbrella mission project scheme that would subsume other existing schemes in the sector.
- The central funding would flow from MHRD to institutions, through the State Councils of Higher Education.
- The funding to states would be made on the basis of critical appraisal of state plans for higher education.
- The plans would describe each state's strategy to address issue of equity, access, and excellence in higher education.
- All funding under the RUSA would be norm-based, and future grants would be outcome dependent. Certain academic, administrative, and governance reforms will be a pre-condition for receiving funding under RUSA.

Centre-state funding for the scheme will be in the ratio of 90:10 for north-eastern states, Sikkim, and J&K, 75:25 for other Special Category States (Himachal Pradesh and Uttarakhand) and 65:35 for other states and UTs. Funding will be available to even private-aided institutions, subject to their duration of existence, for permitted activities (not all) based on certain norms and parameters, in a ratio of 50:50.

The objectives of RUSA would be to achieve the target of GER of 30 percent by the year 2020, which the central government has set for itself. Government of India aims to improve the quality of state universities and colleges by enhancing their existing capacities, so that they become dynamic, demand-driven, quality conscious, efficient, forward looking, and responsive to rapid economic and technological developments occurring at the local, state, national, and international levels. The salient objectives of the scheme can be enumerated as follows:

- Improve the overall quality of existing state institutions by ensuring that all institutions conform to prescribed norms and standards, and adopt accreditation as a mandatory quality assurance framework.
- Usher transformative reforms in the state higher education system by creating a facilitating institutional structure for planning and monitoring at the state level, promoting autonomy in state universities, and improving governance in institutions.
- Ensure academic and examination reforms in the higher educational institutions.
- Enable conversion of some of the universities into research universities at par with the best in the world.
- Create opportunities for states to undertake reforms in the affiliation system in order to ensure that the reforms and resource requirements of affiliated colleges are adequately met.
- Ensure adequate availability of quality faculty in the educational institutions, and ensure capacity building at all levels of employment.
- Create an enabling atmosphere in the educational institutions to devote themselves to research and innovation.
- Expand the institutional base by creating additional capacity in existing institutions, and establishing new institutions in order to achieve enrolment targets.
- Correct regional imbalance in access to education by facilitating access to high quality institutions in urban and semi-urban areas, create opportunities for students from rural areas to get access to better quality institutions, and set up institutions in unserved and underserved areas.
- Improve equity in education by providing adequate opportunities of education to SC/STs, socially, and educationally backward classes; promote inclusion of women, minorities, and differently abled persons.

Scope

All state universities and colleges (both 12B and 2f compliant, and non-12B and non-2f) from all states and Union Territories (UTs) across the country would be eligible for coverage under RUSA. Subject to eligibility, an estimated 286 state universities and 8500 colleges will be covered under this initiative to improve the learning outcomes and employability of graduates, and to scale-up research, development, and innovations. The project will also support these institutions to improve their policy, academic, and management practices. While public funded colleges and universities would be eligible for all the components; the private/aided colleges would be entitled to some components (including infrastructure support) but the funding ratio would be 50:50. Funding to such colleges would be decided based on their antiquity and relevance. Funds would be provided both for infrastructure and quality improvement. Each institution will have to prepare a perspective plan for all the components, which will be then aggregated at the state level, after imposing a super layer of state relevant components.

The project would also enable and empower the states to develop sufficient capabilities to plan, implement, and monitor initiatives for the education sector. Each state must undertake a baseline survey (as illustrated in the institutional and state higher education plan templates) followed by the preparation of state higher education plans, which would be further broken down into annual plans. These annual plans will constitute the basis for determining the funding to states. The plans would have mainly two components, state component and institutional plans aggregated. RUSA will support the states to create new systems and processes.

Approach

RUSA will fund the institutions under a few key components. The yardstick for deciding the quantum of funds for the states and institution will be the norms that will reflect the key result areas—access, equity and excellence. The state higher education plans will capture the current position of the states and institutions on the basis of these norms as well as the targets that need to be achieved. The state Higher Education Council (discussed in following sections) will undertake this process of planning and evaluation, in addition to other monitoring and capacity building functions. The state Higher Education Councils will be the key institutions at the state level to channelize resources to the institutions.

In order to realise the intended outcomes, certain prior commitments towards reform process have to be made by the states. Some of these conditions will be in the nature of apriori and non-negotiable prerequisites, i.e., commitments made by the states as well as institutions for them to become eligible for funding under RUSA. These prerequisites include academic, sectoral and institutional governance reforms, creation of state Higher Education Council, funding commitments by states, filling faculty position (or a commitment to do so within a fixed time frame), etc. Under the scheme an initial, preparatory amount can also be provided to the state government to prepare them for complying with the apriori requirements. Once eligible for funding under RUSA after fulfilling the prerequisite apriori commitments, the states will receive funds on the basis of their achievements vis-a-vis the targets. Future funds' flow would be determined based on outcomes, and achievements against the targets. The emphasis would be not only on physical output, but also on the intended outcomes.

Strategic Focus of RUSA

Strategic funding of state institutions must ensure that the issues of quality and access are addressed in an equitable manner. This would entail encouraging the states to prepare a state higher education plan duly keeping in mind the following aspects:

- Spatial and regional planning after due mapping;
- Programme and discipline planning;
- Mandatory accreditation and quality improvement;
- Reforms—governance and academic;
- Infrastructure saturation;
- Review of the affiliation system;
- Transparent and norm-based funding;
- Outcome-based reimbursements;
- Faculty planning;
- Equity interventions;
- Focus on research and innovations.

Strategy

The projects will be implemented through the Ministry of Human Resource Development (MHRD) of the Government of India as a "Centrally Sponsored Scheme" with matching contribution from the state governments and Union Territories (UTs). Since a five-year time frame may not be adequate for such an ambitious project, the project will be spread over two plan periods of Twelfth and Thirteenth Plans. MHRD and the states will share the project cost.

A set of eligibility criteria for states will be enforced to achieve a high and sustained impact of the project. The criteria will seek to give the states and project institutions adequate decision making powers that will enable and encourage them to deliver quality education, and undertake research and innovation in an efficient manner. The primary endeavour would be to transform the government traditional role of input control into a role of focusing on outcomes, and incentivising improvements in higher education.

The project will require the project institutions to implement academic and non-academic reforms for their self-conceived development programmes that focus on quality and relevance, excellence, resource mobilization, greater institutional autonomy with accountability, research, and equity.

Components of RUSA

RUSA is envisaged as a prime vehicle for strategic funding of state institutions so as to ensure that issues of access, equity, and quality are addressed in an equitable manner with the state as a composite unit of planning. The following are the primary components of RUSA that capture the key action and funding areas that must be pursued for the fulfillment of the targets:

- New universities
- Upgradation of existing autonomous colleges to universities
- Conversion of colleges to cluster universities
- Infrastructure grants to universities
- New model colleges for general streams
- Upgradation of exiting degree colleges to model colleges
- New professional colleges
- Infrastructure grants to colleges
- Research, innovation, and quality improvement
- Equity initiatives
- Faculty recruitment support
- Faculty improvements
- Polytechnic colleges
- Research universities
- Vocationalisation of higher education
- Leadership development of educational administrators
- Medical college upgradation
- Institutional restructuring and reforms
- Capacity building, preparation, data collection, and planning
- Conduct an all India survey of higher education
- Capacity building of central institutions/agencies

The objectives of RUSA would be achieved through need based and customised equity interventions; quality improvement programmes, and obtaining mandatory accreditation. Faculty issues would have to be addressed through creation of new posts, filling existing posts with full time faculty, and faculty improvement programmes.

Equity interventions are being built into the scheme rather than as standalone, low impact interventions. The following components would address the equity issues in a more holistic and integrated manner, thereby making a significant impact on the enrolment of deprived and marginalized sections:

- Building girls' hostels and girls' toilets
- New hostels wherein 50 percent of capacity would be used for SC/ST and socially and educationally backward classes
- Converting existing building into fully disabled friendly environment (e.g. providing ramps, tactile pathways)
- Special facilities/equipments for the disabled (e.g. computers, lab equipments)
- Establishing model colleges in each district
- Special innovative programmes for focus groups and ODL strategies

Guiding Principles of RUSA

RUSA is structured on certain inviolable guiding principles. These tenets constitute the foundational premise and all the decisions taken under the scheme must be guided by them. It is necessary to list these principles clearly at the outset so as to ensure that this scheme does not degenerate into some kind of infrastructure support scheme. The states are expected to keep these principles as guiding posts while formulating their state higher education plans and planning their strategies.

- Performance based outlays, and outcome based reimbursements
- Incentivising and disincentivising
- Apolitical decision-making
- Disclosure based governance
- Streamlining the recruitment process
- Membership of governing bodies
- Institutional leadership
- Changing role perceptions of public representatives and civil servants
- Mandatory accreditation
- Affiliation reforms

Ways to Reform Affiliation System

Under RUSA, the state government's commitment to undertake reforms in the affiliation system is an apriori condition for receiving funds. Following are some suggestions to reform the affiliation system:

- Limit the number of colleges to be affiliated to any university to 100. However, this would mean establishing more affiliating universities than the present numbers.
- Establish campuses of existing universities to better serve colleges in their physical proximity. In this case, all academic and administrative responsibilities and activities regarding colleges will lie with the offices of the various campuses.
- Large autonomous colleges can be encouraged to develop into universities.
- Create college cluster universities by clustering a minimum of 3-5 colleges in the area surrounding a city or in a district, giving the university its own independent establishment, degree granting powers, and governance.
- A number of colleges could be encouraged to merge, to create a larger institution. It is likely that this larger institution would have the capacity to become autonomous. This would also ensure inter-disciplinary and cross-disciplinary learning.
- Establish new constituent colleges where there is a large youth population. A number of constituent colleges can be under a university like the case of Jawaharlal Nehru Technological University in Hyderabad. Unlike the affiliated colleges, which are managed by college management committees, the constituent colleges will be under the administrative control of the university. Recently, Punjab University has followed this model in setting up four constituent colleges in collaboration with the state government.
- Tight regulation and control on establishment of new colleges in the private sector. Prohibiting an already saturated university from further affiliating private colleges may have to be resorted to in extreme cases.
- Every state should be mandated to prepare a road map on higher education which could contribute to the formulation of a scientific policy on affiliation. An effective, and not routine or mechanical, monitoring of the colleges by the affiliating university is urgently required. Conditions are usually laid down while granting affiliation, but the universities are normally not able to monitor the fulfillment of such conditions. This practice needs to be changed. A college not fulfilling the required standards in teaching-learning process and governance should be disaffiliated after giving prior warnings. Of course, in such eventualities, the interest of the students, teachers, and staff have to be protected.

- The acts and statutes of the state universities may be amended suitably to accommodate the vision for a higher enrolment, ensuring social equity as well as quality of education. The existing acts and statutes may have to be fine-tuned to address the educational issues of the present century. The Union Government or the UGC may constitute a committee to frame a model University Act and statutes, on the basis of those existing in the central universities, and institutions of national importance for consideration for adoption by the state universities. A grace period of two to three years can be given to the states within which the amended act and statutes can be brought into force. The UGC can link the eligibility for grants to this provision.
- It is important to ensure that accreditation is not limited to universities and colleges, but is also made mandatory for individual departments and programmes of the university. Funding should be contingent on accreditation. This should lead to more or less uniform quality assurance.
- The Twelfth FYP document of the UGC envisages large scale direct funding for the state universities. Performance-based accreditation should be made mandatory for such funding. A one-time grant amounting to Rs. 100 crore may be made available to the state universities for augmenting academic and infrastructural facilities. The total amount required will be about 15 percent of the total outlay envisaged for Twelfth Plan period by the UGC.
- The states may not be permitted to constitute unidisciplinary universities. Multi-disciplinary synergy is an inalienable element for any university to be worth the name. The UGC and the centre should view this trend of setting up single discipline universities as a matter of concern.
- Colleges in the government and aided sector, having more than 25 years' standing and awarded the National Assessment and Accreditation Council (NAAC) Grade A, may be considered for being given autonomous status. Those with more than 50 years' standing and NAAC Grade A, may be accorded degree-granting status.
- On an average, an Indian university enrolls 3,400 students and a college enrolls 400 students. Hence capacity building in universities and colleges may be encouraged, so that GER may be doubled from the current level. This is a better option than starting new universities since it avoids additional expenses, lapse of time, land acquisition problems, etc.

- Since only self-financing colleges and self-financing programmes of aided colleges have job-oriented inter-disciplinary courses, the students who are economically weaker and enrolled in the state colleges are not getting the opportunity to benefit from such courses. Hence, state colleges and aided colleges must be supported by the state government to introduce job-oriented inter-disciplinary courses.
- The affiliated colleges located in rural areas are unable to attract qualified faculty to serve in them. To overcome this drawback, the faculty should be given incentives by the government to motivate them to serve in the rural areas.
- More than 70 percent of the universities in India have a large number of self-financing colleges. In the absence of any regulatory mechanism, these colleges do not follow the government-laid down reservation policy both in the student admission process and in the faculty selection process. An effective regulatory mechanism must be created for all such institutions to follow.

Critical Reflections

Now the issue of contemplation is whether the RUSA scheme fulfills the higher aspirations of India. The scheme is quite promising, and seems to address the most pertinent questions of Indian higher education. It envisions higher development through an effective system. Let us analyze the pros and cons of the scheme:

- The most important strategic change under the scheme is that it not only covers higher education institution coming under 12B and 2F, but also those institutions not covered by either. This will make hitherto ineligible higher education institutions eligible to reap the benefits of the scheme. Its umbrella structure provides coverage for existing and future demands.
- RUSA scheme ensures funding to higher education on the basis of well-developed norms and criteria. The higher education institutions will have to fulfill mandatory prerequisites to participate in the scheme. This ensures a common minimum level.
- Decentralisation of governance is another feature worth mentioning. The implementation of the scheme will take place at three levels—institutional, state, and central levels. Delegation of powers and decision making will reduce control and provide autonomy.

- Under RUSA the funding responsibility will be shared by centre and state. The project cost will be shared between central government and state government in a defined ratio. This will ensure more resource allocation to higher education sector.
- The state government is free to raise funds with the help of private partners. They can raise funds up to 50 percent in this way, which means greater availability of funds and more public-private participation. This provision is a relief for state governments, and transfers equal responsibility of higher education to social and private organisations and groups.
- RUSA scheme covers sufficiently long period for its functioning. It will ensure that its effect is felt on Indian higher education sector.
- Another important aspect worth mentioning is that the continuity of funds to higher education institutions is based on evolution of work and utilisation of funds already provided. Thus wastage of funds will be reduced to a minimum. There will be proper utilisation of funds and further availability of funds will be conditional.
- Quality issue is dealt with care under RUSA scheme. There are certain prerequisites for the institutions and states to participate in the scheme. Mandatory accreditation and quality parameters are essential steps for institutions to be able to participate. State have to ensure that vacant faculty posts are filled. Apart from this, the scheme provides for many quality improving strategies.
- Preparation of comprehensive state plan and institutional development plan is a unique feature of RUSA. The state plan template is provided in quite a number of details. The institutional development plan outline is also prepared keeping in view the diverse needs of different types of institutions.
- RUSA also provides for evaluation criterion for state plan and institutional development plans. It lays down equalization formula for higher education. The three parameters identified are the population in the 18-23 age group, per capita income, and gross enrollment ratio.
- There is no obvious loophole or limitations in the scheme worth mentioning. It has been worked in minute details by the experts. With these entire distinctive features RUSA scheme looks promising in the draft form. But its effectiveness will depend equally on its successful implementation.

Commissions and Committees

28
Some Important Commissions and Committees

SUMMARY OF RECOMMENDATIONS ON SOME CRITICAL ISSUES OF HIGHER EDUCATION

1. Expansion and Research; Reform and Improvement in Higher Education

University Education Commission, 1949

- To avoid overcrowding, limit enrolment to 3000 in teaching universities, and 1500 in affiliated colleges.
- Mass lecture is the most common form of instruction, and, therefore, should be supplemented by library work, tutorials, and written exercises, ensuring that tutorials do not become "coaching for exams."
- Standards of M.A. and M.Sc. degrees should be raised by regulating admissions as per facilities and faculty.
- Introduce at the earliest, reliable, objective examinations in universities.
- Given the critical role of teacher in transmission of knowledge, replace their differential scales of pay across different disciplines and institutions with uniform scales of pay comparable to provincial services to retain talent, extend PF benefits, retirement age should be 60, and extension till 64 years.

Education Commission, 1964-66

- Plan HE expansion as per manpower needs of next 20 years and enrolment in UG level to double from 1.5 lakhs to 3.5 lakhs and at PG and research level, from 45,000 to 7.5 lakhs.
- Give up open-door policy and adopt selective approach in admissions in Arts and Science courses.
- Establish a second university in a state in case of university with unmanageable under-graduate population in affiliated colleges.
- Specialisation immediately after school at UG level is undesirable and should allow flexibility in choice of courses, like combining physics, chemistry with biology.
- Same should be the approach at PG level.
- Social sciences should be given a significant place in subjects

of study in Indian universities, with adequate provision of scholarships, flexibility in choice of subjects, and higher allocation of funds.

- Develop and promote area studies of different regions like America, China, Asia-West, East, South, South-East, Latin America, etc.
- External examinations will continue for a long time. Introduce more frequent periodic assessment to reduce undue emphasis on external examinations.
- Each department should have a personal advisory committee to search outstanding young persons across India for teaching and research. Teachers must be provided with attractive salaries and research opportunities.
- UGC should sponsor fellowships at Lecturer, Reader, and Professor levels to attract outstanding persons to the teaching profession.

National Commission on Teachers in Higher Education, 1985

- Rigorous merit-based selection crucial for teaching profession and education system should not be fragmented on basis of language, region, caste, and religion.
- Give teachers a place of honour, good salary, prospects of good career development, but also insist on work and accountability from teachers and HE managements.

National Policy on Education, 1986 and POA, 1992

- HE expansion uneven, not conforming to UGC norms, with many universities and colleges without minimum infrastructure. Hence, only consolidation and improvement of facilities rather than quantitative expansion in the previous years.
- Reorganise UG programme on modular pattern with option to combine courses to meet growing demands of specialisation, and facilitate mobility among courses.
- Reorganise boards of studies in universities to facilitate course redesign, and promote inter-disciplinary programmes.
- Recast examination system with continuous comprehensive internal evaluation, introduce semester system, and use of grades in place of marks.
- Specially designed orientation programmes will be organised for professional and career development of teachers.

National Knowledge Commission, 2006 (NKC)

- Open 1,500 universities to boost GER to 15 percent by 2015.
- Reform universities through revision of curricula every three years, supplement annual examination with internal assessment, transit to a course credit system, attract talented faculty by improving working conditions and incentives.

- Through central legislation, form Independent Regulatory Authority for Higher Education (IRAHE) independent of all stakeholders, subsuming regulatory functions of UGC, AICTE, MCI, BCI, etc. such as entry, license, arbitration of disputes, etc. and avoid policy inconsistencies.
- UGC and other regulatory bodies would disburse grants, and maintain public HEIs.
- Enhance quality of education by stringent information disclosure norms, evaluation of courses by teachers and students, retain talented facility by differential salary packages across universities, formulate policies for entry of foreign institutions in India, and promote Indian institutions abroad.
- Syllabi of courses in universities remains unchanged for decades. But they need to be upgraded constantly, and revised frequently, with more autonomy for teachers, through decentralisation to departments.
- Start internal assessment with at least 25 percent weightage, and raise it to 50 percent over time.
- Conscious effort should be made to attract and retain talented students—the potential faculty—and provide them with office and research opportunities along with rewards for performance for individuals and institutions.

Committee on Renovation and Rejuvenation of Higher Education (Yash Pal Committee), 2009

- Form National Commission for Higher Education and Research (NCHER) to subsume academic functions of UGC, AICTE, MCI, BCI, etc. These bodies should conduct regular qualifying examinations.
- Establish a National Education Tribunal to adjudicate on disputes within and between institutions, and reduce litigation in courts.
- NCHER's top priority should be curricular reform, with mobility within a full range of curricular areas.
- Bring vocational education within universities' purview.
- NCHER to create National Research Foundation to promote research in universities.
- Pending NCHER's clear policy stand, stop recognising new deemed universities.
- NCHER to identify 1500 best colleges to upgrade as universities.
- Set up a National Testing Scheme, open to all aspirants of university education, to be held more than once a year.
- Enhance quantum of central financial support to state-funded universities.

Committee on Corporate Participation in Higher Education (N.R. Narayana Murthy Committee), 2012

- India's GER in HE must increase 20 percent by next decade and HE needs additional capacity of 26 million seats.
- For this, remove all barriers to corporate participation.

2. Governance and Reorganisation of Higher Education

Education Commission (1964-66)

- Teaching, research, and service to community, any university's core functions need autonomy from regimentation of ideas and freedom from pressure of party politics.
- Vice-Chancellor, necessarily a distinguished educationist or eminent scholar of any discipline or profession, should embody the spirit of academic freedom, and principles of good management in university.
- Higher appointments should be left to the university, with Chancellor appointing from a panel of three persons.
- Adequate powers should be vested with VC to ensure effective working of the university.
- Important authorities of university include the core policy-making body; the executive council—a small body of 10-15 members, and the academic council which is the sole authority to decide courses of study and standards.

Committee on Governance of Universities and Colleges, (also known as Gajendragadkar Committee) 1972

- Universities and colleges should devise mechanism and machinery to redress grievances of its different constituents, adopt the principle of rotation rather than election to different management bodies.
- UGC as custodian of university autonomy should be consulted before the state enacts or amends any laws on universities.
- Respect autonomy and supremacy of Academic Councils and Boards of Studies in academic matters.

NPE, 1986 and POA, 1986

SCHE a state level body for planning and coordination of HE to protect it from degradation (an euphemism for socio political pressures and interferences).

Gnanam Committee, 1990

- Central government legislated that UGC's regulations are binding on all universities.
- No new university can be established by a state without UGC's

concurrence and without reference to special needs for new university.

CABE Committee on Autonomy, 2005

- In academic matters the universities provide the broad framework, and leave freedom to individual HEIs to design courses, and teachers to try out pedagogical innovations.
- UGC and AICTE should guide curriculum revision ensuring inclusion of frontier areas in curriculum.
- All universities quickly shift towards adoption of choice-based credit courses and semester system.
- All universities establish linkages with open and distance learning universities to enhance enrolment.
- Disband teacher appointment on contract, and allow institutions to fill up vacancies expeditiously.
- Allow universities to offer courses as per emerging realities of the region.
- In administrative matters, it called for a review of all university acts and statutes periodically for better management, and to grant autonomy to affiliated colleges.
- Let institutional heads decide number and rank of faculty positions.
- University and college authorities and bodies to have a mix of elected and nominated persons.
- VC's selection only by search-cum-selection process.
- Recognised the need for training and development of academic administrators of HEIs to improve quality of governance.
- In financial matters, it recommended that one third investment on education should be for HE.
- Bring all government universities and government-aided colleges under UGC funding pattern, and increase allocations to UGC.
- Full public funding of HEIs no longer possible, and alternative fund generation needed to encourage and incentivise.
- Set a ceiling on fee levels and ensure HEIs do not indulge in malpractices in fees.
- Give HEIs autonomy to take up consultancy and sponsored research projects. Make UGC more effective for maintenance of standards. HEIs need to be given full autonomy for academic and research collaborations with their counterpart industry and professional organisations in India and abroad.
- Need to encourage private participation in HE with adequate social control.
- Need professional ethics and norms of accountability from teachers.

3. Privatisation and Private Higher Education

NPE, 1986 and POA, 1986

- State Council of Higher Education (SCHE) cannot legislate creation of colleges without UGC's consent and sanction.
- Statutory bodies like UGC would regulate admission as per physical facilities and faculty strength.
- SCHE would prepare coordinated plans of HE development in a state which would be endorsed by UGC.

NPE, 1986 and Revised POA, 1992

- Government of India should set up a High Powered Committee for mobilisation of resources for higher education; and also a High Powered Committee on Technical Education for the same purpose.

Punnaya Committee 1992

- Rather than penalise any university or college, the UGC should incentivise them with a matching grant. Universities and colleges need to generate own funds for development purposes.
- Cent per cent income tax exemptions to endowments and contributions to HEIs.
- Self-financing courses only for those who can afford to pay, and adequate subsidy loan provisions for economically weaker students unable to pay high fees.
- Funding for HE is essentially the state's responsibility.

Swaminathan Committee on Technical Education, 1994

- Public technical education institutions should raise internal and external resources from industry, alumni, consultancy, sponsored research/projects, etc.
- Fix fees at a higher level, and revise them periodically.

Ambani-Birla Group, 2000

- Establish world-class HE facility at each district HQ.
- Foster a healthy mix of state and affordable private initiatives.
- Enforce strictly "user pays" principle in HEIs with state support for economically weaker sections.
- Complete freedom to private agency without reference to UGC, AICTE, etc. to establish HEIs.
- HEIs to be out of bounds for politics and political parties.

NKC, 2009

- Private investment in HE is welcome, and should be encouraged by offering land grants and other facilities.

Yash Pal Committee, 2009

- To double the current capacity of HEIs all three approaches are necessary, viz., public, private, and PPP, but with consistent ground rules to do away with ills associated with private initiatives.
- Private initiatives should not be driven by profit motives and confine attention to commercially viable sectors like professional courses, but should also offer social and natural science courses.
- Given considerable misuse of provisions and pending decisions of Tandon Committee on Deemed Universities, UGC should suspend sanction or recognition of new deemed universities.

Tandon Committee on Deemed Universities, 2009

- Abolish 44 out of 126 deemed universities, which neither on past performance nor on future potential, hold hope and deserve their status, and a national committee needs to be set up to salvage future of affected students.
- VCs, as in traditional universities, should head governing bodies of deemed universities like Board of Management, Executive Council, and Governing Council, and its membership should include more than 50 percent of academicians and with not more than one or two of Trust/President's representatives.
- Trust/President can't nominate VC, PVC, etc.
- Centralised admission test to govern admissions.
- Fees should be reasonable to the cost of the course.
- Ensure that private participation does not slip into crass commercialisation.

Narayan Murthy Committee, 2012

- Create enabling conditions to make HE system robust and useful to attract private investments.
- Improve quality of HE with corporate participation.
- Engage corporate sector to invest in existing institutions, set up new ones, and develop new knowledge clusters.

FICCI Education Summit, 2013

- Create enabling environment with fewer barriers for private and foreign participation.
- Change from government as a single provider of funds to a situation where students, researchers, and faculty can source funds from multiple sources to ensure autonomy and freedom from any control or accountability.

References

Agarwal, P. (2013). *Indian Higher Education: Envisioning the Future.* New Delhi: Sage.

Ahmed, F. and Garg, S. (2015). *Higher Education in Knowledge Era: Innovation, Excellence and Values.* New Delhi: Viva Books.

AIU (2001). Round Table on Internationalisation of Indian Higher Education (The Mysore Statement) New Delhi: AIU.

Ali, Z. and Jamal, R. (2006). An Impact Study of UGC Academic Staff College, AMU. *Journal of All India Association for Educational Research*, (18).

Annual Status of Higher Education (2014) New Delhi: AIU.

Antony, S. (2001). Impact and Assessment and Accreditation on Institutions of Higher Learning. *University News*, 39(8).

Arya, S. (1995). University-Industry Linkage. *University News,* 33 (15).

Arya, A. (2000). *Indian Women-Education and Empowerment*. Delhi; Gunjan Publishing House.

Asha, K. and Neela, J. (eds.) (1995). *Speaking for Ourselves: Women in Distance Education*; New Delhi: Manohar.

Asha, K. and Margaret, T. (eds.) (2001). *Brave New Women of Asia: How Distance Education Changed Their Lives.* Vancouver: COL.

Bhatti, S.S. (1994). Universities and Industrial Development: Bridging the Gap. *University News* 32 (14).

Dasgupta, S. (2014). Reforms in Medical Education: Optimising Quantity and Quality. *Indian Journal of Public Health*, 58.

Deo, M.G. (2012). Research Training for Medical Students in Developing Nations. *Medical Education,* 46.

Deo, M.G. (2009). Need for Research Oriented Medical Education in India. *IJMR,* 130 (2).

D'Mello, B. (1999). Management Education: A Critical Appraised. *Economic and Political Weekly,* 34 (48).

Elton, L. (1998). Dimensions of Excellence in University Teaching. *International Journal of Academic Development.* 3 (1).

FICCI (2014). *Higher Education in India: Moving Towards Global Relevance and Competitiveness*. New Delhi: FICCI.

Govt. of India (1971). *Report of the Committee on the Status of Women in India: Towards Equality*. New Delhi: Ministry of Education and Social Welfare.

Goel, C. and Goel, D. (2014). Teacher Education in India: Issues and Concerns. *University News*, 52 (23).

Goyal, D. and Goyal, C. (2012). Teacher Education Scenario in India. *MIER Journal of Educational Studies*, 2 (2).

GOI (1968). *National Policy on Education,* 1968. New Delhi: Govt. of India.

GOI (1986). *National Policy on Education* New Delhi: Govt. of India.

Gupta, M. (2003). *Women and Educational Developments*. Mumbai: Swarup and Son Publishers.

Janaki, D. (2006). *Empowering Women through Distance Learning in India*. A Paper to 4th Pan Commonwealth Forum on Open Learning.

Kamat, R. and Sharma (1999). Industry-University Partnerships. A Double Benefit. *University News*. 37 (52).

Kailas, A. and Khajurkar, D. (2014) Varma Commission Work Plan and Recommendations for Teacher Education Institutions and Strengthening NCTE. R*esearch Front*.

Kumar, S. (2004). Report Highlights Shortcomings in Private Medical Schools in India. *British Medical Journal,* 328:70

Maslak, M.A. and Singhal, G. (2008). The Identity of Educated Women in India: Confluence or Divergence. *Gender and Education,* 20 (5).

Mishra, K. (2007). *Encyclopedia of Women.* Calcutta: Omega Publishers.

Mellor, J. (2011). Interrupted Journey of Agriculture Education. *Economic and Political Weekly,* 46 (4).

Nayar, U. Verma, K. and Adkoli, B.V. (eds.) (1955). *Driven Strategies in Medical Education in India: Curricular Reforms.* New Delhi: AIMS.

National Knowledge Commission (2007). *Report to the Nation—2006.* New Delhi.

NAAC (2012). *Report of NAAC Review Committee on Academic Staff Colleges.* Bangalore: NAAC.

NCTE (2009). *National Curriculum Framework for Teacher Education.* New Delhi: NCTE

Pai Panandiker, V.A. (1991). Management Education: A Long Term View. *Economic and Political Weekly*, 26 (48).

Passi, B.K. and Sahoo, P. K (1998). Academic Staff Colleges: Some Experiences. *University News,* 26 (31).

Powar, K.B. (1998). *Accountability in Higher Education,* New Delhi: AIU.

Powar, K.B. (1997). *Higher Education in India: Retrospect and Prospect*. New Delhi: AIU.

Ramabrahmam, I. (1995). Accountability of Teaching Profession—Role of Academic Staff Colleges. *University News,* 33 (28).

Report of the Task Force on Medical Education for the National Rural Health Mission. (2005) Ministry of Health and Family Welfare. Govt. of India.

Saha, K.C. (1991). Reorienting Management Education. *Economic and Political Weekly,* 26 (48).

Sesharatnam, C. (2001). Distance Education Promoters Women's Educational Advancement. *New Frontiers in Education,* 31 (4).

Shehanaz, S.I. (2011). Privatisation of Medical Education in Asia. *South Asian Journal of Medical Education,* 5 (1).

Singh, G. (2015). *New NCTE Regulations for setting up New Teacher Education Colleges.* Tribune News Service.

Singh, L.C. (2015). NCTE Regulations-2014: a Few Reflections on Their Impact and Prospects. *University News,* 53 (40).

Singh, A. (2005). Restructuring Medical Education. *Economic and Political Weekly.* 40 (34).

Srivastava, M. (2012). *Open Universities: India's Answer to Challenges in Higher Education.* New Delhi: Vikas.

Stromquist, N. (1968). Women's Education in Development: From Welfare to Empowerment: *Convergence,* 2 (3).

Swaminathan, D. (1990). A Model for University-Industry Symbiosis. *University News,* 31 (28).

Supe, A. and William, P. (2006). Challenges and Issues in Medical Education in India. *Academic Medicine,* 81 (2).

Sharma, S. (2004). *History of Education.* New Delhi: Anmol Publications.

Sushma, S. (1998). *Women and Empowerment: Approaches and Strategies.* New Delhi: Discovery.

Tamboli, P.M. and Nene, Y.L. (2013). Modernising Higher Agricultural System in India to Meet Challenges of 21st Century. *Asian Agri History,* 17 (3).

Tilak, J.B.G. (2014). Private Higher Education in India. *Economic and Political Weekly,* 49 (40).

Twelfth Five Year Plan (2012-17), New Delhi: Govt. of India.

Verma, J.C. (2012). *Vision of Teacher Education in India: Quality and Regulatory Perspective. Volume. I.* New Delhi: Govt. of India.

Vision of Teacher Education in India (2012). Quality and Regulatory Perspective, Govt. of India, Ministry of HRD.

Yash Pal Committee (2009). *Report of the Committee to Advise on Renovation and Rejuvenation of Higher Education.* New Delhi. MHRD, Govt. of India.

Index

Academic councils, 157, 246
Academic framework, 88–89
Academic freedom, 14, 149, 191–92, 246
Academic programmes, 131, 151, 160–61, 189
Academic quality, 125, 161, 180
  norms of, 125
Academic Staff Colleges (ASCs), 25, 54–55, 57–61
Accountability, 16, 26–27, 107–8, 115, 149, 154–57, 161, 163, 174, 225, 234, 244, 247, 249
Accreditation
  agencies, 160, 165
  body, 160
  standards, 165
  status of Autonomous Colleges, 157
Adult education, 15, 130
  promotion of, 15
Advanced learning technology (ALT), 198
Advocates Act, 121–23, 125
Agricultural education, 102–7
Agricultural Research Education, 103
Agricultural universities, 102–4, 106–8, 137
Agriculture education, 106
AICTE Act, 177
Ambani-Birla Report, 172–73, 207
American management education knowledge, 95
Arthashastra, 4
Asia-Pacific Region, 164
Assessment, 19, 43, 45, 79, 82, 84, 102, 159, 161–64
Association of Indian Universities, 188, 190–91, 193
Autonomous colleges, 24, 36, 43, 88, 151–54, 157
Autonomous research organisation, 223
Autonomy
  academic, 26, 89, 153
  of higher education institutions, 155, 174
  institutional, 234

B.R. Ambedkar Open University (BRAOU), 136, 140–41
Bachelor of Law, 120
Banaras Hindu University (BHU), 32–34, 66, 85–86, 92
Bar Council of India (BCI), 121–23, 125, 177, 245
Bengal Engineering College, 103
Bethune College for Women, 151
Bharati Vidyapeeth College, 70
Birla Institute of Technology and Sciences (BITS), 66, 179
Brahminical education, 3
British market in India, 6
B-Schools in India, Growth of, 96
Buddhist education, 3–4
Budget grants, 105
Business education, 99

Career development, 54, 59, 244
Caste system, 212
Central Advisor Board of Education, 168
Central Advisory Board of Education, 16, 136, 155, 168–69, 173–75
Central Council of Homeopathy, 177
Central Education Institutions, 214
Central Institute of Education, 109
Central Power Research Institute (CPRI), 222
Centre for Distance Engineering Education Programme, 202
Centre-state
  funding, 230

relationships, 106
Chemical Technology, 66, 91
College Development Councils, 27
Colleges
accredited, 24, 202
agricultural, 105
aided, 232, 238
autonomy, 151, 153
cluster, 184
Commerce, 95
government-aided, 247
government-funded, 70
home science, 129
legislate creation of, 205, 248
medical, 73
model, 23–24, 27, 234
private professional, 206
public funded, 232
regional, 85
residential undergraduate, 103
self-financing, 205, 238
traditional, 41
Colonial Times, 3, 6
Commercialization, 193–94
Communication technology, 22, 93, 197, 201–2, 218, 224–25
Compulsory Education Act, 113
Computer Based Training (CBT), 200
Confederation of Indian Industries (CII), 88, 186
Consortium for Educational Communication (CEC), 201
Constitution of India, 123
Continuing Medical Education, 80–81
Corporate participation, 209, 246, 249
Corporate Social Responsibility, 219
Cost recovery, 173–74
Council of Scientific and Industrial Research (CSIR), 220–22

Deemed universities, 31, 37, 83, 157, 178, 206–8, 249
Defence Research and Development Organisation (DRDO), 222
Degree colleges, 234
Delhi University, 32–34, 66, 136
Dental Council of India, 78, 80, 177
Differently-abled students, 25
Digital library, 199–200, 221
Disadvantaged students, 63
Distance education, 132–33, 136–37, 140–44, 177, 198, 203
benefits of, 137
Distance learning, 82, 134, 138, 200–203
Doctoral Research Programme, 224
Doctoral students, 224, 226
DST Policy Statement, 182–83

East Indian Company, 6
Economic development, 16, 85, 127, 144, 159, 220
Economic empowerment, 127
Education Commission, 11, 14, 104, 151–52, 167, 243
Education/Educational
adequate, 131
broad-based, 86
college, 176
compulsory, 13–14
computer, 144
conferences, 8
cost of, 170, 188, 206
democratization of, 136, 198
elementary, 5, 15, 116, 167, 172
female, 127
finances, 167
formal, 138
gender, 118
girl, 14, 132
high-touch remedial, 41
integrated, 41
justice-oriented, 123
loan, 170, 214
management, 18
minimum standards of, 178
non-formal, 133
policy, 6, 14–15, 172
pre-primary, 12
psychology, 54
religious, 5, 13
skill-based, 26
state-supported, 207
traditional, 199
yoga, 118
Educational Satellite (EDUSAT), 201–2
E-education, 199
E-learning, 82, 198–99, 202
Employability, 185–86, 232
Engineering colleges, 85–86, 91, 93, 103, 184

private, 86
regional, 86, 183
Engineering Education, History of, 85
Engineering students, 90
English style of higher education, 7

Faculty Student Ratio (FSR), 63
Fake universities, 40
Feminist learning, 134
FICCI Education Summit, 210, 249
Five Year Plans, 21, 119, 193, 217
Foreign Direct Investment (FDI), 194
Formal system, 103, 133, 136
Free education, 12

GATS, 191–93
Gender equality, 127–28, 130
Gender gap, 213
General education, 42, 45
Girl students, 24
Global Initiative of Academic Network (GIAN), 194
Gnanam Committee, 167, 206, 246
Governance, 26, 43, 107–8, 157, 178, 210, 233, 236, 238, 246–47
Government funding, 160, 165, 205–6, 216
Government of India Act, 33
Gross Domestic Product (GDP), 13, 102, 167–68, 176
Gross Enrolment Ratio (GER), 23, 210, 213, 216, 230, 237, 244

Haryana Agricultural University (HAU), 104
Health education, 128
Higher Education Management, 128
Higher education, 4–5, 7–8, 19–20, 22–27, 41–42, 54–55, 57–59, 128–31, 138–40, 158–61, 166–80, 184–96, 213–20, 238–39, 243–46
cost of, 168
defining, 173
international, 187–88
mass-based, 159
quality in, 164
quality of, 202, 208
reclassified, 173
socio-historical journey of, 3
stakeholders of, 162, 192
standards of, 178, 180
state funding of, 174
Higher Educational Institutions Bill, 180
Higher learning, 4–5, 140, 229
Human Resource Development Centres (HRDCs), 60–61

Imperial Agricultural Research Institute (IARI), 103–4
Implementation Core Committee (ICC), 63
Incubation funds, 184–85
Independent Regulatory Authority of Higher Education (IRAHE), 124, 178, 245
India Council for Technical Education, 27, 86, 184
India Institute of Medical Sciences, 32
India Meteorological Department (IMD), 222
India Space Research Organisation (ISRO), 87, 222
Indian Agricultural Research Institute, 104
Indian Citation Index, 64, 67
Indian Council of Agricultural Research (ICAR), 102, 104, 106–7, 177
Indian Council of Medical Research (ICMR), 222
Indian Council of Social Science Research (ICSSR), 222–23
Indian Institute of Management, 66
Indian Institute of Science (IISc), 32, 66, 85, 179
Indian Institute of Social Welfare and Business Management (IISWBM), 95
Indian Institutes of Science, Education and Research (IISERs), 157
Indian Institutes of Technology (IITs), 19–20, 32, 64, 86, 91, 157, 179, 214, 225–26
Indian Medical Association (IMA), 80
Indian Medical Council Act, 79, 84
Indian National Science Academy (INSA), 222
Indian Nursing Council, 79
Indian School of Business (ISB), 101
Indian Space Research Organisation, 222
Indian Veterinary Institute, 105

Indira Gandhi Centre for Atomic Research, 32
Indira Gandhi National Open University (IGNOU), 15, 32, 136–37, 140–42, 201–2
Industrial Training Institutes (ITIs), 129
Information and Communication Technology (ICT), 18, 55, 92, 118, 197–202
Information and Library Network (INFLIBNET), 202
Information Resource Centre (IRC), 229
Information technology, 56, 84, 143, 217, 219
Institute of Chemical Technology, 66, 91
Institutional
  bottlenecks, 181
  capacity, 116
  leadership, 235
  mechanisms, 62
  pattern, 29
  platform, 115
Institution-building, 96, 187
Institution-industry collaboration, 181
Institutions
  accredited, 88
  aided, 171
  autonomous, 41, 155, 161
  central, 234
  distribution of, 23, 158
  financial, 173
  foreign, 188–90, 245
  grant-in-aid, 170
  international, 229
  nonprofit, 19
  private-aided, 230
  private self-financed, 23, 158
  private-sponsored, 209
  private unaided, 207
  professional, 183
  research-informed, 89
  vocation-focused, 216
Intake capacity, 24, 74–75
Internal Quality Assurance Cell (IQAC), 163
International Management Institute, 65–66
International Network for Quality Assurance Agencies in Higher Education (INQAAHE), 160, 164
International standards of education, 188
Internationalisation, 187–88, 193, 195, 220
  higher education, 187, 189, 191, 193–95
  effects of, 188
Inter-University Centre, 25, 118, 202

Jawaharlal Nehru University (JNU), 32, 34, 66
Job-oriented inter-disciplinary courses, 238

Knowledge society, 55, 202
Kothari Commission, 11, 13–14, 59, 152, 167

Law Commission of India, 121–23
Learning materials, 200–201, 204
Legal education, 120–26
  vision of, 123
Liberalization, 184, 195, 205
Literacy rate, 134
Local bodies, 13

Madrasas, 5
Magna Carta of English education, 7
Maktabs, 5
Malnutrition, 106
Management education, 95, 99–101, 169
  professionalise Indian, 96
  specialised, 96
Management institutions, 65, 181
  premier, 101
  private, 65
Management research, 98
Medical colleges, 74, 78–80, 83–84
Medical Council of India (MCI), 78–80, 82–84, 177, 245
Medical education, 4, 73–76, 78–81, 83–84
Medical Education, Task Force on, 84
Medical Grants commission (MGC), 84
Millennium Development Goals, 130
Mobilisation of additional resources, 170, 174, 206
Multi-lingual country, 203
Mysore Statement, 188, 190

NAAC Accreditation, 162–63

National Agricultural Research System (NARS), 103
National Assessment and Accreditation Council (NAAC), 19, 24, 60–61, 161–65, 177, 237
National Board of Accreditation (NBA), 63, 87, 165, 177
National Commission for Higher Education and Research, 245
National Commission for Human Resources for Health (NCHRH), 83
National Commission on Teachers in Higher Education, 244
National Council for Educational Research and Training, 16, 222
National Council for Teacher Education (NCTE), 17, 112–18, 163–64
National Council for Teacher Educational Research, 17
National Curriculum for Teacher Education (NCFTE), 112–14, 117
National Curriculum Framework, 113
National Education Policy, 16, 59
National Eligibility Entrance Test, 83
National Institute for Transforming India, 21
National Institute of Design (NID), 179
National Institute of Fashion Technology (NIFT), 179
National Institute of Technology, 92–93
National Institutes of Technology (NITs), 32, 64, 86, 157
National Institutional Ranking Framework (NIRF), 62, 64, 67, 70
National Knowledge Commission (NKC), 14, 37, 83, 99, 123–25, 157, 175–76, 178, 180, 207, 227, 244, 248
National Occupational Standards (NOSs), 42, 45
National Policy of Education, 14, 59
National Policy on Education (NPE), 13–16, 37, 54, 59, 128–29, 152, 161, 167–70, 181, 205, 207, 244, 246, 248
National Policy on Education Review Committee (NPERC), 168–69
National Quality Framework, 189
National Skill Qualification Framework, 41, 215
National University of Educational Planning and Administration, 194
National Vocational Education Qualification Framework, 26, 185
Navratna Universities, 40
NIRF rankings, 70
NITI Aayog, 21, 79
Nodal agencies, 190, 201
Non-merit goods, 172

ODL system, 142
Off-campus centres, 38
Open Distance Learning, 136, 142
Operation blackboard, 15
Organisation for Economic Cooperate and Development (OECD), 40

Pedagogy, 18, 54, 57, 112, 200
Personal development, 41–42
Pharmaceutical Council of India, 177
Pharmacy Council of India (PCI), 78, 177
Planning Commission, 21, 41, 192, 209, 230
Pre-service teacher education, 119
Primary healthcare, 83–84
Prime Minister Council on Trade and Industry (PMCTI), 172
Private institutions, 39, 65, 83, 165, 205, 207, 209–10
Private Medical Colleges in India, 76
Product specification, 98
Professional disciplines, 106–7
Programme accreditation, 87
Promotion of Indian Higher Education Abroad (PIHEAD), 193
Public Private Partnership (PPP), 26, 176, 208, 218, 227, 249
Punnayya Committee, 170–71, 206, 248

Quality assessment, 159
Quality Assurance, 143, 159–62, 164
Quality education, 17, 109, 195, 215–16, 219, 233
Quality improvement, 21, 232–34
Quality reform, 194
Quality teaching-learning materials, 161

Ramamurti Review Committee, 168
Ranjit Roy Committee, 83
Rao Committee, 87–88, 99

Rashtriya Uchch Shiksha Abhiyan, 24, 37, 39, 230–35, 238–39
Recognition of Prior Learning (RPL), 45
Regional Engineering Colleges (RECs), 86, 183
Regulatory framework, 83, 177
Rehabilitation Council of India (RCI), 177
Remedial coaching, 214
Research Productivity, Impact, and IPR (RPII), 63
Rig Vedic education, 3
Right to Education (RTE), 112
Royal College of Surgeons, 73
Rural Medical Practitioners (RMPs), 78

Salary differentials, 124
Sarkar Committee, 85–86
School management committee, 112
School teacher training, 115
Science and Technology Application for Rural Development (STARD), 222
Science and Technology for Weaker Sections (STAWS), 222
Science education, Growth of, 14
Self-evaluation, 161, 163
Skill competency, 45
Skill development, 185, 213, 215
Social gap, 213
Soft loans, 170–71, 174
State Agricultural Universities (SAUs), 102, 104–8
State Council of Higher Education (SCHE), 37, 246, 248
Statutory councils, 38, 189
Structural adjustment programme, 74, 169
Student assessment, 82, 160
Student loans, 168–69, 216
Student mobility, 190
Student performances, 13
Student-teacher ratio, 80, 215, 217
Swaminadhan Committee, 171, 248

Tandon Committee, 207–8, 249
Tata Institute of Social Science (TISS), 179
Teacher Education Assessment and Accreditation Centre (TEAAC), 114
Teacher Education Institutions (TEIs), 112, 114–17, 163–64
Teaching and Innovation (TI), 63
Teaching Learning Centres (TLCs), 61
Teaching shops, 19
Technical institutions, 157, 170, 177, 181
Tele-education system, 202
Tertiary education, 138, 174
Theology, 5

Under-represented communities, 215, 217, 219
Universities, 7–8, 19–20, 31–41, 43–44, 122–24, 151–54, 156–57, 170, 173–78, 182–84, 188–90, 205–9, 227, 236–38, 243–48
  accredits, 177
  best, 20, 140
  deemed multidisciplinary, 39
  exclusive, 24
  government-aided, 194
  multi-disciplinary, 66–67
  multi-faculty, 157
  parent, 152
  public, 23, 31, 158, 205
  rural, 103
  single discipline, 237
  unidisciplinary, 237
  world class, 40, 108
University education, Expansion of, 15
Upanishads, 4–5

Value-education, 27
Vedic period, 3
Vellore Institute of Technology, 64–65
Video conferencing, 142
Visva Bharati, 34, 66

Washington Accord, 88
Women's studies centres, 131
World Bank, 88, 166, 171–72, 174
World Declaration on Higher Education, 190

Xavier Labour Relations Institute (XLRI), 65, 95

Yash Pal Committee, 37–38, 156, 176, 180, 209, 245, 249